JACK B. YEATS

A Celtic Visionary

MANCHESTER CITY ART GALLERIES
ORMEAU BATHS GALLERY, BELFAST

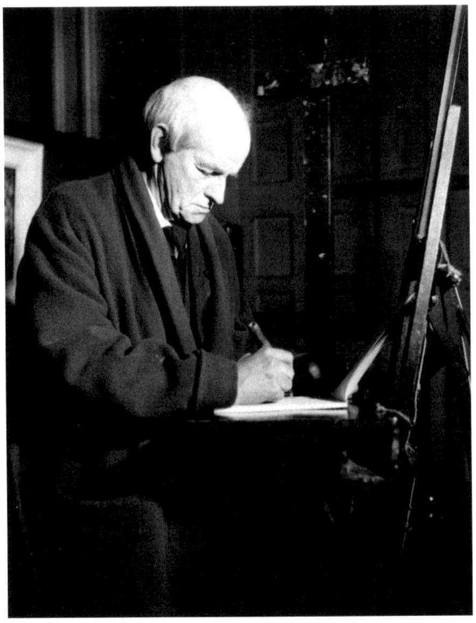

Jack B. Yeats in his Dublin studio, 1950
photograph taken by William MacQuitty

HOMAGE TO JACK B. YEATS

What is incomparable in this great solitary oeuvre is its insistence upon sending us back to the darkest part of the spirit that created it and upon permitting illuminations only through that darkness.

Hence this unparallelled strangeness which renders irrelevant the usual tracing of a heritage, whether national or other.

What is less magic than this extraordinary craftsmanship, as if inspired by the thing to be done in its own urgency?

As for references that have been unearthed – Ensor and Munch at the top of the list – the least that can be said is that they are not much help.

The artist who stakes his being comes from nowhere. And he has no brothers.

Shall I embellish? There is neither place nor time for reassuring notes on these desperately immediate images. On this violence of need which not only unleashes them but disrupts them beyond their vanishing lines. On this great internal reality which incorporates into a single witness dead and living spirits, nature and void, everything that will cease and everything that will never be. And finally on this supreme master who submits to what cannot be mastered, and trembles.

No.

One can simply bow, wonder-struck.

Samuel Beckett

Les Lettres Nouvelles, April 1954, Paris

FOREWORD

This exhibition focusses on Jack B. Yeats's late paintings when his work consists of an extraordinarily vivid panorama of Irish life, imbued with a strong sense of the visionary. It is a deeply personal Celtic mysticism in which the forces of nature appear to shape man's destiny. The figures in his paintings are often set against, and intimately bound up with, the landscape and constantly changing light of the Irish sky. Yeats was a contemporary of Picasso and Matisse and indeed showed alongside them in the seminal Armory exhibition of 1913 in New York. He was never a part of the vigorous debates about modern art, as he himself was elusive, tending to remain apart from other artists and visiting few exhibitions. Yeats's style can be associated with the European Expressionism of Munch, Nolde, Ensor and Kokoschka. By allowing himself to be carried away by what he saw and fusing it with his memory, great paintings of a magical and mysterious quality were created. We hope that this exhibition will show that Yeats deserves to be considered not just as the greatest Irish artist of modern times, but also as one of the great European painters of the twentieth century.

The exhibition has benefitted from several extremely generous loans, without which it would not have been possible. We would like to thank the following for their very positive response to our requests for loans: Alan and Mary Hobart of Pyms Gallery, London; Leslie Waddington, Thomas H. Lighton and Sarah Tooley of Waddington Galleries Ltd and Theo Waddington and Magdalen Evans of Theo Waddington Fine Art Ltd. With their help, important loans have been secured from private collectors, to whom we are also grateful. Thanks are due to Francis Greenacre, Bristol Museums and Art Gallery; Brian Kennedy of the Ulster Museum, Belfast and Richard Green of York City Art Gallery for agreeing to lend works from their collections. We are delighted that lenders have agreed to part with their works for the entire duration of the tour, and we recognise that this is often not an easy decision.

We have received significant sponsorship towards the exhibition from Bank of Ireland and we wish to record our appreciation of their generosity and thank Michael Feely for his personal cooperation. The publication of this catalogue has also been assisted by the generous support of Pyms Gallery. It is very appropriate that this exhibition should be presented as part of the first Manchester Irish Festival and we thank them and their sponsors, Guinness, for their help in promoting it. We should particularly like to thank P. J. Leydon and Councillor Dorothy Rathbone, Chair of the Galleries and Museums Committee of the City Council, who have both contributed valuable advice and encouragement. We also wish to thank Sandra McCormack, Nigel Walsh, Nikos Papastergiadis and Virginia Tandy for their support.

The exhibition has been selected by Stephen Snoddy and it benefits from his considerable knowledge of and enthusiasm for the artist's work. As well as his essay, the catalogue includes two texts by Samuel Beckett and John Berger. We are grateful to Edward Beckett of the Samuel Beckett Estate and John Berger for giving us permission to republish them. Thanks are also due to Anne Yeats and Michael Yeats for allowing us to reproduce works by Jack B. Yeats.

Finally, although the exhibition was initiated and organised by Manchester City Art Galleries, it has developed into a collaboration with the Ormeau Baths Gallery, Belfast. This is the first exhibition of Yeats's work in Belfast since the Yeats Centenary Exhibition in 1971. We both welcome this opportunity to work together and bring Yeats's paintings to the attention of new audiences in both England and Northern Ireland.

Richard Gray
Director, Manchester City Art Galleries

Noreen O'Hare
Director, Ormeau Baths Gallery, Belfast

'NEVER HAVE A NARROW HEART'

Jack B. Yeats believed that to love life is to capture some intense moment of the enjoyment of life and to pass it on to others who can share it if they so wish. In the era of the internet and the information superhighway this may seem a romantic notion but it is an engagingly and typically human characteristic of Yeats. 'No one creates... the artist assembles memories'[1] seems to me to be about this intense moment that is always past but can be recaptured by trained observation, memory and technique. This is the job of the artist and in Yeats's words he spoke of painting as 'the fairest and the finest means of communication humanity has yet found because it is the most simple.' But memory, although its basis is on the feelings of the heart and the acute observation of the eye, is not easily indexed into an ordered file. Each individual memory has its own associations but also brings with it other memories and associations. Yeats brings his multitude of memories and fuses them, consciously and subconsciously, into symbolic and majestic subjects.

In his late oil paintings from about 1924, he parallels James Joyce whose use of language in Ulysses combines mythical, legendary, historical, symbolic and realistic styles into astonishing evocative narratives. So themes which Yeats has treated naturalistically or with clear definition in his early work – horses, fairs, travelling players, crowds – acquire symbolic overtones in the late oil paintings.

The similarities in Yeats's and Joyce's creative parallels can be demonstrated by a story of how both painter and writer used chance as part of their creative process. 'It is natural that an artist should change incessantly in his style like Joyce. It is an inevitable process.'[2] Yeats explained to Shotaro Oshima that the size of Joyce's handwriting was because his sight was failing and how Joyce dictated his works to a copyist he employed.

'One day he was dictating to the copyist as usual, when there was a knock at the door. Joyce said, "Come in!" and the copyist wrote down "Come in!" The next day when Joyce was listening to the copyist reading the manuscript he had dictated, he was surprised to hear the words "Come in!" in an unexpected place. He said to the copyist that he couldn't have dictated such words. The copyist answered that he had certainly heard them. Joyce laughed and said "Ah! I remember. Please leave the words as they are. I said those words to the knocking at the door. Don't cross them out. There is some meaning even in words uttered casually!"'

Yeats ended this story with a hearty laugh, 'There may be some people who will laugh at such a piece as mine as the product of mere phantasy. But even in mere phantasy there often are things inseparable from truth, or things more real than reality itself. It is the very world a true artist lives in.'

In the late oil paintings colour now dominates, it acquires a fluidity reflecting the emotional drive which is evident in the vigorousness of the brush, palette knife, brush handle, the paint tube itself or sometimes even the artist's fingers. Human figures merge with the landscape or emerge from within the landscape echoing the constantly changing nature of land, sea and sky. It is Yeats's colour that explodes magnificently into light or fades into darkness. His emotional use of paint was moulded by the physical nature of the west of Ireland where great roaring winds sweep in from the Atlantic to drench the land with spray and weaken the spirit before the drifting clouds threaten further havoc. Yeats experienced this sense of wildness and freedom, the untamed forces of nature and interpreted this through his paint until the paint itself escapes its own material.

His idealistic vision is best revealed in paintings of single characters alone. The curiousity of the viewer is tempered so as not to violate the privacy of the individual. The individual or 'traveller' remains mysterious, a tension exists between the 'traveller' and viewer. The viewer wishes he had the freedom of the 'traveller' so that he could avoid the responsibility of modern life. However, this is nostalgia and it is dangerous if it encourages a longing for the past. To look back is also to ignore and lose sight of the viewer's desires for the future. Yeats's paintings are a celebration of an heroic and legendary past but also an affirmation of the future. They hold latent memories and attendant hopes for anyone who wants to reflect upon and explore their own imagination.

As the viewer we are caught in an imaginary journey between fantasy and reality, between the past and the future. This is the essence of Yeats's late painting.

It is the enigma of the traveller, on a journey not sure whether to go back or move forward. For Yeats and perhaps the viewer, 'the finest picture in the world will give the finest moment finest felt by the finest soul with the finest memory.'[3]

For Yeats, a painting was complete if it was interpreted in many different ways by everybody who looked at it. It didn't matter to him whether anybody understood his paintings and he was quietly amused at the various interpretations and meanings that collectors and critics placed on his work. At his exhibition openings he always wore a rose in his buttonhole, not as a sentimental gesture but as an indication of a particular poetic notion. The symbolism of the rose was that the viewer's interpretation was only one of many and the true meaning of the work was the artist's secret.

James White, past Director of the National Gallery of Ireland, recalls,[4] 'I received a letter from the artist inviting me to his studio in Fitzwilliam Place. He received me with his usual old-world courtesy and took me in to the private place where the painting was done – always in electric light I had heard previously and never in the presence of any one else. Tied to the top of his easel was a pink paper rose. He then recalled to me a dinner at which I was present and which I left in a blazing temper. It was given in the United Arts Club in Dublin in honour of Jack B. Yeats and it had seemed to me that our greatest artist had been damned with faint praise by a number of condescending speakers. Later that night when he arrived home his wife gave him a pink paper rose with which someone had presented her at the dinner. He went into his studio and thereupon tied the rose to an easel. "I made a vow then," he told me, "that from thence forward all my work would be sub rosa; I would never again discuss the meaning of my pictures."'

Yeats never showed or discussed his work in the studio and it was only revealed when it was ready for showing in an exhibition. He refused permission for his work to be reproduced and he disliked references to his age, his family background, his opinions or his way of life. "It doesn't matter who or what I am. People may think what they will of the pictures." Yeats felt that his paintings were all important and that they would speak for themselves. His pictures do not need translation; that would be to undo his own creation. He was an artist of contemplative detachment, he was elusive and deliberately remained aloof from other artists and no one was allowed to see him paint. Yeats's inner vision was only communicated to the viewer when poetry and paint, memory and imagination coalesced *sub rosa*. The privacy of his practice became public.

Yeats's everyday scenes in the late paintings take on the vibrancy and majestic grandeur of epic art. They combine the classical world and contemporary world, aesthetic life and daily life, symbolism and realism; all co-exist on the canvas. It is in this combination that the truth of a Yeats painting exists and it is realised through the imagination of the viewer. There is an equidistance between painter, viewer and event depicted and it is this relationship that reveals Yeats's humanity. He expresses a true visionary idealism and optimism that is rare in artists today. He used paint to catch moments of great emotion which renew us and lift up our hearts to face an ever changing world.

When we look at his work let us hope for a moment of *radiance* and in Yeats's own words, 'Never have a narrow heart.'[5]

Stephen Snoddy

NOTES

[1] Hilary Pyle, *Jack B. Yeats: A biography*, Andre Deutsch Limited, revised edition, 1989, p.128

[2] Roger McHugh, editor, *Jack B. Yeats A Centenary Gathering*. An interview with Jack Butler Yeats by Shotoro Oshima, The Dolmen Press, 1971, p.54

[3] *Ár nÉire*, Vol. IX, No 12 p.189 – 190

[4] James White, *Jack B. Yeats, 1871 – 1957, A Centenary Exhibition*, Secker & Warburg, 1971, p.14

[5] Hilary Pyle, op.cit., p.139

1

THE TRAIN THROUGH THE WOOD

oil on slateboard 1925

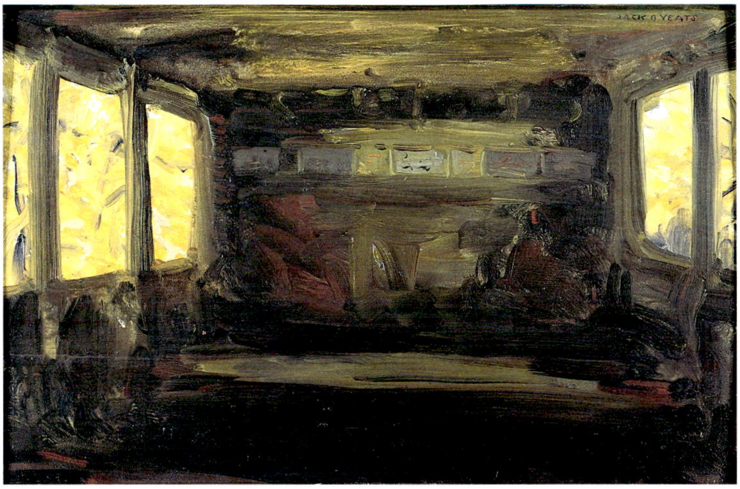

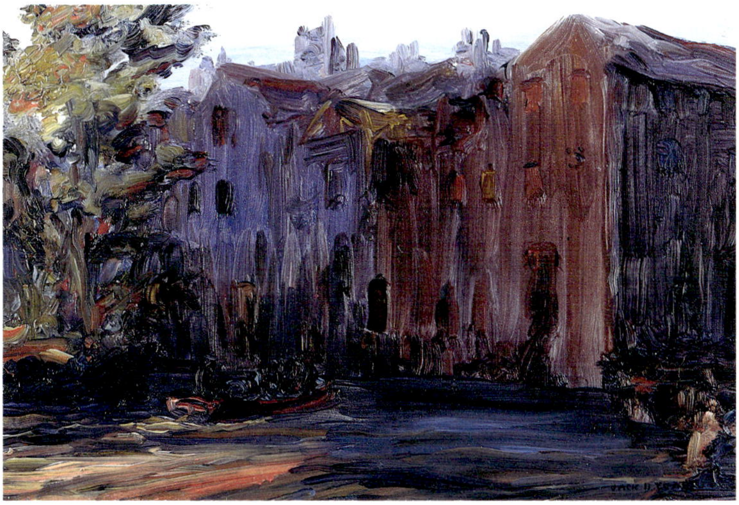

2

THE RETURN FROM THE PICNIC

oil on slateboard 1925

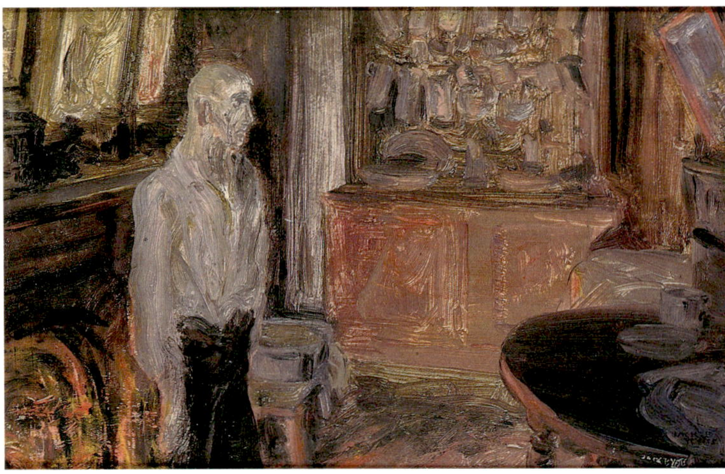

3

QUAY WORKER'S HOME

oil on slateboard 1927

4

THE EMIGRANT

oil on slateboard 1927

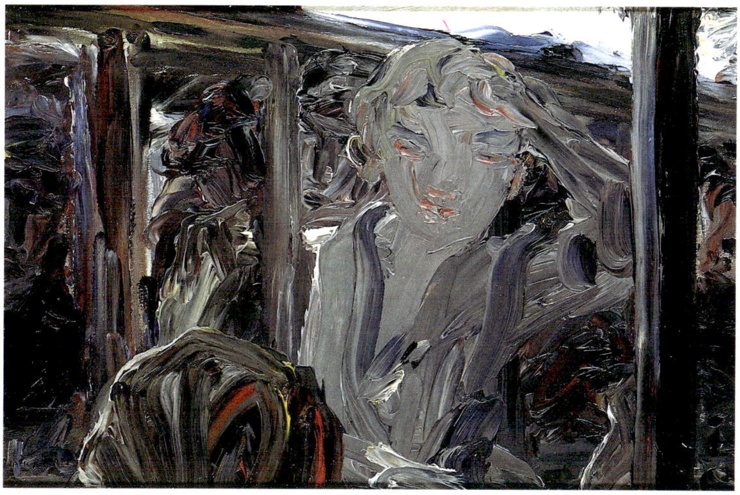

5

O'CONNELL BRIDGE

oil on canvas 1927

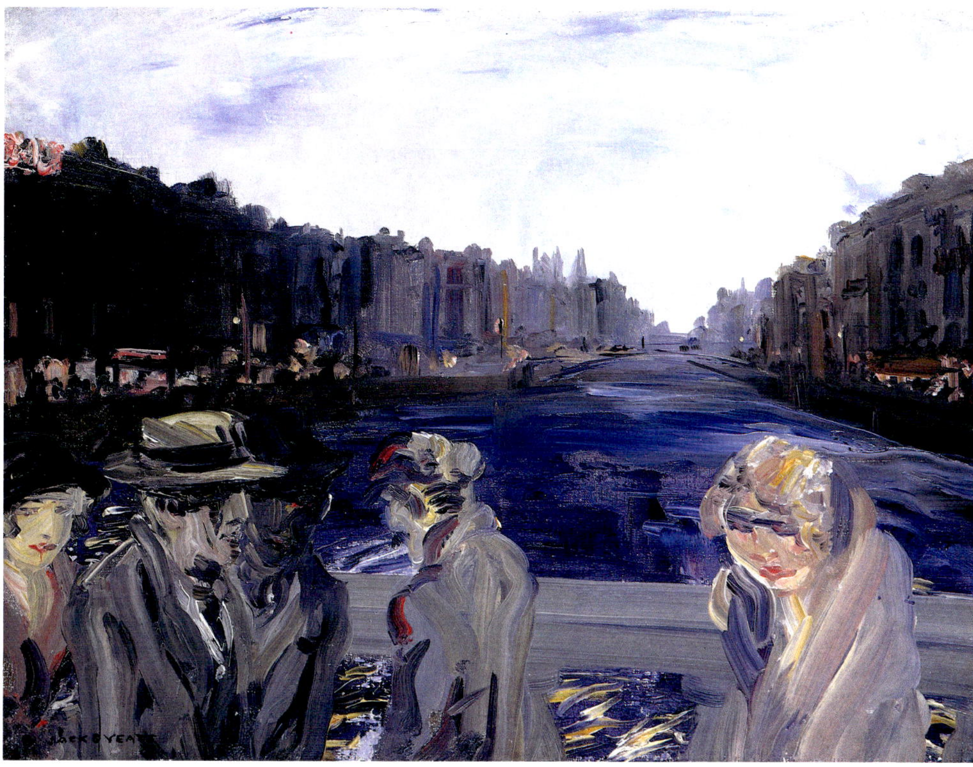

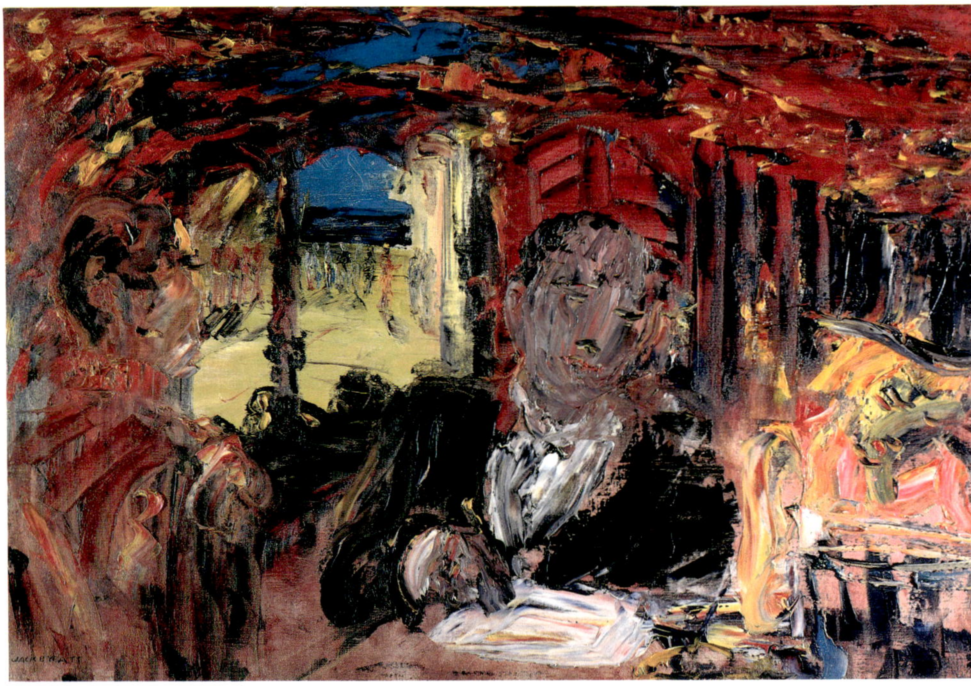

6

THE AVENGER

oil on canvas 1928

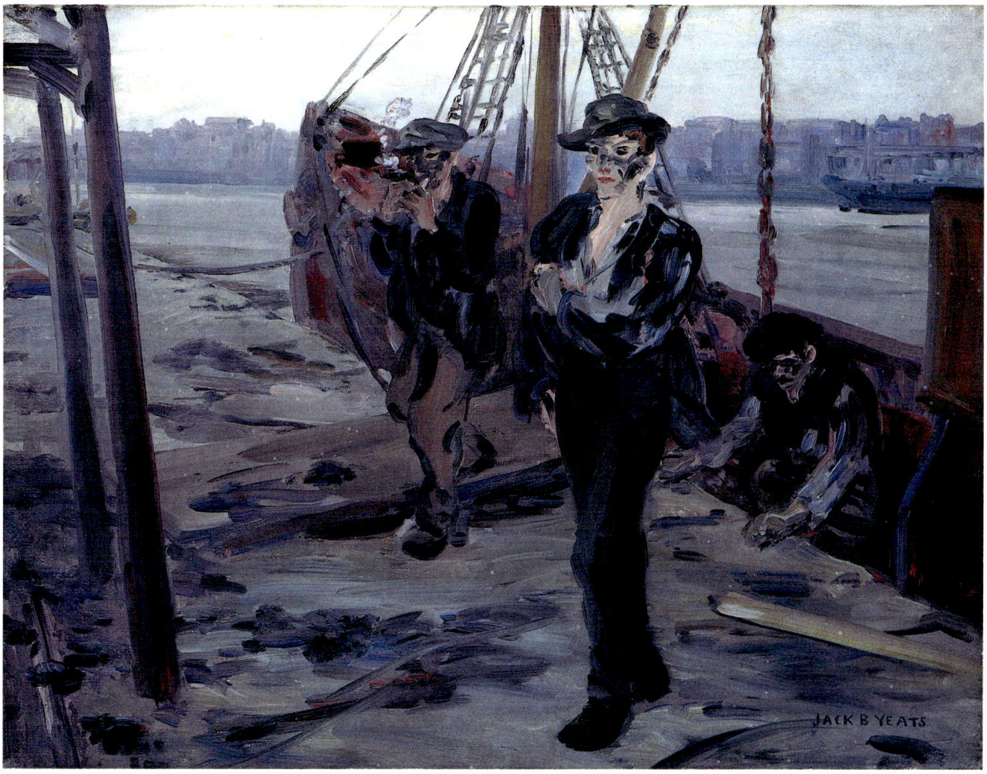

7
COAL BOAT

oil on canvas 1929

8

GOING TO WOLFE TONE'S GRAVE

oil on canvas 1929

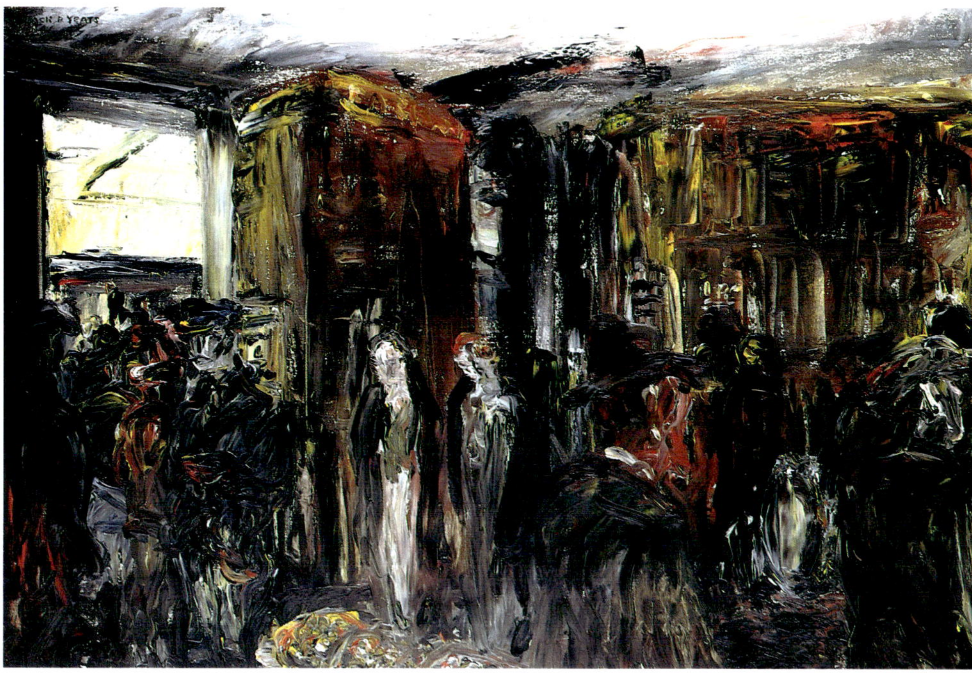

9

THE SWAN

oil on board 1936

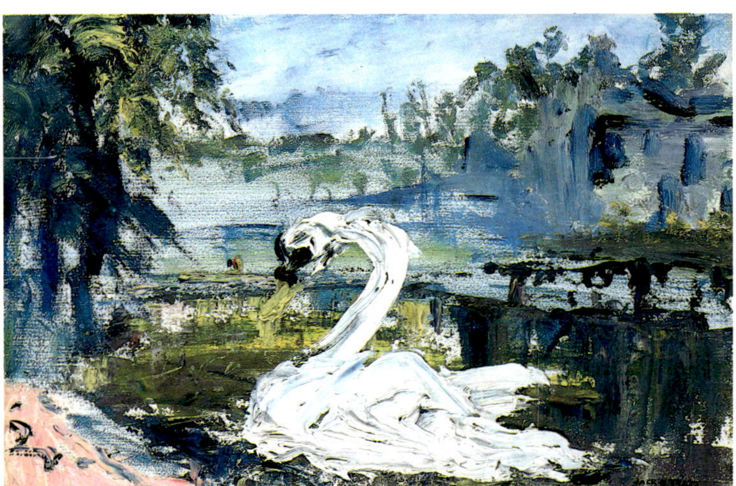

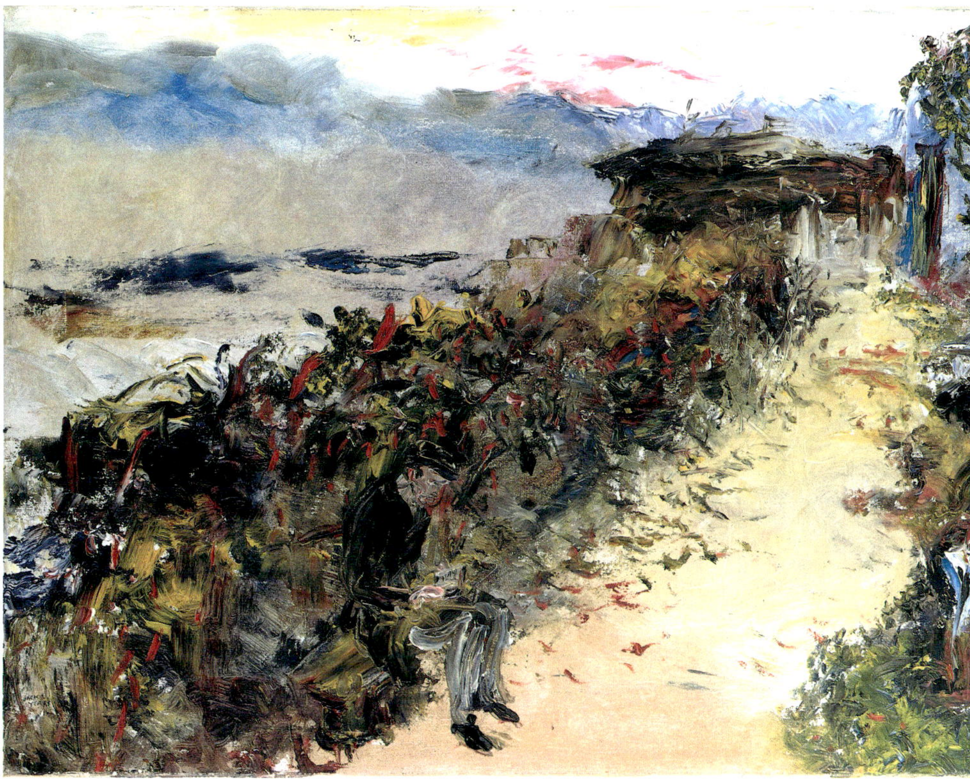

10

A STORM/GAILLSHION

oil on canvas 1936

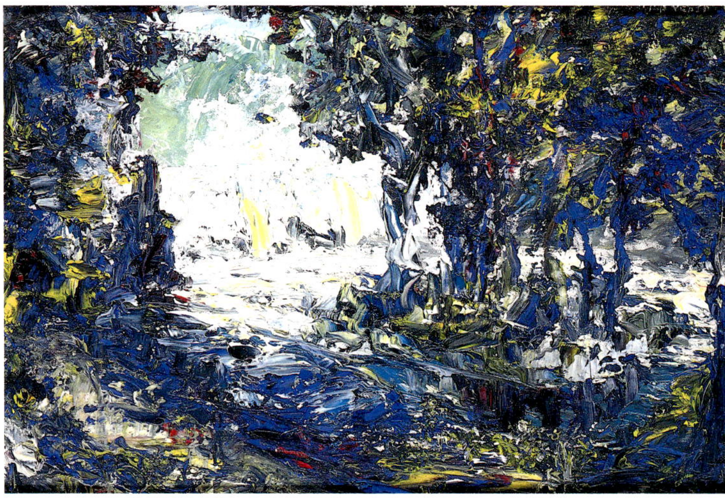

11

A LITTLE WATERFALL

oil on board 1941

12

SLEEP

oil on canvas 1944

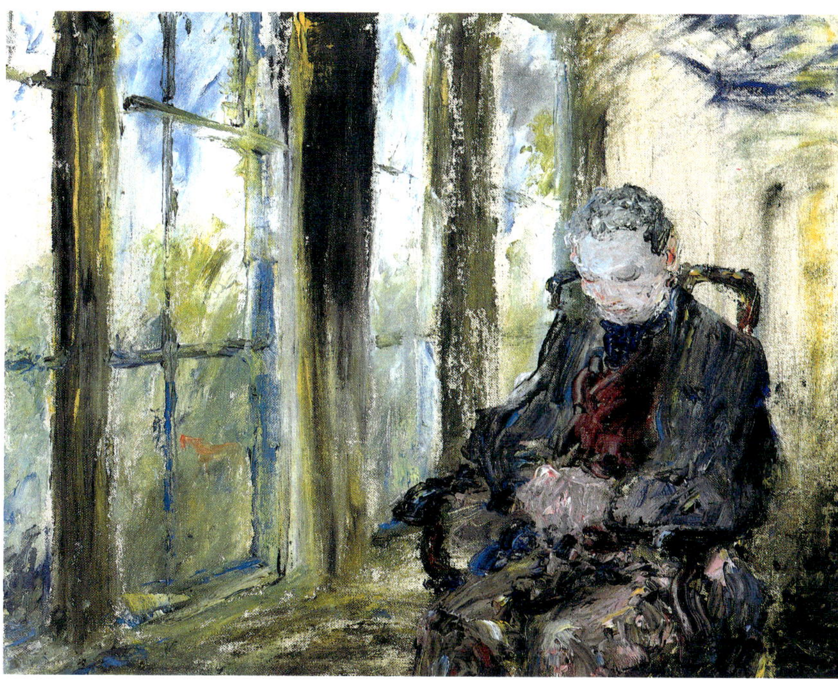

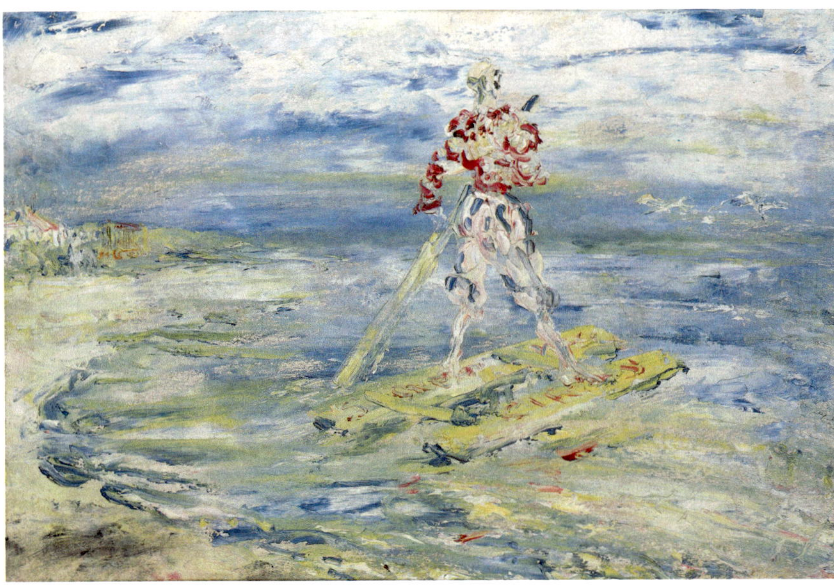

13

THE CLOWN OF OCEAN

oil on canvas 1945

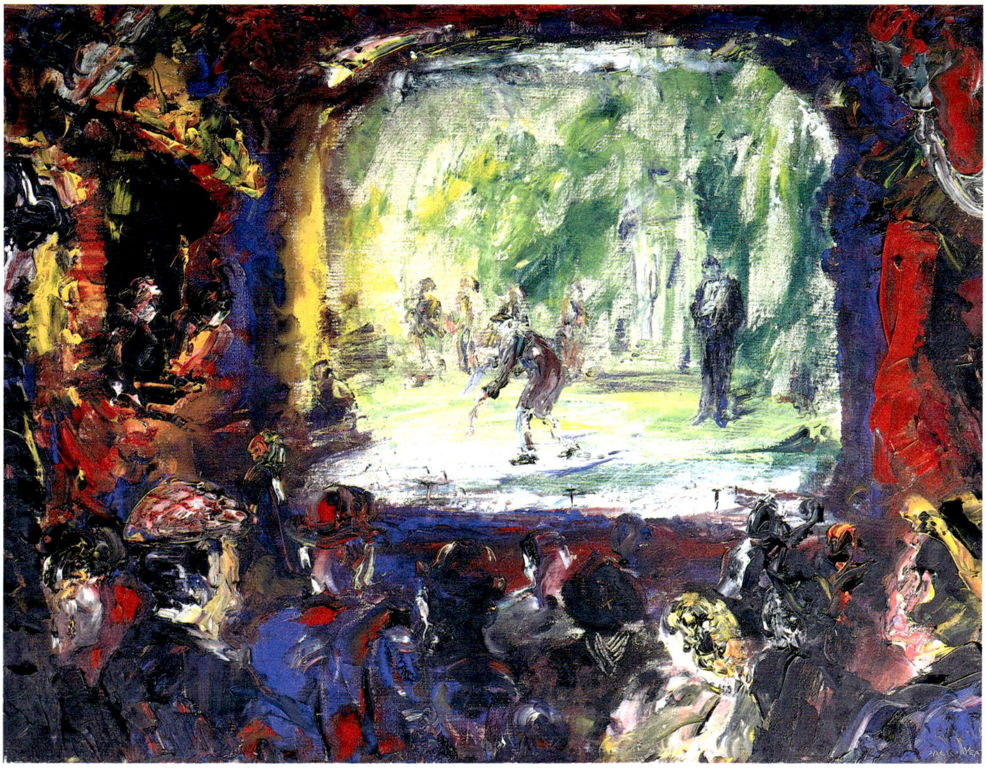

14

THE AMATEUR VENTRILOQUIST

oil on canvas 1945

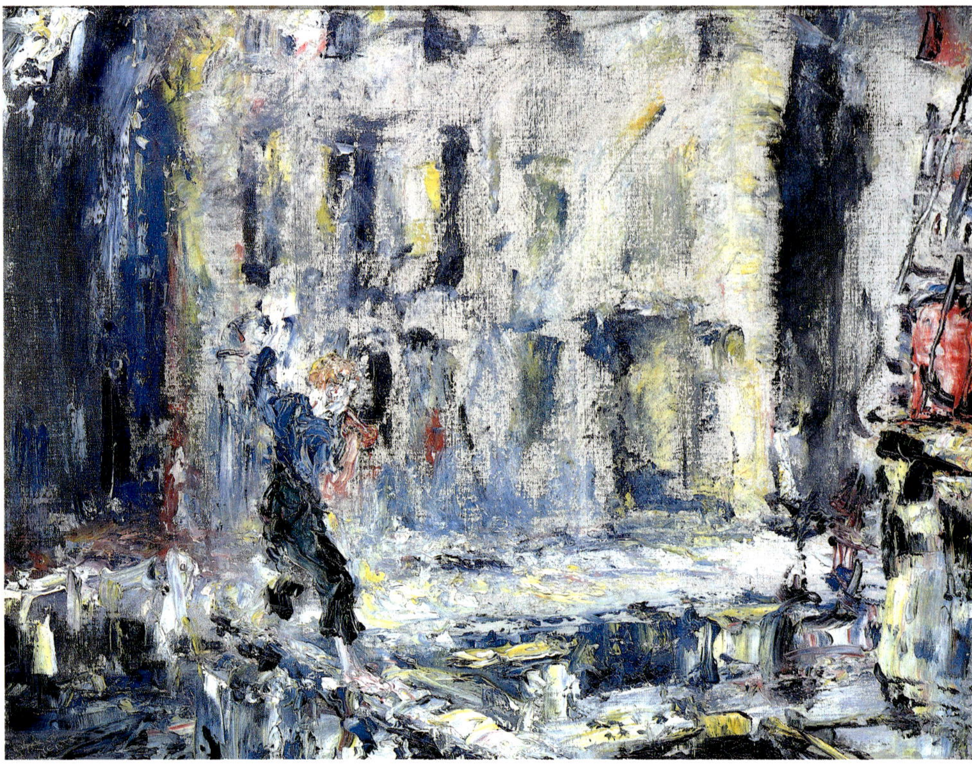

15
THE DERELICT SHIP

oil on canvas 1946

16

FRETTED TREES

oil on canvas 1947

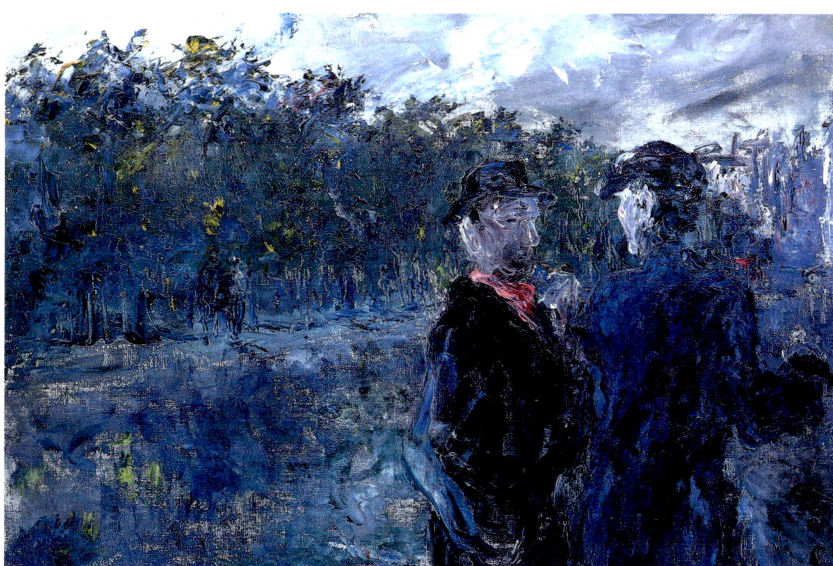

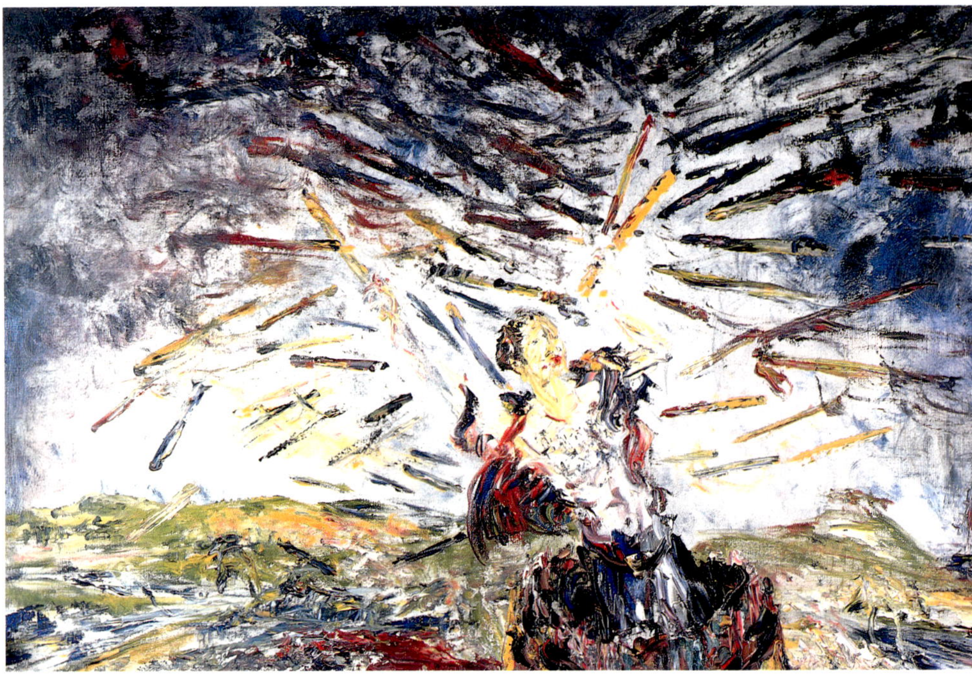

17

HUMANITY'S ALIBI

oil on canvas 1947

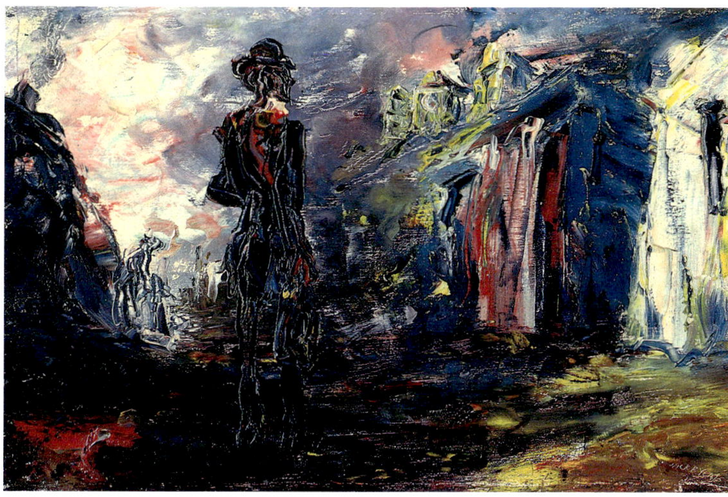

18

A NEW TOWN

oil on board 1947

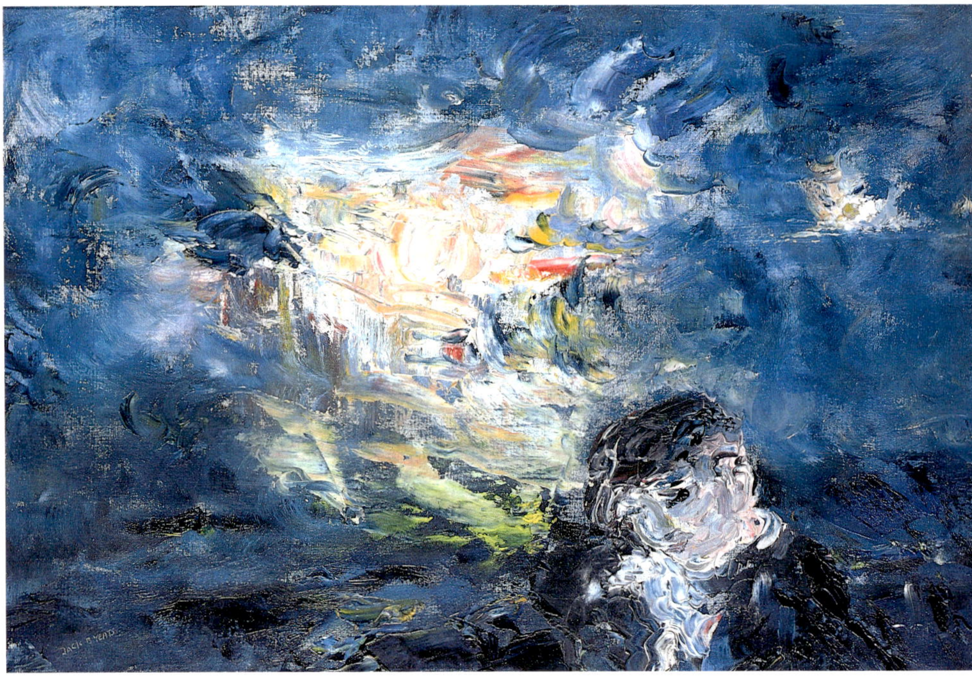

19

THE SUN

oil on canvas 1947

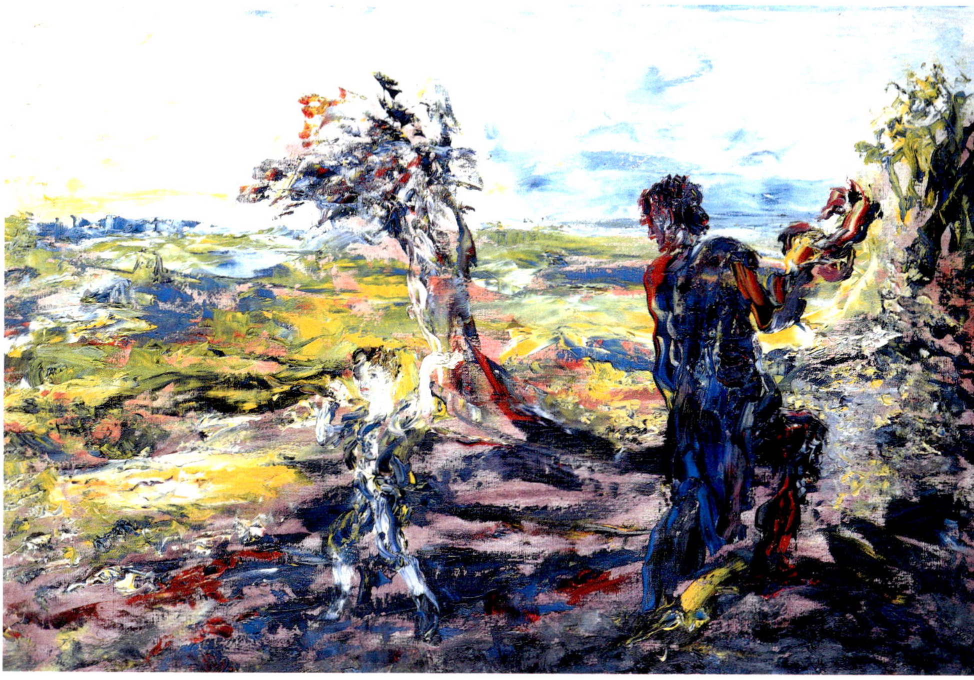

20

ON THE MOVE

oil on canvas 1950

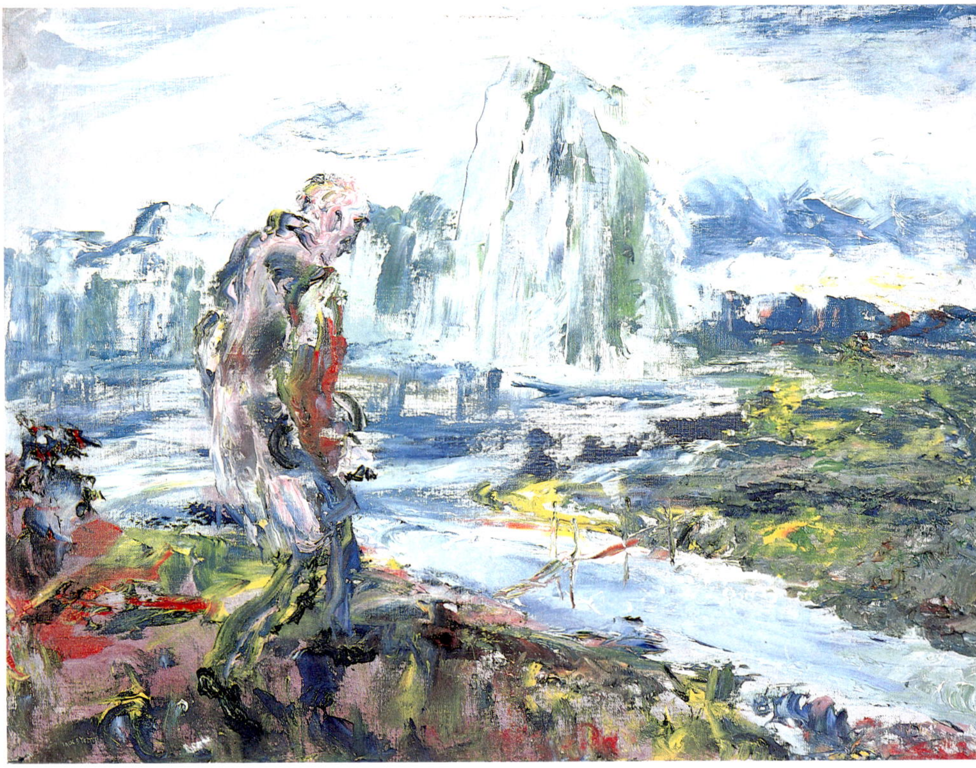

21

ON THROUGH THE SILENT LANDS

oil on canvas 1951

22

THERE IS LIFE IN THE FIRE YET

oil on canvas 1951

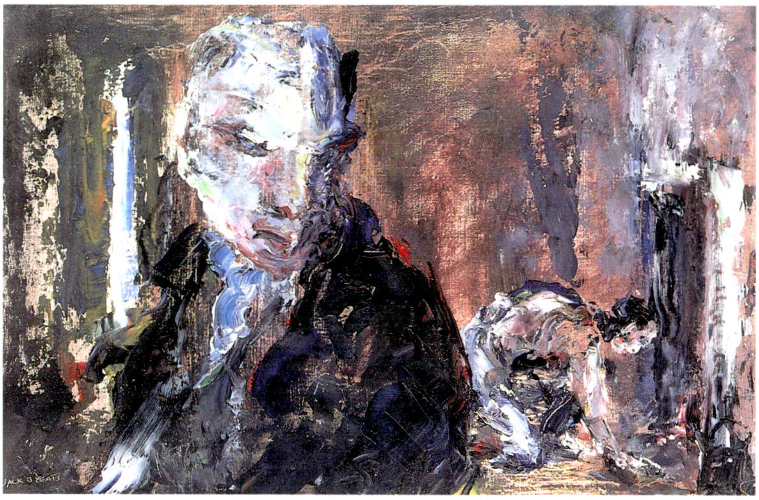

23

THE CIRCUS HAS COME

oil on canvas 1952

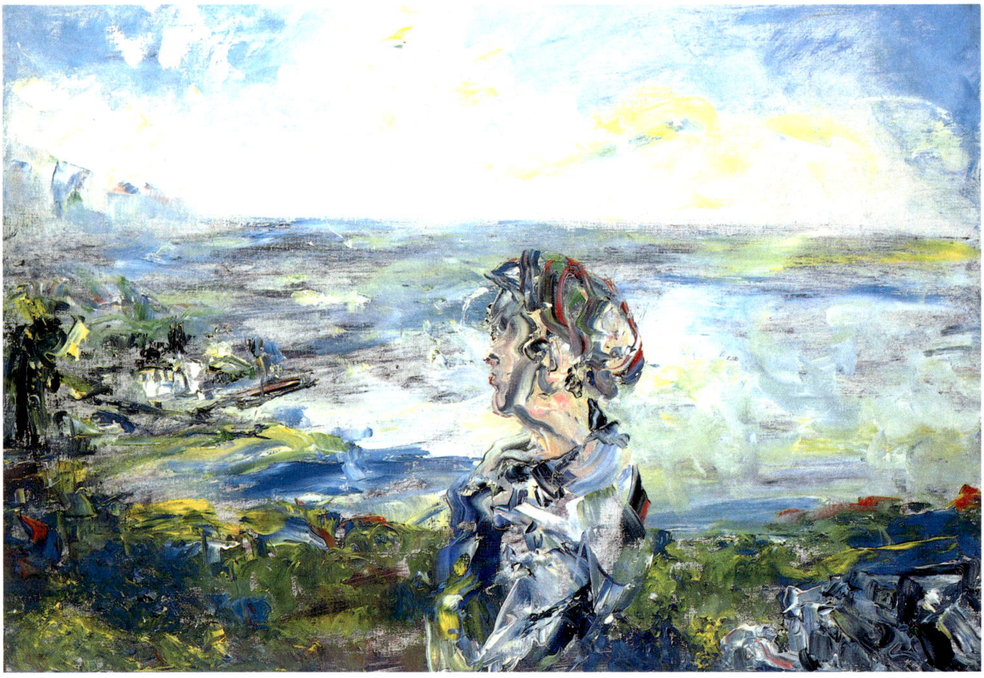

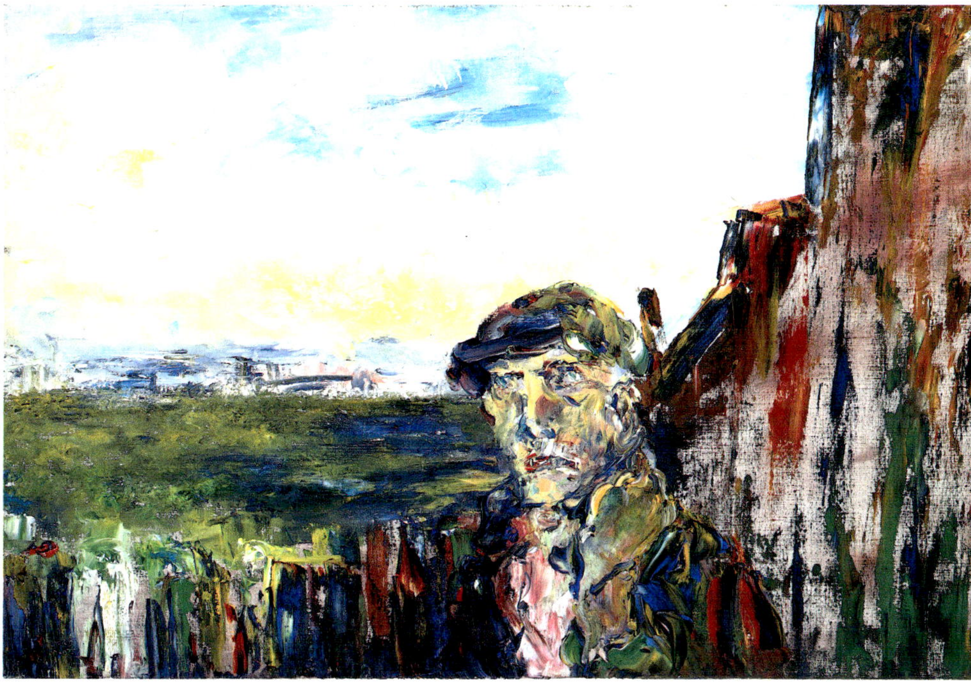

24
THE GROUND MAN

oil on canvas 1952

25

STRANGE MEETING

oil on canvas 1953

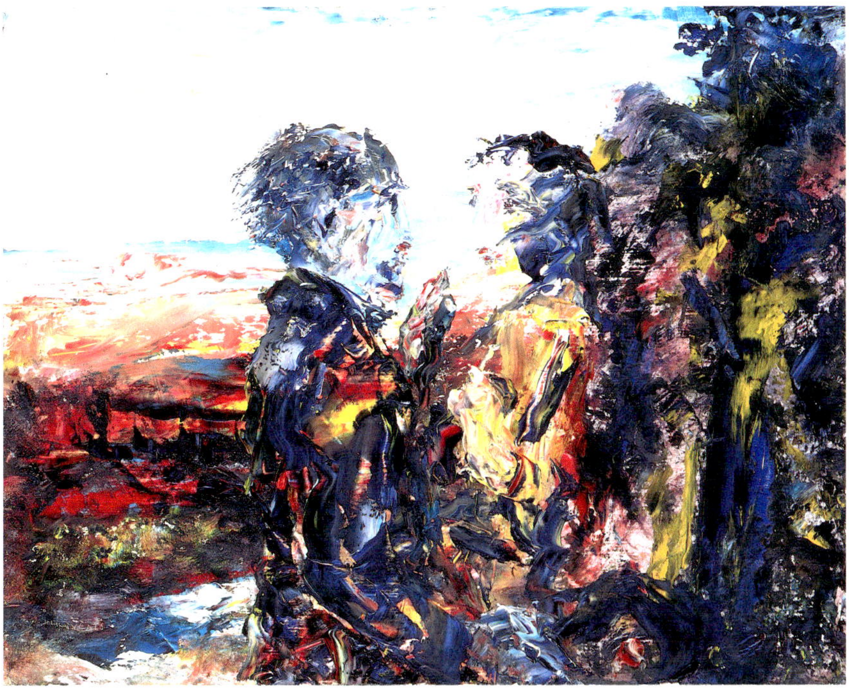

26

A SPECKLED MEMORY

oil on board 1954

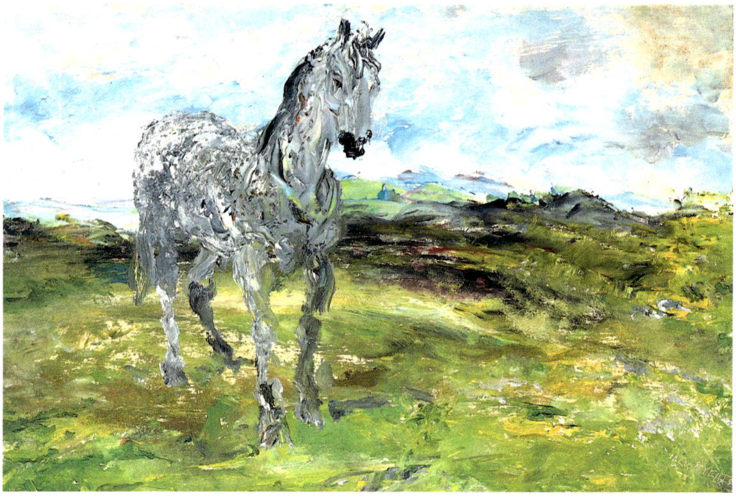

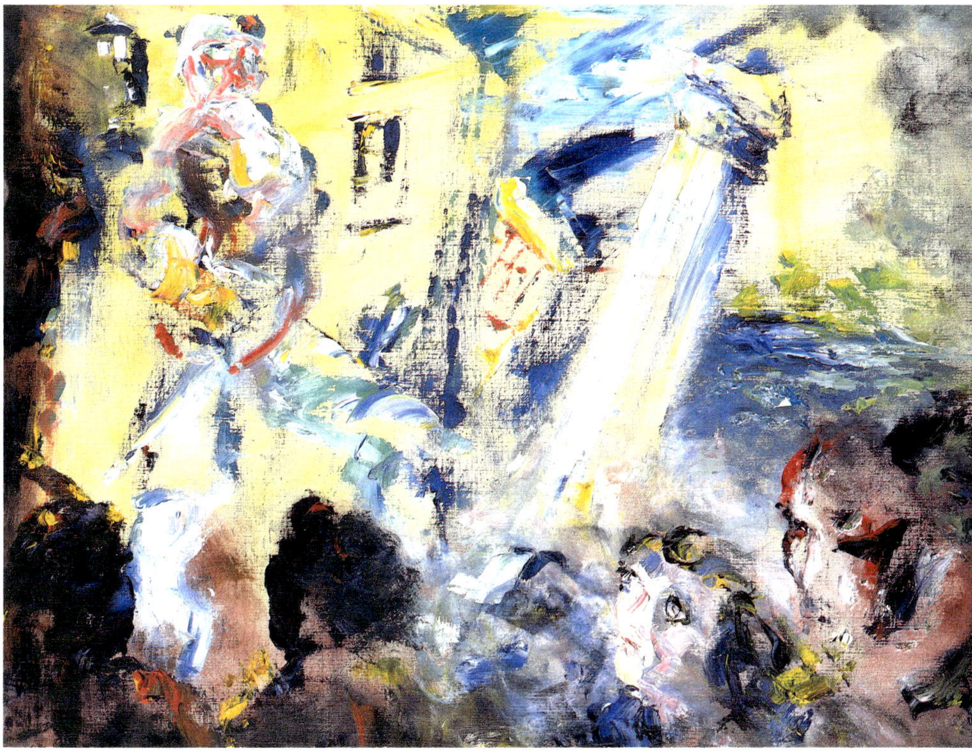

27

FORGIVE HIM

oil on canvas 1954

28

THAT WE MAY NEVER MEET AGAIN

oil on canvas 1955

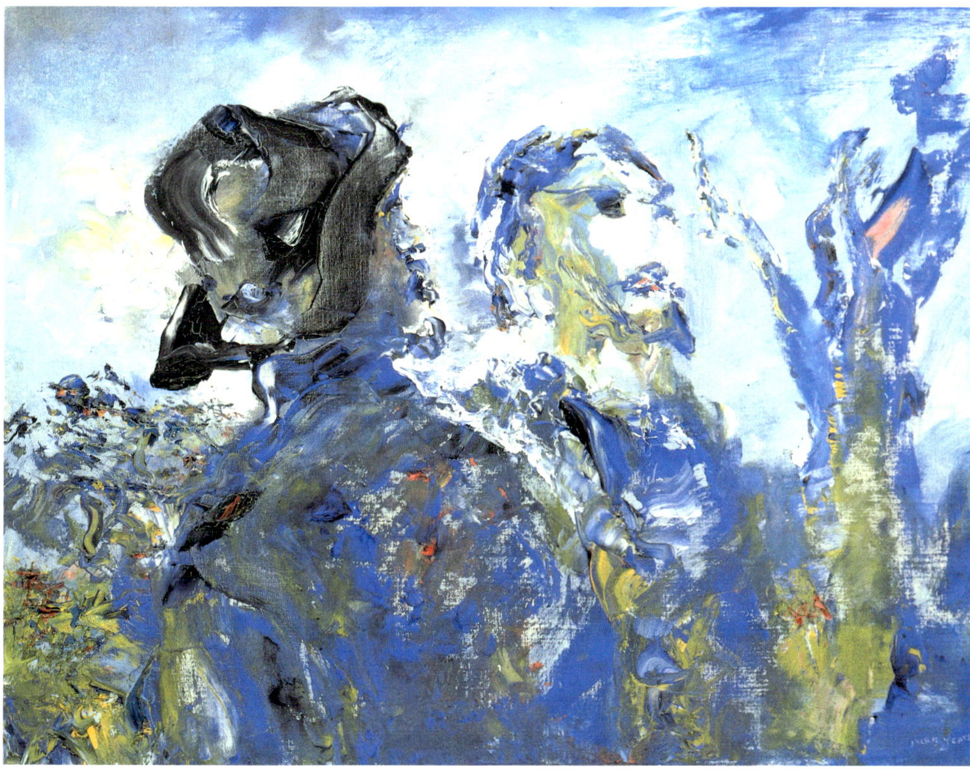

THE LIFE & DEATH OF AN ARTIST

He is an old, very tall, thin man. His face is that of an old, tall, upright man; no literary image should be used to describe the face of this life-long image maker. And when I told him, thinking of how many tinkers, and horse traders and wanderers he had painted, that Léger had said that the artist was in the same class as the *clochard*, because in their common desire for the danger of maximum freedom they backed the same horse, the only difference being that the artist won and the *clochard* lost – when I told him this, he smiled, sharing his own experiences with himself, and added like an old man, and exactly like an old man and nothing else – except that he was attentive enough to nod at the speed with which I was drinking his Irish whiskey – he added, 'Yes, but some of the best people are losers. I've known some terrible brilliant men – all brilliance on the outside, and all morality inside, as a second line of defence.'

How he hates morality, this octogenarian. For him morality is a foreign imposition brought on the point of the bayonet. A romantic conception? But this man is one of the last living romantics – not because he is still alive, but because he lives his philosophy. On the periphery of the twentieth century, he has challenged Thoreau's nineteenth century remark, 'It is now noble to profess because it was once noble to live.' He has not played with the light effects so that the critics, goggling, search for the right word, earn their money by their hard struggle, and eventually spell out the label Romanticism; he is a romantic who has always walked out into the darkness, so that when he meets his travellers there is no need to portray them in fancy dress, for they already wear all that he has imagined in his own previous dark solitary journey. When a man advances into a cave, the dark winds round his throat and trails behind him like a scarf. When a girl stands on the shore, look how the sea becomes her – in both palpitating senses of that word *become*. When soldiers are seen striking camp for the *second* time, all movements are automatic and even the dawn is tarnished, because 'supposing you know you must die at dawn and you prepare yourself, and supposing you are reprieved and then have to face another dawn with the same knowledge – that is hard indeed.'

No one has ever been allowed to watch him paint. Before his wife died he used to take a white pipe-cleaner – 'like a sheep's leg' – and bend it into a circle and put it on the knob of his studio door to warn her that he was at work. A question of professional secrets? No, a question of his being desperately – and to us rational materialists, almost incomprehensibly – anxious that he might not be able to rediscover his own secrets. 'And Carlyle,' he laughs, 'thought ninety-nine per cent of genius was taking pains. I am sure now his poor wife had something to say about that. A painting is an event. And that's what that old Gamp Fry – do you still read him? – a grey-minded man and a timid painter, too – that's what he never understood. You can plan events, but if they go according to your plan they are not events.'

I disagreed with him about art being amoral and said that I thought the artist had a moral obligation: namely, to identify himself to the full with his subject.

His reply was to fill up my glass, refocus his eyes and tell me about his subjects. He sang, 'The boy I love is in the gallery' with Marie Lloyd, he showed me with his long, thin hands the secrets of the grabbing, conjuring tricks plied at the horse fairs, he fought old fights in the ring, he brought in a horse suspiciously offered for sale in the middle of the night, and examined it with a lantern, he kept a late rendezvous in the East India Docks, and then coming back to my point he said: 'Maybe. But too many moral people expect you to be respectful to your subjects. And how can you be that if you identify yourself with them? And then these same people come along and ask you, 'How long did it take you to do that painting?' and if you say months, they think it's worth a lot. That's morality for you.'

Referring to Jack Yeats's paintings, Samuel Beckett wrote, 'He grows Watteauer and Watteauer.' That is a perceptive stimulating remark. The differences are obvious: the folds in the silk have become tears in rough cloth: the artificial gestures of the *fête* in the enclosed garden have become the so similar but *naturally* exaggerated gestures with which travellers greet each other on a deserted open plain. The nervousness of the technique has become magnified, as though one square centimetre of Watteau were painted to the scale of a square foot: Yeats is coarser – and gayer. But their subjects – transience, mortality – are the same, and, although Watteau's vision was melancholically ironic and Yeats's, just because it is coarser, is heroic – death for him is the condition for human consciousness and therefore for freedom – there has been no artist between these two who has specifically dealt with the same subject so poignantly and unsentimentally.

Thus Yeats's theme is universal. That is not to say that his works would fit easily into the modern cosmopolitan museum. They would not, for the works which are pre-fabricated for that museum are by artists who prefer to 'profess' rather than live. And it is because Yeats realizes that this profession of being all things to all men means the denial of living art, that he has always refused to allow his work to be reproduced in colour and bound in sumptuous volumes. The fact that he has consequently lost international recognition means less to him than the fact that each painting is an event – a single event. And when publishers have promised him the most accurate and faithful reproductions, he has replied: 'The better they are the worse they are.'

Like all artists who achieve a degree of universality, Yeats is closely bound with the local and particular. Cézanne seems formalized until one has seen Provence through his eye. Yeats seems too 'mobile', over-spontaneous, until one has watched the west coast of Ireland. And watched is the word, for the landscape there is a fast series of events, not a view – an unchanging structure. The land is as passive as a bog can be. The sky is all action. I am told that the sky is similar in California, and perhaps along any ocean coast facing west. But in Ireland the sky is a dancer, tender and wild alternately, and then furious, ripping her clothes and parading her golden body to get just one glimmer of response from the peat. And she gets it. For in the ruts and bog puddles and along the wet shoulders of a tarpaulin the water flashes back, seeming by contrast with its surroundings even brighter than her. And it is this wild dancing and wilder response that Yeats has painted. This is how the green lying on a distant hill is pulled, by the sheer movement of a foreground head turning, into that head's eyes, whilst the miles between the head and the hill remain. This is how a red streak in the sky becomes the gauntlet of a rider and the belly of his horse below.

Not that Yeats has ever been a literal landscape painter. He transforms everything within his imagination. And if I had to give a single reason why I believe he is a great painter I would cite the consistency of this power of his to transform. Like Giorgione or Delacroix, he can cast his spell even over the foreground of his pictures. Most modern romantics because they do not live their philosophy can never bring their romantic vision nearer than the middle distance: the foreground simply remains a frame. Yeats – and in this he is unlike his brother – has never stepped out of his vision. He has continued to embrace mortality in the face of every moral warning. But he has been able to do this because his vision has its roots in his country: visually in the Irish landscape: poetically in Irish folklore: and ideologically in the fact that Ireland has only up to now been able to fight English imperialism with the image of the independent individual Rebel.

* * *

Jack Yeats is now dead. For those who are at all aware of an artist as a man his paintings change after his death. Whilst he is alive all his works, even those that are declared finished, are seen to some extent as works in progress; as you look at them you relate them to an imagination that still exists and is still working; his works then chart a progress. After his death they become final and definitive; they no longer chart his progress, they gather together to form his destination. In Dublin I wanted to ask Yeats about his paintings. Today similar questions do not even come to mind. The living artist is either more or less open to intervention, persuasion, influence, questioning, which is why his work can have an urgency for us which is different in kind from anything we can get from works of the past. From them we can only learn. There is thus a logic in the fact that only when an artist is dead can he be fully recognized as great, as a source of understanding and inspiration, but this is different, for our relationship with him then cannot be purely a pupil-teacher one: we are also related to him by a hundred and one other mutual responsibilities because both he and we are alive. Yeats has now become a master.

Very many of Yeats's last pictures are implicitly, but not explicitly, concerned with death. *Sleep Sound*: two figures lie on a moor, the sky above them heavy as the breathing of those who might keep their wake. *The Hour of Sleep*: a man nods in a mountain field of gentians and behind him is a monolithic, immovable, dead block of stone. *The Nights are Closing In*: two figures talk against a sky being torn to tatters. *Tir-na-n-Og*: which means the country where neither age nor death exists and where the Irish peasant believes 'you will get happiness for a penny'.

How is it then, the reader may ask, that I, a Marxist, can find so much truth and splendour in the art of an arch-romantic such as Yeats? Professor George Thomson has already answered this question by quoting the painter's brother:

Sing on: somewhere at some new moon,
We'll learn that sleeping is not death,
Hearing the whole earth change its tune.

What, in other words, we have in common with the genuine romantic is a sense of the future, an awareness of the possibility of a world other than the one we know. (I say *genuine* romantic to distinguish men like Yeats or Géricault, who lived their romanticism, from those who merely use romantic poses.) Strange as it may sound, no European country had until recently a greater sense of the future than Ireland. This was partly because no bourgeoisie had destroyed its popular art, which was an art of longing, and partly because its colonial status bred rebels. Even the fairies, the ghosts, the banshees, the famous songs, the notorious and magnificent edifices of words that could be built in a few moments out of nothing, were partly expressions of an Irish conviction that there was something beyond the facts of that poverty which quite simply halved their population in the second half of the nineteenth century. Even today the IRA flickers with something of the same spirit. Ireland has not yet reached that critical point where she can only defend her way of life: she is still striving, staggering, suffering and dreaming towards one. And however much the keep-art-pure-sirs may hate it, it is impossible to appreciate Yeats fully without understanding something of this.

It is this which explains how Yeats was a modern painter – he had no nostalgia for the art styles of the past – and yet was apparently quite uninfluenced by Cubism and Abstract art. It is also this which explains why his work, which is expressionist in character, is nevertheless quite free from the sense of personal desperation found in mid-European Expressionism. (In this Yeats resembles the Indonesian painter, Affandi, and it may well be that this kind of romantic but outward-facing expressionism is the natural style of art for previously exploited nations fighting for independence – modern classicism requires an industrial society.) Yeats's romantic view of life brought him closer to his subjects – his horsemen, actors, lovers, talkers, beggars – instead of separating him from them. His paintings, as opposed to the landscapes they include, do not convey loneliness; on the contrary, they appear to be made out of the stuff of legends that have been as much handled and commonly slept in as the blankets on the inn's bed for travellers. Further, it is Yeats's Irish background which explains why his direct influence on younger European painters would be a dangerous one, leading to theatrical mannerism.

What his background cannot directly explain is Yeats's pictorial genius as a painter: his sense of colour, like a Venetian's, but derived from rags and a lean shimmering world, instead of from velvets and mellow feasts: his draughtsmanship, nervous, spontaneous – sometimes achieved, I suspect, by painting with the very nozzle of the tube of pigment, occasionally becoming incoherent, but at its best describing forms breaking against the surface of the mist, the dusk, the sunlight, like fishes breaking the surface of water as they leap across it: his sense of pictorial unity, so that for all the shreds of colour and the shimmer and the speed, his canvases as a whole are permanently calm.

Both Yeats's pictorial genius and his spirit can be epitomized by a small canvas called *The First Away*. It represents simply a man's head and shoulders against the sky. The way in which the smooth milky surface of the sky and the curdled paint describing the man's features are held together in unity is a miracle of tonal and colour adjustment, as refined as any passage in Braque. As for the content: the man's eyes in his pale shriven face are closed in rapture. Is it he or is it the horse who is first away? And away to where?

To where:

Delight makes all of the one mind,
The riders upon the galloping horses
The crowd that closes in behind.

Now that he is dead, Yeats has become a master: he teaches us to hope.

John Berger

LIST OF WORKS

1
THE TRAIN THROUGH THE WOOD
oil on slateboard 1925
9 X 14 INS, 22.9 X 35.6 CM
Waddington Galleries Ltd

2
THE RETURN FROM THE PICNIC
oil on slateboard 1925
9 X 14 INS, 22.9 X 35.6 CM
Waddington Galleries Ltd

3
QUAY WORKER'S HOME
oil on slateboard 1927
9 X 14 INS, 22.9 X 35.6 CM
Waddington Galleries Ltd

4
THE EMIGRANT
oil on slateboard 1927
9 X 14 INS, 22.9 X 35.6 CM
Waddington Galleries Ltd

5
O'CONNELL BRIDGE
oil on canvas 1927
18 X 24 INS, 45.7 X 61 CM
Pyms Gallery, London

6
THE AVENGER
oil on canvas 1928
24 X 36 INS, 61 X 91.5 CM
Pyms Gallery, London

7
COAL BOAT
oil on canvas 1929
18 X 24 INS, 45.7 X 61 CM
Waddington Galleries Ltd

8
GOING TO WOLFE TONE'S GRAVE
oil on canvas 1929
24 X 36 INS, 61 X 91.5 CM
Pyms Gallery, London

9
THE SWAN
oil on board 1936
9 X 14 INS, 22.9 X 35.6 CM
Waddington Galleries Ltd

10
A STORM/GAILLSHION
oil on canvas 1936
18 X 24 INS, 45.7 X 61 CM
Waddington Galleries Ltd

11
A LITTLE WATERFALL
oil on board 1941
9 X 14 INS, 22.9 X 35.6 CM
Waddington Galleries Ltd

12
SLEEP
oil on canvas 1944
14 X 18 INS, 35.5 X 46 CM
Theo Waddington

13
THE CLOWN OF OCEAN
oil on canvas 1945
14 X 21 INS, 35.6 X 53.3 CM
Waddington Galleries Ltd

14
THE AMATEUR VENTRILOQUIST
oil on canvas 1945
18 X 24 INS, 46 X 61 CM
Private Collection, courtesy of Pyms Gallery

15
THE DERELICT SHIP
oil on canvas 1946
18 X 24 INS, 45.7 X 61 CM
Theo Waddington Fine Art Ltd

16
FRETTED TREES
oil on canvas 1947
14 X 21 INS, 35.6 X 53.3 CM
Private Collection

17
HUMANITY'S ALIBI
oil on canvas 1947
24 X 36 INS, 61 X 91.4 CM
Bristol Museums and Art Gallery

18
A NEW TOWN
oil on board 1947
9 X 14 INS, 22.9 X 35.6 CM
Waddington Galleries Ltd

† *only showing at Leeds*

19
THE SUN
oil on canvas 1947
14 X 21 INS, 35.6 X 53.3 CM
Pyms Gallery, London

20
ON THE MOVE†
oil on canvas 1950
24 X 34 INS, 60.9 X 88.9 CM
Leeds Museums and Galleries (City Art Gallery)

21
ON THROUGH THE SILENT LANDS
oil on canvas 1951
20 X 27 INS, 50.8 X 68.6 CM
Collection Ulster Museum, Belfast

22
THERE IS LIFE IN THE FIRE YET
oil on canvas 1951
9 x 14 ins, 22.9 x 35.6 cm
Theo Waddington Fine Art Ltd

23
THE CIRCUS HAS COME
oil on canvas 1952
24 X 36 INS, 61 X 91.4 CMS
Waddington Galleries Ltd

24
THE GROUND MAN
oil on canvas 1952
24 X 36 INS, 61 X 91.5 CM
Private Collection, Ireland

25
STRANGE MEETING
oil on canvas 1953
14 X 18 INS, 35.6 X 45.7 CM
Private Collection, London

26
A SPECKLED MEMORY
oil on board 1953
9 X 14 INS 22.9 X 35.6 CM
Private Collection, courtesy of Pyms Gallery

27
FORGIVE HIM
oil on canvas 1954
20 X 27 INS, 50.8 X 68.6 CM
Waddington Galleries Ltd

28
THAT WE MAY NEVER MEET AGAIN
oil on canvas 1955
18 X 24 INS, 45.7 X 61 CM
York City Art Gallery

CHRONOLOGY JACK B. YEATS
1871 - 1957

For a detailed list of exhibitions, publications, etc see Hilary Pyle, *Jack B. Yeats: A Biography*, Andre Deutsch Limited, revised edition, 1989.

1871

Jack Butler Yeats, third son and youngest of six of John Butler Yeats, the portrait painter and Susan Pollexfen of Sligo, 23 Fitzroy Road, Regent's Park, London, born on August 29. Younger brother of William Butler Yeats, poet, born 1865.

John Butler Yeats, 'It was my father who made me the artist I am, and kindled the sort of ambition I have transmitted to my sons ...'

1879 – 1887

Lives mainly with his grandparents, William and Elizabeth Pollexfen, at Merville, and then Rathedmond, Sligo. Jack was to inherit the great love of boats and sailing from his grandfather.

1887

Joins his family in London at 58 Eardley Crescent, Earls Court. Attends art classes at South Kensington School of Art, at Chiswick School of Art, and at Westminster School of Art.

1888

Yeats family moves to 3 Blenheim Road, Bedford Park. He starts work as a black and white artist for *The Vegetarian*.

1891

Works as an illustrator for the first time for *Ariel* and *Paddock Life*.

1892

Designs posters for David Allen & Sons in Manchester. Illustrates *Irish Fairy Tales* by his brother, W. B. Yeats.

1894

Staff artist on *Lika Joko*. Marries Mary Cottenham White (Cottie) on August 23, at Emmanuel Church, Gunnersbury, Middlesex and goes to live at Chestnuts, Eastwort, Chertsey, Surrey.

1895

Strand Races, West of Ireland exhibited at the Royal Hibernian Academy in Dublin.

1896

First drawing accepted by *Punch* (appeared regularly in *Punch* from 1910 – 41 under the pseudonym W. Bird).

1897

Moves to Strete, Devon to their own house, Snail's Castle (Cashlauna Shelmiddy). The motif of a round tower rising out of a snail's shell was often employed to embellish books and envelopes. Begins to work consistently in watercolour. First solo show in November, at the Clifford Gallery, Haymarket, London.

1898

Visits Venice. Present at the 1798 Celebrations of the Battle of Carricknagat, Sligo.

1899

First exhibition devoted to Irish subject-matter held at Walker Art Gallery, London and Leinster Hall, Dublin. Visits Coole at the invitation of the playwright, Lady Gregory, and visits Aran Islands. Visits Paris in June.

1900

Death of his mother, Susan Pollexfen Yeats. Paints *Memory Harbour*. Shows plays in his miniature theatre at Cashlauna Shelmiddy.

1901

Presents his first miniature play.

1902

First issue of *A Broadsheet* with Pamela Colman Smith. Ran for twenty four numbers. John B. Yeats and the rest of the family move back to Dublin.

1903

Edits *A Broadsheet* alone until the final number in December. John Masefield, the poet, visits Strete.

1904

Visits New York for his exhibition at the Clausen Galleries, *Recent watercolours*. Contributes to Hugh Lane's Exhibition of Irish Art, Royal Hibernian Academy, Dublin. Publishes *The Bosun and the Bobtailed Comet*. Exhibits as Associate of RHA in November, but allows his associate membership to lapse.

1905

Tours South Connemara with the dramatist, J. M. Synge, to prepare articles for the *Manchester Guardian*.

1906

Illustrates Synge's book, *The Aran Islands*. Paints his first landscape in oil, and continues to paint regularly in oil.

1907

Sees the London performance of *The Playboy of the Western World*, by J. M. Synge. Holidays on The Rhine, visits Rotterdam.

1908

Yeats's father visits New York and settles there permanently. First issue of *A Broadside*, published at Dun Emer Press by Elizabeth Yeats, who founds the Cuala Press, and publishes *A Broadside* there until 1915.

1909

Publication of *A Little Fleet*. Death of Synge.

1910

Sells Cashlauna Shelmiddy and goes to live at Red Ford House, Greystones, Co. Wicklow. Last visit to Sligo for many years for the funeral of his uncle, George Pollexfen.

1911

Visits London. Begins to contribute to RHA again.

1912

Publishes *Life in the West of Ireland*, an album of line drawings, watercolours and oils. Visits Donegal.

1913

Learns Irish and visits Kerry to further his studies. Yeats illustrates the poet Padraic Colum's book, *A Boy in Erinn*. Oil illustrations for Canon Hannay's, *Irishmen All*. Exhibits in International Exhibition of Modern Art, at the Armory, New York and Whitechapel Art Gallery, London, *Summer Exhibition: Irish Art*.

1914

Re-elected Associate Royal Hibernian Academy. Solo exhibition, Walker Art Gallery, London in July is the last occasion that he shows his work until 1920.

1915

Elected to Royal Hibernian Academy. Beginning of illness and depression. First 'half-memory' sketches.

1916

The Easter Rising. Yeats's pictures among those destroyed in the burning of the Royal Hibernian Academy.

1917

Visits his brother W.B. at Thoor, Ballylee, and paints in Roundstone. Moves to 61 Marlborough Road, Donnybrook, Dublin. He found the city less lonely than Greystones. Yeats loved to walk along the canal, 'It was an honour to think that every step was a step nearer the west. Where ever I am I always want to walk towards the west. As well as from a desire to get to an ocean coast, from a wish to be going with the sun.'

1919

Paints landscapes in Skibbereen and Schull.

1920

Closes his Dublin exhibition in sympathy with the national strike protesting against the refusal of the British authorities to recognise the status of political prisoners. Visits Tawin and the Burren.

1921

Member of the Glasgow Society of Painters and Sculptors. Exhibits with Society of Independent Artists, Annual Exhibition, New York, and continues to do so until 1926.

1922

Contributes to the Exposition d'Art Irlandais in Paris and lectures there to the Irish Race Congress. He spoke of painting as 'the fairest and the finest means of communication humanity has yet found because it is the most simple'. Death of John Butler Yeats in America.

1923

Paints *The Liffey Swim* (National Gallery of Ireland, Dublin).

1925

Disassociates himself from Cuala Press and devotes himself entirely to painting. First of three exhibitions at Tooth's, London. Exhibits for first time at the Carnegie International Exhibition, Pittsburgh, continues to exhibit there regularly until 1939.

1927

Exhibition at Ruskin Galleries, Birmingham, *Paintings of Ireland*.

1929

Moves to 18 Fitzwilliam Square in the centre of Dublin. James Joyce (1882 – 1941) buys two of his Liffey paintings and says that 'he and Jack have the same method'.

1930

Publishes his first important prose work, *Sligo*. Exhibits in Toronto. Visit from Samuel Beckett (1906 – 1989) who later buys two paintings. 'I'm glad you liked him', (Beckett) Thomas MacGreevey wrote to Yeats. 'He was completely staggered by the pictures and though he has met many people through me he dismissed them all in his letter with the remark, "and to think I owe meeting Jack Yeats *and* Joyce to you!"'

1931

Included in Barbizon Museum of Irish Art, New York, *Opening Exhibition*.

1932

Exhibition at Ferragail Galleries, New York and Barbican Museum of Irish Art, New York.

1933

Publishes *Apparitions* and *Sailing, Sailing Swiftly*.

1936

Publishes *The Amaranthers*.

1938

Contemporary Art Society Exhibition, London.

1939

Appointed a governor of the National Gallery of Ireland. *Harlequin's Positions* produced by the Abbey Experimental Theatre. Death of W. B. Yeats.

1940

Member of the London Group. Contributes to *British Painting since Whistler* at the National Gallery, London. Death of his sister, Elizabeth Yeats. He returns to the practice of sketching regularly.

1942

Nicholson and Yeats at the National Gallery, London. *La La Noo* performed by the National Theatre Society at the Abbey. Publishes *Ah Well: A Romance in Perpetuity*.

1943

First exhibition with Victor Waddington, Dublin. Exhibits at inaugural show of the Irish Exhibition of Living Art.

1944

Publishes *And To You Also*.

1945

Jack B. Yeats National Loan Exhibition held in Dublin.

1946

D. Litt. Dublin University. Paints *Men of Destiny* (National Gallery of Ireland). Special invitation to exhibit with The Society of Scottish Artists at Royal Scottish Academy, Edinburgh.

1947

Death of his wife Mary Cottenham Yeats. Publishes his last novel, *The Careless Flower*.

1948

Solo exhibition, Temple Newsam House, Leeds. Major retrospective at the Tate Gallery, London, organised by the Arts Council of Great Britain and toured to Aberdeen Art Gallery and RSA, Edinburgh.

1949

In Sand produced at the Abbey Experimental Theatre. Diploma of the Accademia Culturale Adriatica, Milan. Death of his sister, Lily Yeats. Paints *There is No Night* (Hugh Lane Municipal Gallery of Modern Art, Dublin).

1950

Invested as Officer of the Legion of Honour at the French Embassy in Dublin.

1951

American retrospective exhibition opens at Philips Gallery, Washington. Tours to Colorado, Toronto, Detroit and New York. Begins to spend winters in the Portobello Nursing Home, Dublin.

1953

Sketchbooks continue until this year.

1954

Exhibition at the Galerie Beaux Arts in Paris, Samuel Beckett writes homage (see frontispiece)

1955

Goes to live permanently at Portobello Nursing Home. Last exhibition at which Yeats was present, Waddington Galleries, Dublin.

1956

Last exhibition takes place at Belfast Museum and Art Gallery. Visit of John Berger. In November Oskar Kokoschka, who was a great admirer, wrote to 'Jack B. Yeats the great painter (may be the last!)' begging him not to leave his brush idle. 'Please, after having had your rest, let your unruly soul for another turn out in the wonderfull (sic) world of your sagas and take up painting again! You alone can to-day tell in painting such touching stories!'

1957

Dies on March 28.
Buried at Mount Jerome Cemetery, Dublin.

ACKNOWLEDGEMENTS

Catalogue published for the exhibition
Jack B. Yeats: A Celtic Visionary
organised by Manchester City Art Galleries in collaboration with
the Ormeau Baths Gallery, Belfast

City Art Galleries, Manchester 9 March – 21 April 1996
Leeds City Art Galleries 27 April – 2 June 1996
Ormeau Baths Gallery, Belfast 7 June – 6 July 1996

Exhibition administration by Howard Smith; thanks to Tracey Walker
Catalogue edited by Howard Smith and Stephen Snoddy

ISBN 0 901673 49 8

Samuel Beckett (1906-1989) Homage to Jack B. Yeats written April 1954 on the occasion of Yeats's exhibition at Galerie Beaux Arts, Paris; translated by Ruby Cohn.

John Berger The Life and Death of an Artist
(from the book Permanent Red, first published by Methuen & Co, 1960) © John Berger

Photographic credits: lenders and Prudence Cuming Associates

Catalogue designed by Alan Ward @ Axis, Manchester
Typeset in FF Quadraat
Printed by Jackson Wilson Printers Ltd, Leeds
Stochastic Randot Colour Screening by Leeds Photo Litho, Leeds

Manchester City Art Galleries
Mosley Street
Manchester
M2 3JL

Ormeau Baths Gallery
18A Ormeau Avenue
Belfast
BT2 8HS

Exhibition sponsored by Bank of Ireland

Bank of Ireland

Catalogue supported by Pyms Gallery, London

En Toi je me confie

– Pour méditer avec les Psaumes –

Psaumes sélectionnés et commentés par

John Stott

Éditions
EXCELSIS

Édition originale publiée en anglais sous le titre :
Favourite Psalms, par Angus Hudson, Angleterre.

ISBN : 1-85985-036-7

Traduit de l'anglais par Michèle Schneider

ISBN : 2-911260-86-4

La présentation des passages poétiques se calque sur la structure des vers hébraïques – tout en conservant aux lecteurs francophones la possibilité de lire ces textes de manière rythmée (par l'adjonction du signe ˡ à l'intérieur des vers).

Couverture : Jacques Maré – Iota Création –France
Mise en page : Eliette Teissier – Excelsis Sarl

EXCELSIS
Boîte Postale 11 – 26450 Cléon d'Andran – France
Télécopieur : 04 75 90 43 18
Librairie sur site Internet : WWW.XL6.COM

Dépôt légal : Juillet 2000

Imprimé à Singapour

Table des matières

Préface

Que serait l'expression de la foi chrétienne sans les chants ? Un signe infaillible de la plénitude du Saint-Esprit est, justement, que vous louiez « le Seigneur de tout votre cœur par vos chants et vos psaumes » (Éphésiens 5.19). Qui pourrait imaginer un culte d'adoration, où l'on ne chanterait pas ? Il convient de nous exhorter mutuellement. « Venez, crions (ou : « chantons ») notre joie en l'honneur de l'Éternel ! Louons le Seigneur ! Acclamons notre rocher, car il est notre Sauveur ! » (Ps 95.1).

Chaque génération de croyants a composé et publié de nouveaux hymnes et pourtant, le plus ancien recueil de l'Église, le Psautier, ou Livre des Psaumes, n'a jamais perdu de son attrait. Jésus aimait les psaumes. Il les citait souvent. Il s'est même approprié certaines de leurs affirmations : c'est lui le fils et le seigneur de David (Ps 110) et la pierre rejetée, devenue la pierre d'angle (Ps 118). Il s'est également reconnu dans la victime innocente endurant des souffrances atroces, évoquées, par exemple dans les psaumes 22, 31, 41 et 59.

Si les Psaumes ont toujours eu la faveur des chrétiens, c'est qu'ils parlent le langage universel de l'âme humaine. « Le livre des Psaumes, écrivit Rowland E. Prothero dans *The Psalms in Human Life* (1904), contient toute la musique du cœur de l'homme. » Quelle que soit notre humeur spirituelle, il se trouve toujours un psaume qui, en harmonie avec notre cœur, exprime le triomphe ou la défaite, l'enthousiasme ou la dépression, la joie ou le souci, la louange ou le repentir, l'émerveillement ou la colère. Par-dessus tout, les psaumes proclament la grandeur du Dieu vivant, Créateur, Soutien, Roi, Auteur de la Loi, Sauveur, Père, Berger et Juge. Nous ne pouvons que tomber à genoux et adorer ce Dieu que nous révèle le Psautier.

Dans leur collection « Prayer Book Commentaries », les éditions Hodder and Stoughton ont publié en 1966 un ouvrage intitulé *The Canticles and Selected Psalms.* Il est resté longtemps épuisé. Je suis donc reconnaissant à Tim Dowley pour son idée de faire paraître une version modernisée de certains chapitres de cette belle édition illustrée.

John Stott

Psaume 1

La voie des justes et la voie des méchants

Selon Jérôme, ce psaume représenterait pour certains « la préface du Saint-Esprit au Psautier. » Il en constitue certainement une très bonne introduction et développe deux thèmes parmi les préférés des Psaumes.

Le premier est l'opposition entre *le juste* et *le méchant*. Le message de la Bible dans son ensemble, et plus particulièrement celui des écrits de Sagesse, est que les êtres humains entrent dans l'une ou l'autre de ces deux catégories ; il n'en existe pas une troisième. On retrouve ce même contraste entre le juste et le méchant dans les psaumes 32, 36 et 112.

Le second thème concerne le bonheur terrestre et la destinée ultime des êtres humains. Le premier et le dernier mot du psaume 1 posent les termes de l'alternative. Le juste qui met sa joie dans la Loi de Dieu est *heureux*, tandis que l'homme sans Dieu va à *la ruine*. Cette « bénédiction » ou cette « malédiction », selon les termes employés par Jérémie, l'auteur probable de ce psaume (voir Jérémie 17.5-8), transparaissent déjà dans cette vie.

Le Mur Occidental, ou Mur des Lamentations, à Jérusalem, tire son nom des lamentations des Juifs déplorant la destruction du Temple. C'est la seule partie du Temple à laquelle ils avaient presque toujours eu accès.

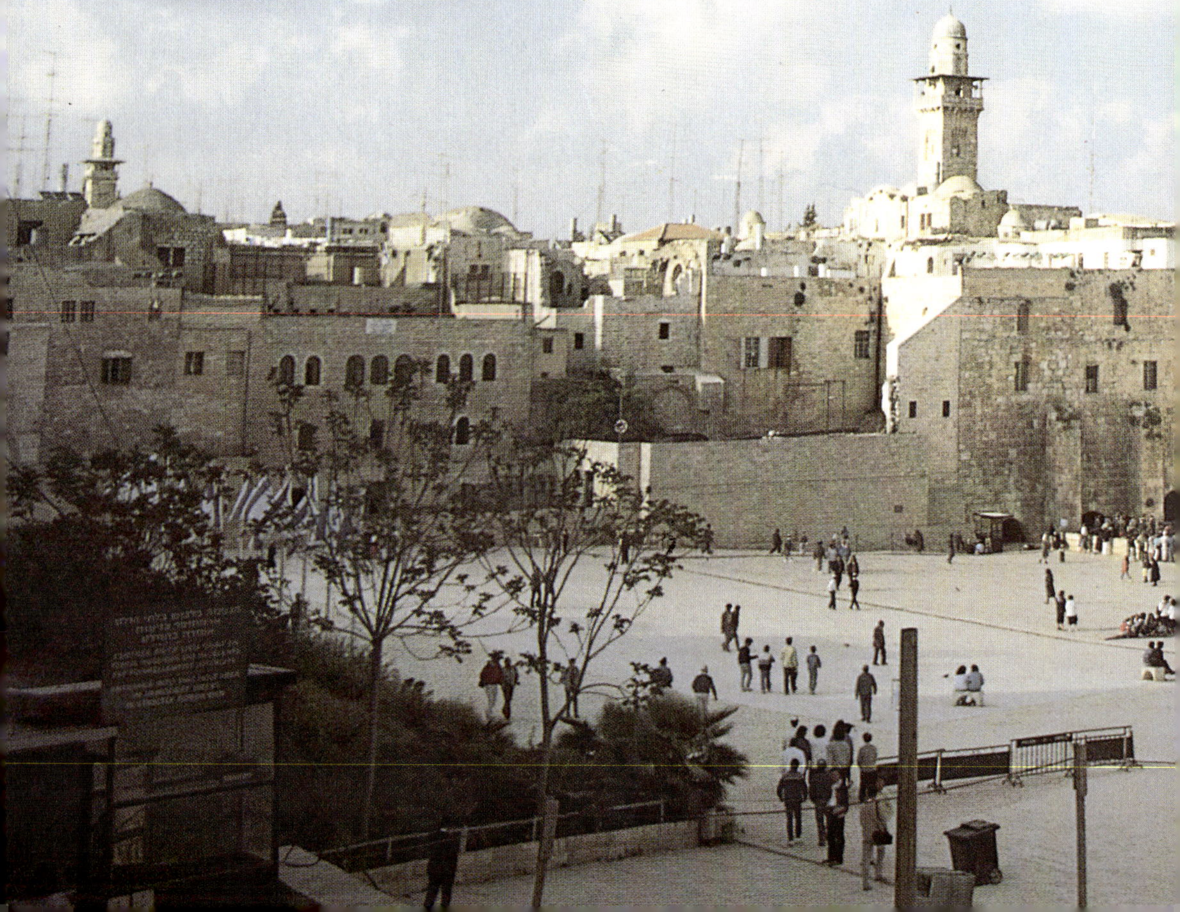

Ces deux thèmes annoncent déjà l'enseignement de Jésus, à savoir que les êtres humains se trouvent, soit sur la route large qui conduit à la perdition, soit sur le chemin étroit qui mène à la vie (Matthieu 7.13, 14).

Le juste prospérera (v. 1-3)

Le juste est d'abord défini par ce qu'il ne fait pas, avant de l'être par ce qu'il fait. Il ou elle *ne marche pas selon les conseils des méchants… ne va pas se tenir sur le chemin des pécheurs… ne s'assied pas en compagnie des moqueurs.* On remarquera avec quel soin les termes ont été choisis, pour composer trois séries de mots parallèles : « marche, se tient, s'assied », « conseil, chemin, compagnie » et « méchants, pécheurs, moqueurs ». De plus, ils évoquent une progression dans le mal. Les hommes qui craignent Dieu ne prennent pas conseil des méchants

1 Heureux l'homme | qui ne marche pas | selon les conseils | des méchants,
qui ne va pas se tenir | sur le chemin des pécheurs,
qui ne s'assied pas | en compagnie des moqueurs.
2 Toute sa joie il la met | dans la Loi de l'Eternel
qu'il médite jour et nuit.
3 Il prospère comme un arbre | planté près d'un courant d'eau ;
il donne toujours son fruit | lorsqu'en revient la saison.
Son feuillage est toujours vert ;
tout ce qu'il fait réussit.
4 Tel n'est pas le cas | des méchants :
ils sont pareils à la paille | éparpillée par le vent.
5 Aussi, lors du jugement, | ils ne subsisteront pas,
et nul pécheur ne tiendra | au rassemblement des justes.
6 Car l'Eternel veille | sur la voie des justes ;
mais le sentier des méchants | les mène à la ruine.

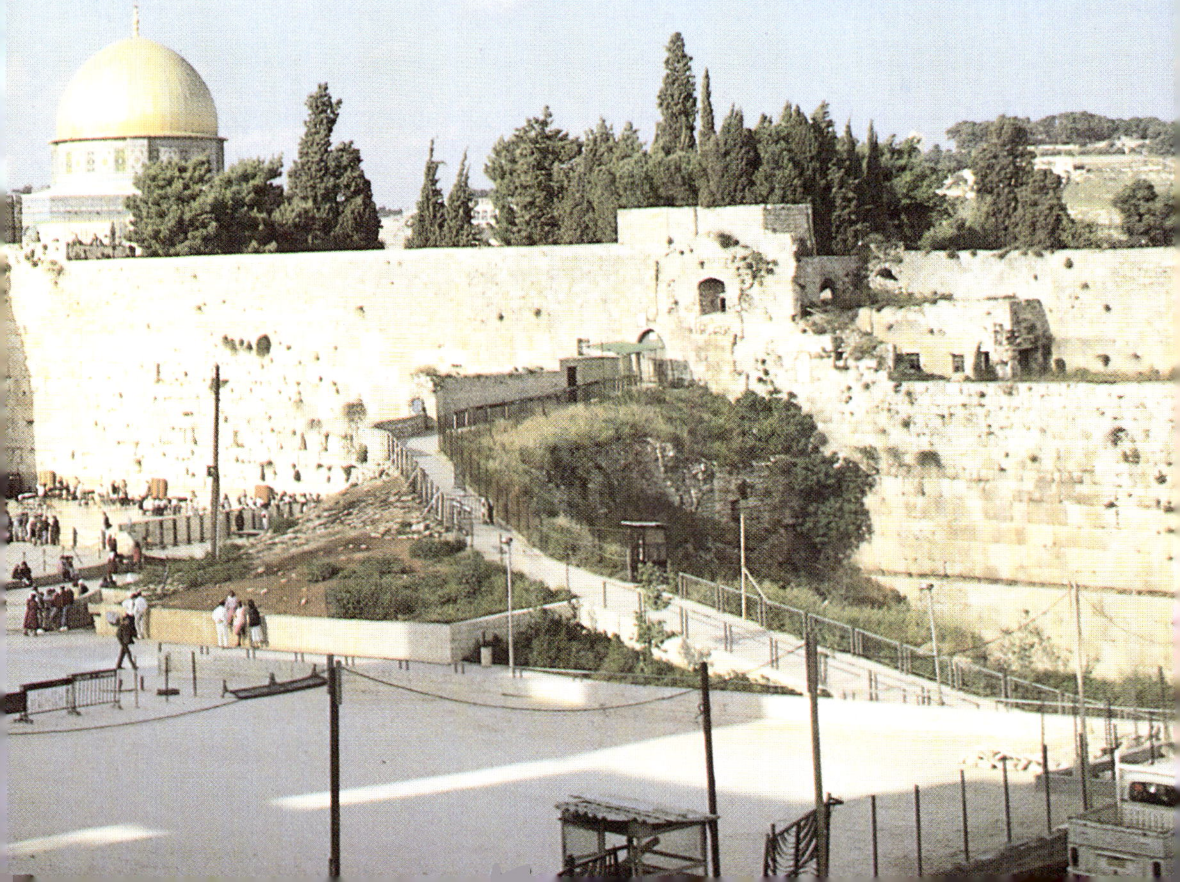

pour conduire leur vie, ils ne s'attardent pas non plus avec ceux qui font constamment le mal ; encore moins restent-ils continuellement parmi les hommes cyniques qui se moquent ouvertement de Dieu.

Plutôt que de suivre l'exemple de telles personnes, les hommes justes prennent comme référence *la Loi de l'Éternel* (v. 2). Cette *Loi* (Torah) qui doit être notre guide, ne désigne pas les seuls Dix commandements, ni même toutes les règles et ordonnances de la Loi de Moïse, mais englobe toute la révélation de Dieu. En effet, bien qu'elle ait été donnée à travers Moïse et les prophètes, elle n'en est pas moins *la Loi de l'Éternel*, c'est-à-dire « la Parole de Dieu ».

La Loi de l'Éternel fait la *joie* de juste, qui témoigne par-là de sa nouvelle naissance, car « ...la nature humaine... n'est que haine de Dieu : elle ne se soumet pas à la Loi de Dieu, car elle ne le peut pas » (Rm 8.7). Mais lorsque leur être intérieur a été régénéré par le Saint-Esprit, les hommes pieux se mettent à aimer la Loi de Dieu, qui leur révèle la volonté de leur Seigneur. Ils ne se révoltent pas contre ses exigences, tout leur être l'approuve et y adhère (voir Ps 19 ; 40.8 ; 112.1 ; 119). Ils vont *méditer* cette Loi qui fait leur joie, s'y plonger jour et nuit.

On s'accorde à dire que ce psaume était le texte préféré de Jérôme, l'auteur de l'ancienne version latine de la Bible. Il l'a sans nul doute mis en application dans sa vie, étudiant sans relâche les Écritures, d'abord dans le désert, puis dans la grotte où il habita pendant près de trente cinq ans, près du site de la nativité à Bethléhem. En fait, l'expérience du psalmiste est celle de tous les chrétiens. La méditation quotidienne de la Bible est pour eux source d'une joie sans fin.

Tels sont donc les justes. Ce n'est pas auprès de l'opinion publique, ni des modes changeantes d'un monde sans Dieu qu'ils recherchent jour après jour la direction pour leur vie, mais dans la Parole révélée de Dieu, à laquelle ils prennent plaisir et qu'ils méditent. Ils sont par conséquent *comme un arbre planté près d'un courant d'eau* (v. 3).

Cette métaphore se retrouve souvent dans la Bible. L'arbre, de quelque espèce qu'il s'agisse ici, connaît de toute évidence le secret d'une santé et d'une vigueur permanentes, donnant son fruit en sa saison, son feuillage restant vert sous les plus terribles ardeurs du soleil. De même que l'arbre tire régulièrement sa nourriture de l'eau par ses racines, les justes, par une méditation quotidienne de la Loi de l'Éternel, rafraîchissent et renouvellent leur âme en Dieu. Un tel arbre est solidement *planté* ; un tel homme, à l'image de Josué, prospère dans tout ce qu'il entreprend.

Les méchants périront (v. 4-6)

Tel n'est pas le cas des méchants. Autant leur condition actuelle que leur destinée sont totalement différentes. Loin de ressembler à un arbre productif, ils sont comme de la paille sèche et inutile. Au lieu d'être plantés au bord de l'eau, ils sont emportés par le vent.

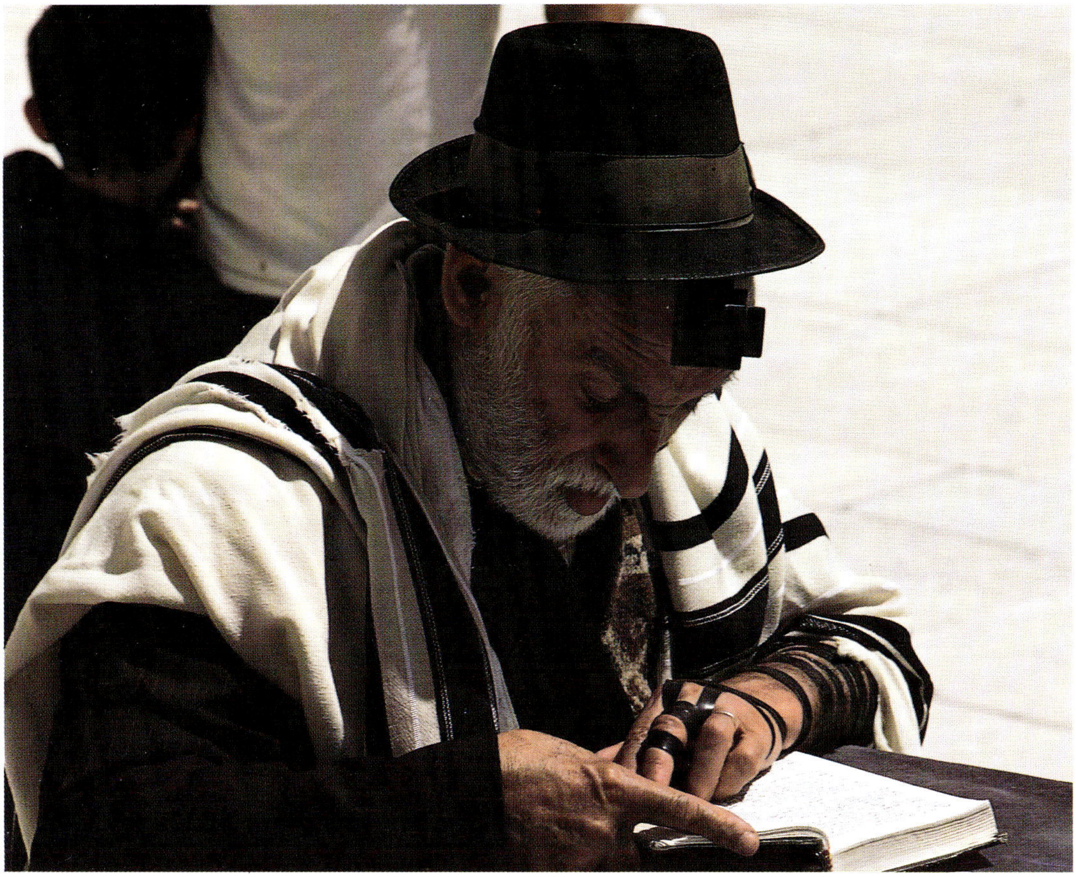

Un Juif pratiquant lit les Écritures devant le Mur des Lamentations à Jérusalem. Depuis 1967, l'espace devant le mur a été aménagé en une grande esplanade ouverte à tous.

Cette métaphore renvoie à une scène de vie courante aux temps et dans les pays bibliques (voir Ps 35.5 ; Es 17.3 ; Mt 3.12). L'aire de battage était généralement un terrain plat bien exposé au vent, au sommet d'une colline. On ramassait le blé à l'aide de grands vans ou de pelles et on le jetait en l'air. Le grain précieux retombait, prêt à être engrangé, tandis que la bale, plus légère, était dispersée aux quatre vents.

Les méchants sont *pareils à la paille*, par deux aspects. Ils sont secs et inutiles en eux-mêmes et ils ne pèseront pas lourd lors du jugement de Dieu. Le mot hébreu traduit par *méchants* évoque une idée d'instabilité (cf. Es 57.20, 21). Autant l'arbre est planté solidement, autant la paille, elle, est instable. Les méchants ne résisteront pas à l'épreuve du jugement de Dieu ici-bas, et encore moins quand viendra le jour du jugement dernier. Ils ne subsistent pas même maintenant dans le *rassemblement des justes*, car ils n'appartiennent pas au reste du peuple de Dieu.

Le verset 6, qui oppose *la voie des justes* au *sentier des méchants* résume et conclut ce psaume. L'Éternel, nous est-il dit, *veille sur la voie des justes*, alors que *le sentier des méchants les mène à la ruine.*

Crépuscule sur les collines. « Éternel, notre Seigneur, que ta gloire est admirable sur la terre tout entière ! Au-dessus du ciel, on célèbre ta splendeur. »

Psaume 8

Qu'est-ce que l'être humain ?

Le premier et le dernier verset de « ce petit poème exquis », comme l'a appelé C.S. Lewis, se font écho : *Éternel, notre Seigneur, que ta gloire est admirable sur la terre tout entière !* Ce psaume est une confession de la majesté du nom, ou de la nature de Dieu, majesté que ses œuvres révèlent tant sur la terre qu'au ciel. Les ennemis de Dieu, aveuglés par l'orgueil et la révolte, ne peuvent voir sa gloire, mais sont *confondus* par les *enfants* et les *nouveau-nés*. Jésus a cité ces paroles dans le Temple, alors que les enfants l'acclamaient de leurs *hosanna*, sous les protestations indignées des chefs des prêtres et des scribes (Mt 21.15, 16). Aujourd'hui de même, la foi simple des enfants et l'humilité des

2 Eternel, notre Seigneur,
que ta gloire est admirable | sur la terre tout entière !

Au-dessus du ciel, | on célèbre ta splendeur.
3 De la bouche des enfants | et des cris des nouveau-nés,
tu fais jaillir la louange | qui confond tes adversaires,
pour imposer le silence | à ceux qui, chargés de haine, |
se rebellent contre toi.

4 Quand je contemple le ciel | que tes doigts ont façonné,
les étoiles et la lune | que tes mains ont disposées,
5 je me dis : Qu'est-ce que l'homme, | pour que tu en prennes soin,

chrétiens qui leur ressemblent glorifient Dieu (voir Mt 11.25, 26 ; 1 Co 1.26-29).

Que Dieu se soit abaissé vers les êtres humains, d'une part (v. 4, 5), et qu'il leur ait accordé une position de domination sur la terre, de l'autre (v. 6-9), voilà qui remplit le psalmiste d'adoration et d'émerveillement. La somme de ces deux vérités nous aide à avoir une vision équilibrée de l'être humain et à apporter une réponse juste à la question éloquente du psalmiste, à savoir, *Qu'est-ce que l'homme ?*, autrement dit, quelle est la valeur d'un être humain ?

L'insignifiance des êtres humains (v. 4, 5)

La question du psalmiste a surgi de l'observation du ciel nocturne. Si David est l'auteur de ce psaume, il pense sans aucun doute à sa jeunesse, alors que, jeune berger, il dormait souvent à la belle étoile, pour garder le troupeau de son père sur les collines proches de Bethléhem. Couché sur le dos, il contemplait l'immensité insondable au-dessus de lui, cherchant à pénétrer les profondeurs lumineuses du

et qu'est-ce qu'un être humain | pour qu'à lui tu t'intéresses ?
6 Pourtant, tu l'as fait | de peu inférieur à Dieu,
tu l'as couronné | d'honneur et de gloire.
7 Tu lui donnes de régner | sur les œuvres de tes mains.
Tu as tout mis sous ses pieds :
8 tout bétail, gros ou petit,
et les animaux sauvages,
9 tous les oiseaux dans les airs | et les poissons de la mer,
tous les êtres qui parcourent | les sentiers des océans.

10 Eternel, notre Seigneur,
que ta gloire est admirable | sur la terre tout entière.

ciel oriental. Il savait que les cieux, la lune et les étoiles, avaient été façonnés par les doigts de Dieu (v. 4) et, de la contemplation de leur grandeur et de leur mystère, jaillit ce cri : *Qu'est-ce que l'homme, pour que tu en prennes soin, et qu'est-ce qu'un être humain pour qu'à lui tu t'intéresses ?* (v. 5).

Si telle fut la réaction de David, il y a près de trois mille ans, ne devrait-elle pas à plus forte raison être la nôtre, à nous qui vivons à l'époque de l'astrophysique et de la conquête de l'espace ? Si nous considérons les planètes de notre système solaire, d'une taille infinitésimale par rapport aux innombrables galaxies à des millions d'années-lumière, il peut nous paraître incroyable que le grand Dieu de l'univers, non seulement nous remarque, mais encore s'intéresse à nous. C'est pourtant ce qui se passe. Jésus nous a même affirmé que tous les cheveux de notre tête étaient comptés.

La grandeur des êtres humains (v. 6-9)

Par rapport à l'immensité de l'univers, l'homme est certes insignifiant, mais il n'en est pas de même sur terre, où Dieu lui a accordé une position d'importance : *Pourtant, tu l'as fait de peu inférieur à Dieu, tu l'as couronné d'honneur et de gloire. Tu lui donnes de régner sur les œuvres de tes mains* (v. 6, 7).

La domination qui nous est impartie manifeste pleinement que nous ne sommes que légèrement inférieurs aux êtres célestes, voire à Dieu. Il a investi les êtres humains d'une souveraineté royale, les couronnant d'honneur et de gloire (v. 6) et leur confiant le contrôle de ses œuvres. Il est même affirmé que Dieu a « tout mis sous ses pieds » (Segond).

Le psalmiste fait essentiellement allusion au règne animal, aux bêtes tant sauvages que domestiques, aux *oiseaux dans les airs* et aux *poissons de la mer*, ainsi qu'à tous les êtres peuplant le fond des océans (v. 8, 9). Il ne s'agit pas là de fiction poétique. Notre domination croît au fur et à mesure que l'univers livre ses secrets à la recherche scientifique. Toutefois, même de nos jours, l'homme n'est pas véritablement le maître de la création, dominant sur tout, comme l'indiquent les trois citations de ces versets dans le Nouveau Testament.

Dans Hébreux 2.5 et les versets suivants, il nous est dit : « Or actuellement nous ne voyons pas encore que tout lui soit soumis ». Cependant, l'auteur s'empresse d'ajouter : « Mais (...) Jésus se trouve maintenant (...) couronné de gloire et d'honneur. » À cause de son péché et de sa chute, l'humanité a perdu une partie de la domination que Dieu lui avait confiée, mais celle-ci a été rétablie par Jésus, le second Adam. C'est en lui plutôt qu'en nous, que se manifeste cette domination. Par sa mort il a même détruit le diable, dont il a délivré les esclaves (He 2.14, 15). Il est à présent « couronné » et élevé à la droite de Dieu.

Bien que la domination dont parle ce psaume concerne plutôt l'homme Jésus-Christ que l'être humain, elle s'applique aussi à nous qui avons pris par la foi part à son élévation. L'apôtre Paul a écrit que l'extraordinaire grandeur de la puissance de Dieu qui a élevé Jésus et

« a tout placé sous ses pieds » est aussi pour nous qui croyons (Ep 1.19-22). Nous avons fait l'expérience, en effet, de cette puissance qui nous a arrachés à la mort due au péché, nous a élevés avec le Christ et fait siéger avec lui dans les lieux célestes, où nous participons à sa victoire et à sa domination (Ep 2.5, 6).

Mais tout n'est pas encore fini. Bien que le Christ soit élevé loin audessus de toute loi et de toute autorité et que toutes choses soient potentiellement sous ses pieds, tous ses ennemis n'ont pas encore reconnu leur défaite pour se soumettre à lui. Ce n'est qu'au jour où il apparaîtra dans sa gloire et où les morts ressusciteront, qu'il anéantira « toute Domination, toute Autorité et toute Puissance hostiles. Il faut en effet qu'il règne jusqu'à ce que Dieu ait mis tous ses ennemis sous ses pieds. Et le dernier ennemi qui sera anéanti, c'est la mort. Car, comme il est écrit : « Dieu a mis toutes choses sous ses pieds » (1 Co 15.24-26).

Un jeune garçon juif lit les Écritures à la synagogue près du Mur des Lamentations, à Jérusalem. La synagogue est située près de l'arche Wilson, par où l'on pouvait jadis accéder au Temple.

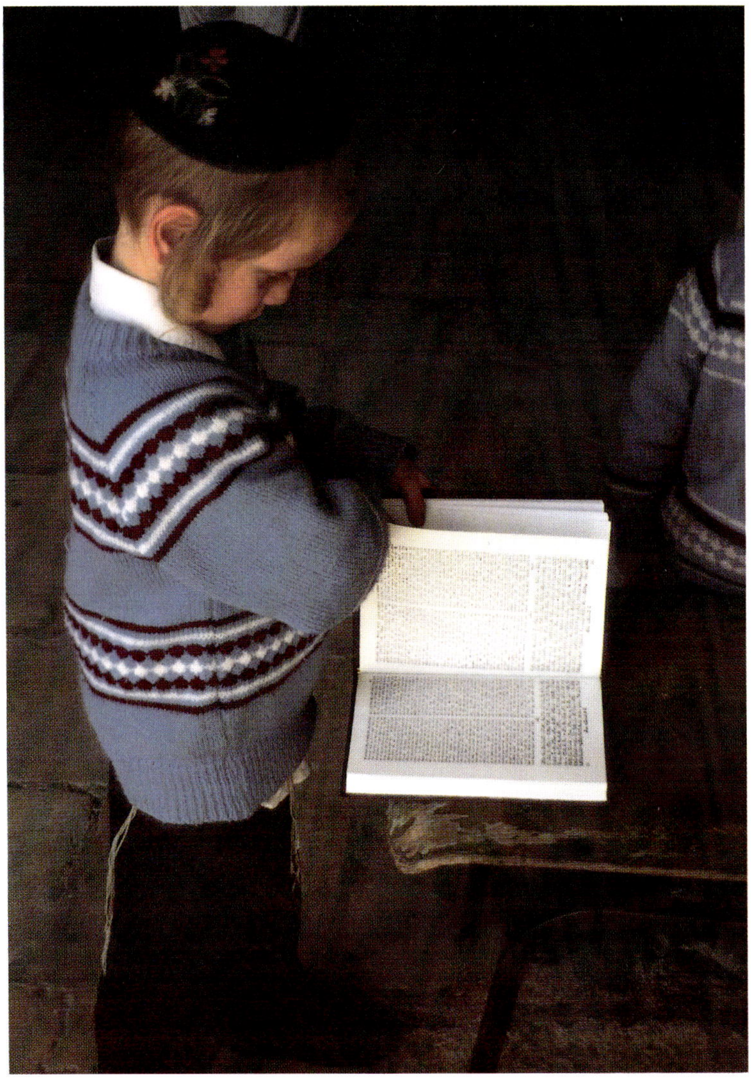

Page suivante :
Des Juifs orthodoxes prient devant le Mur Occidental, à Jérusalem. Beaucoup d'entre eux portent encore les manteaux et les chapeaux noirs caractéristiques de leurs ancêtres d'Europe centrale.

Psaume 15

Une vie droite

Le psaume 15 définit les conditions selon lesquelles un homme ou une femme peut vivre dans la présence de Dieu. Il est intéressant de noter qu'il établit un lien indissociable entre religion et moralité. Il est construit autour d'une question et de sa réponse, et s'achève par une déclaration solennelle qui dépasse de loin les termes de la question de départ.

La question (v. 1)

Éternel, qui peut rester dans ton sanctuaire ? Et qui donc peut demeurer sur ta montagne sacrée ? La *montagne sacrée* de Dieu désigne bien entendu Jérusalem, et son *sanctuaire* probablement la tente qui abritait l'arche avant que Salomon ne construisît le Temple. On pense en effet que, de même que le psaume 24, ce psaume fait allusion à l'événement rapporté dans 2 Samuel 6.12-19 et 1 Chroniques 15 et 16, où l'on voit David faire transporter l'arche depuis la maison d'Obed-Edom jusque sur la colline de Sion, la « cité de David » et la placer sous la tente qu'il avait dressée à cet effet. Ce psaume mettrait alors l'accent sur le défi moral que représentait pour les habitants de Jérusalem la présence de Dieu au milieu d'eux.

Eternel, qui peut rester | dans ton sanctuaire ?
Et qui donc peut demeurer | sur ta montagne sacrée ?
2 L'homme à la conduite intègre : | il pratique la justice,
et il dit la vérité | qu'il pense au fond de son cœur,
3 il n'insulte pas son frère,
et il ne raconte rien | qui déprécie son prochain
ou lui cause un préjudice.
4 Il méprise l'homme vil,
mais il honore celui | qui respecte l'Eternel.
Il tient toujours ses serments | même s'il doit en pâtir.
5 Lorsqu'il prête de l'argent, | c'est toujours sans intérêt,
il refuse qu'on l'achète | pour condamner l'innocent.

Qui se conduit de la sorte | rien ne pourra l'ébranler.

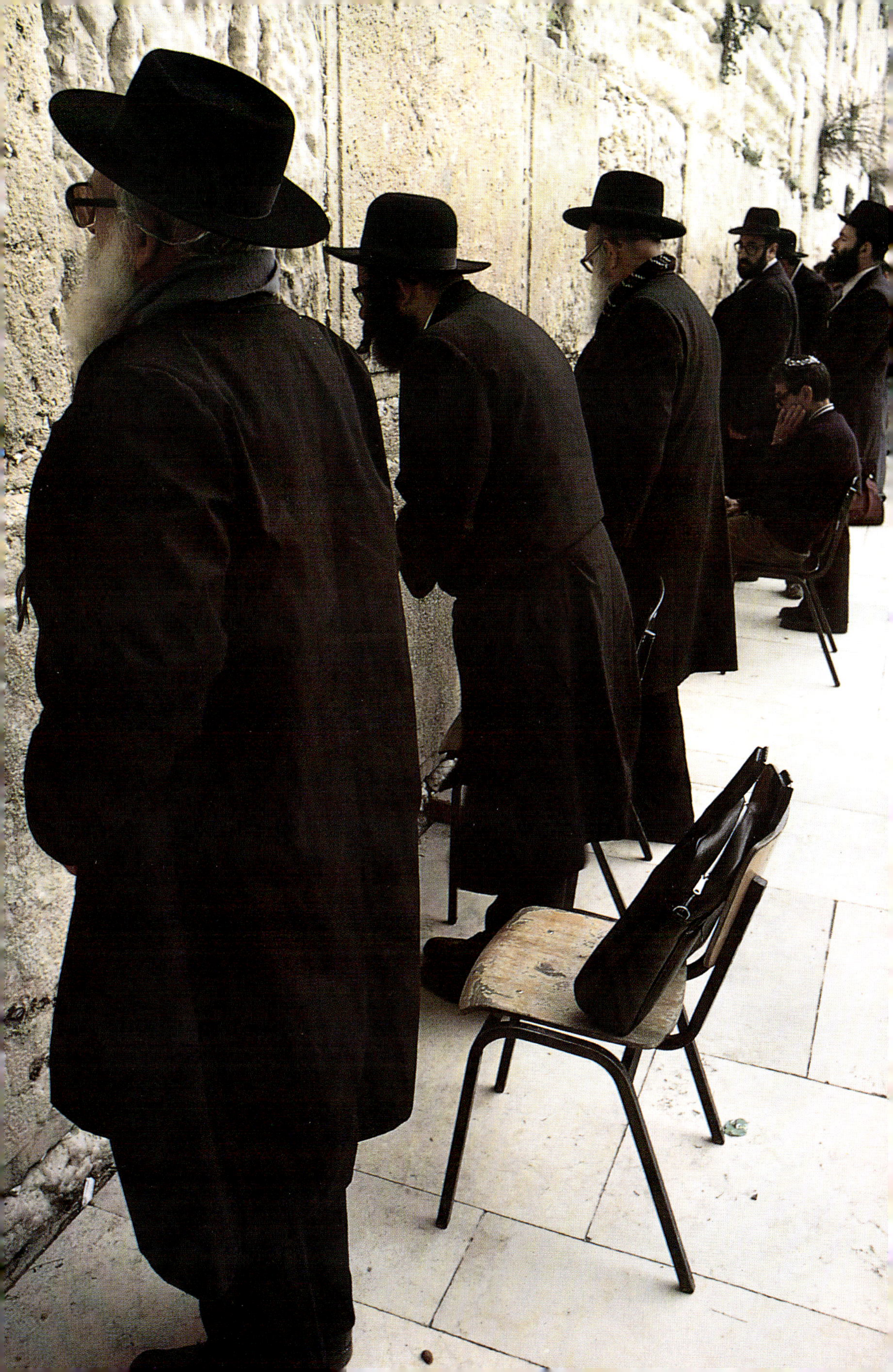

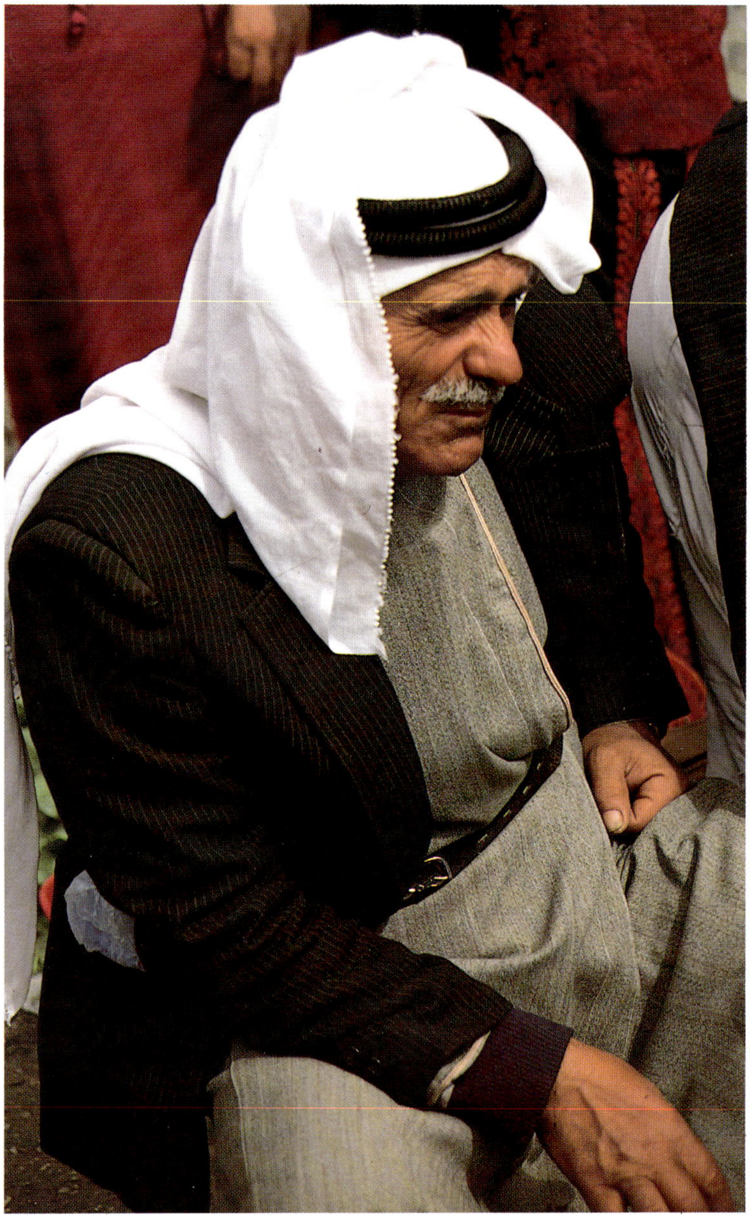

Un marchand du marché aux légumes de Bethléhem.

Mais ce psaume a une portée plus étendue. Il tente de définir les termes selon lesquels un être humain peut demeurer dans la présence de Dieu, dans cette vie comme dans celle à venir. Le psalmiste sait pertinemment que Yahvé est un Dieu saint et que le péché sépare les pécheurs de Dieu. « Car tu n'es pas un Dieu qui prend plaisir au mal. Celui qui est méchant n'est pas reçu chez toi » (Ps 5.5). Qui, alors, peut demeurer dans la présence de Dieu ?

La réponse (v. 2-5a)

En réponse à sa propre question, le psalmiste dresse un portrait de la personne qui peut s'approcher de Dieu. C'est un portrait modèle, un idéal auquel personne ne ressemble parfaitement, sinon l'homme Jésus, le Christ. Jésus seul est entré dans la présence de Dieu au ciel sur la base de son mérite propre ; quant à nous, nous ne pouvons accéder à Dieu que par le Christ.

Mais, réconciliés avec Dieu par le Christ, nous pouvons jouir d'une communion constante avec lui à condition que, par sa grâce, nous menions une vie sainte telle que la décrit ce psaume. C'est une sainteté sociale, qui se rapporte exclusivement à notre devoir envers notre prochain, puisqu'une bonne relation avec Dieu est nécessairement conditionnée par une bonne relation avec les autres. Il est inutile d'espérer vivre près de Dieu si nous ne recherchons pas le bien de notre prochain.

Les personnes dignes de jouir de la présence de Dieu sont donc *intègres* (v. 2). Leur droiture de caractère est telle, qu'elles font ce qui est juste et disent ce qui est vrai. Bien plus, la vérité qu'elles expriment vient de leur *cœur*, car leurs paroles reflètent toujours leurs pensées. Elles sont conséquentes dans leurs pensées, leurs paroles et leurs actes.

Cette affirmation positive d'ordre général va être illustrée par des exemples précis et pour la plupart négatifs, qui ont pour effet de faire ressortir d'autant mieux l'excellence des hommes justes.

Premièrement, ils ne disent ni ne font rien qui pourrait nuire à leur prochain (v. 3). Pas d'insulte, rien qui porte atteinte à l'honneur du prochain, pas de calomnie. Ce dernier terme peut vouloir dire deux choses, soit qu'ils ne répètent pas de mauvais propos concernant leur prochain, soit qu'ils ne profitent pas injustement de ce que celui-ci se trouve dans une situation difficile, pour l'abaisser. Deuxièmement, ils font preuve de discernement à l'égard des autres. Ils n'ont pas peur d'exprimer leur désapprobation envers les hommes vains, et ils montrent clairement qu'ils honorent ceux qui respectent Dieu (v. 4a). Troisièmement, ils restent fidèles à leurs engagements, même s'ils doivent y perdre. Ce sont des hommes de parole (v. 4b). Quatrièmement, enfin, ils n'exploitent jamais le pauvre, ni n'oppriment l'innocent (v. 5a).

Cela revient à dire, par exemple, qu'ils ne prêtent pas d'argent avec intérêt et ne se laissent pas corrompre. Nous sommes ici en présence de figures bien connues dans l'Ancien Testament, à savoir le prêteur cupide et la magistrat injuste qui accepte des cadeaux contre un innocent. Ces deux pratiques étaient condamnées par la Loi (Ex 22.25 ; Lv 25.35-38 et Ex 23.6-8 ; Dt 16.19 ; 27.25) et dénoncées par les prophètes (voir, par ex., Ez 22.12).

Une déclaration solennelle (v. 5b)

Voilà donc qui est digne de demeurer dans la présence de Dieu, l'homme ou la femme qui aime son prochain. Mais le psalmiste va encore plus loin. Non seulement ces personnes habiteront près de Dieu, mais, qui plus est, rien ne pourra les ébranler. Bien au contraire, elles traverseront toutes les vicissitudes de la vie d'un pas ferme et assuré, jusqu'au jour du jugement.

Psaume 16

La foi et l'espérance

Malgré la prière initiale (*O Dieu, protège-moi*), ce psaume est en réalité la confession de la foi et de l'espérance d'un croyant. Réfugié en Dieu (v. 1), il a trouvé en lui son bonheur (v. 2, 6, 7) et il a la certitude que même la mort ne peut lui ravir cette vie véritable qui se trouve dans la communion avec Dieu (v. 10, 11). Pierre, le jour de la Pentecôte, et Paul, dans la synagogue d'Antioche de Pisidie, ont tous deux repris les derniers versets du psaume pour les appliquer à la résurrection de Jésus (Ac 2.24-31 ; 13.34-37).

La foi (v. 1-6)

Le verset 2 explique ce que veut dire mettre sa confiance, ou « se réfugier », en Dieu (v. 1 ; cf. Ps 73.24). Le croyant s'est détourné des plaisirs du péché et des vanités du monde, pour chercher et trouver son bien en Dieu. Aimant Dieu, il aime aussi les siens, *ceux qui lui appartiennent* (v. 3).

Par contre, il ne prend aucun plaisir à la compagnie des incroyants, de ceux qui délaissent le Dieu vivant et vrai pour *d'autres dieux* (v. 4). Il sait qu'ils vont au-devant de graves problèmes, qu'ils *ne font qu'augmenter leurs tourments*. Il est bien décidé à ne prendre aucune part *à leurs sanglantes libations*, ni même à prononcer le nom de leurs idoles (v. 4). Une telle conduite serait incompatible avec son attachement sans partage à l'Eternel, dont il se met à parler avec exaltation (v. 5,

O Dieu, protège-moi, | car je me réfugie en toi.
2 Je dis à l'Eternel : | « Tu es mon maître,
et tout mon bonheur est en toi. »
3 Je suis plein d'affection | pour ceux qui t'appartiennent | dans le pays :
ce sont eux qui sont vraiment grands.
4 Mais tous ceux qui s'affairent | à chercher les faveurs | des autres dieux
ne font qu'augmenter leurs tourments.
Je ne prendrai pas part | à leurs sanglantes libations.
Le nom de ces idoles | ne passera pas sur mes lèvres.

5 L'Eternel est ma part | et la coupe où je bois.
Tu garantis la part que j'ai reçue.
6 Tu en as fixé les limites, | c'est un jardin plein de délices,
mon héritage est merveilleux.

7 Oui, je loue l'Eternel | qui me conseille,
qui, la nuit même, | éclaire ma pensée.
8 Je garde constamment | les yeux fixés sur l'Eternel.
Puisqu'il est près de moi, | rien ne peut m'ébranler.
9 Mon cœur est dans la joie,
mon âme exulte d'allégresse,
mon corps repose dans la paix :
10 tu ne m'abandonneras pas | dans le séjour des morts,
tu ne laisseras pas | ton serviteur fidèle | se décomposer dans la tombe.
11 Tu me feras connaître | le chemin de la vie :
plénitude de joie | en ta présence,
et bonheur éternel | auprès de toi.

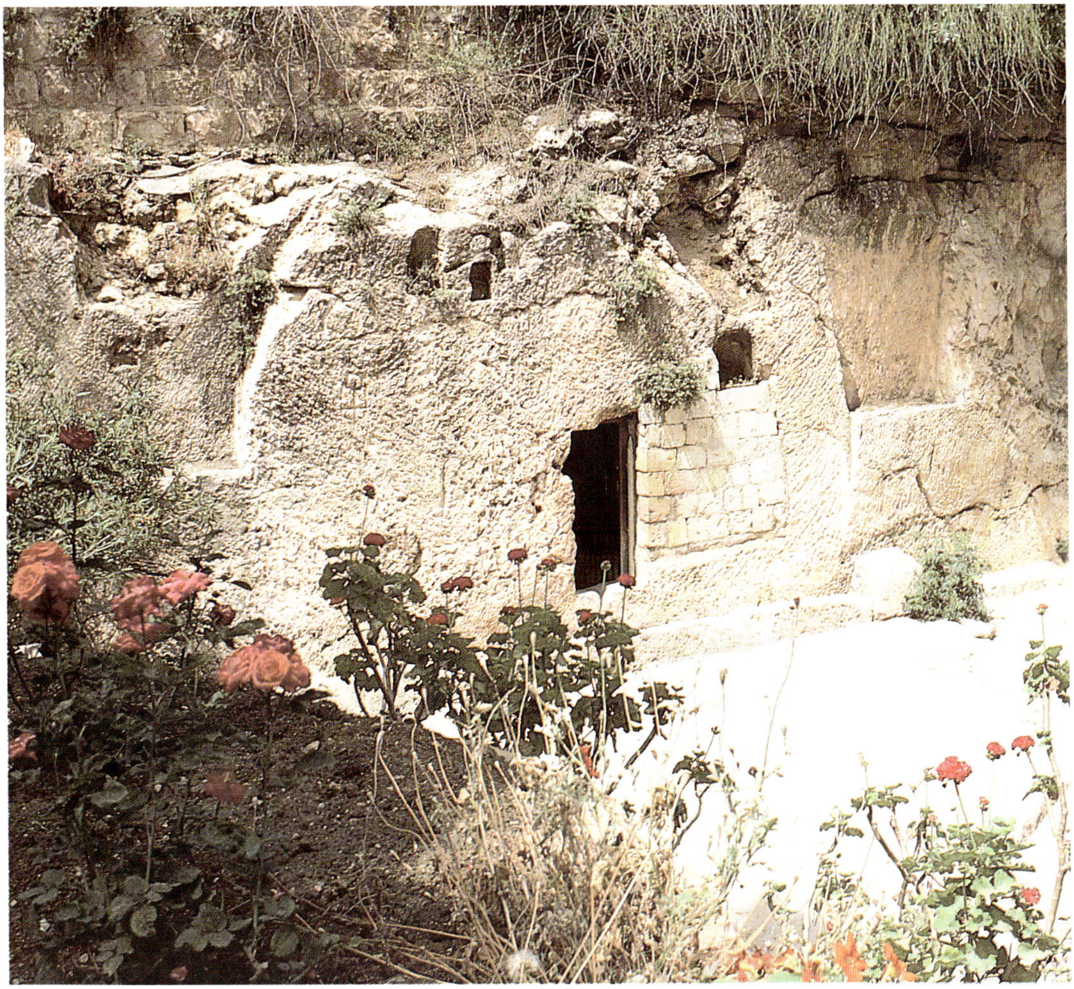

Le tombeau dans Jérusalem Est. Il est peu probable que ce soit ici le lieu où Jésus a été enseveli et d'où il est ressuscité. Ce jardin offre néanmoins un havre de paix à de nombreux visiteurs.

6). En lui donnant une *part* (probablement de nourriture plutôt que de pays), ainsi qu'une *coupe*, l'Eternel a pourvu à ses besoins fondamentaux de nourriture et de boisson. Bien plus, Dieu est pour lui un *héritage…merveilleux*, à l'image des prêtres lévites dont l'héritage était l'Éternel et qui n'avaient, de ce fait, pas reçu de possession dans le pays de Canaan (voir, par ex., Nb 18.20).

L'espérance (v. 7-11)

David, à qui Pierre et Paul attribuent ce psaume, se répand en actions de grâce (v. 7) envers l'Eternel qui le *conseille* et qui, *la nuit même, éclaire sa pensée.* Il ne précise pas la nature de cet enseignement divin, qui se rapporte probablement à la fin de ce psaume.

Dieu s'approche de David pour lui parler ; c'est son propre cœur qui l'instruit alors que, dans le silence de la nuit, il médite sur sa communion intime avec son Dieu. Son expérience lui permet d'affirmer avec confiance que, si Dieu est toujours près de lui (v. 8 ; en hébreu « à sa droite »), *rien ne peut l'ébranler*. En d'autres termes, les bénédictions liées à sa communion avec Dieu ne sauraient se limiter à son seul bien-être, mais sont aussi gage de sécurité. Sa foi engendre une espérance.

David se réjouit à présent en son cœur et son âme de ce qu'il a la certitude que son corps aussi *repose dans la paix* (v. 9). Fort de cette nouvelle assurance, il s'adresse directement à Dieu (v. 10, 11).

Trois interprétations sont possibles pour ces versets, toutes trois bien fondées. Au sens littéral, ils expriment la conviction de l'auteur qu'il ne mourra pas, que son âme n'ira pas dans *le séjour des morts* et que son corps ne va pas *se décomposer*. L'arrière-plan historique de ce psaume n'est pas connu, mais il se peut que David, alors hors-la-loi et en fuite devant Saül, ait exprimé là sa confiance qu'il ne serait pas livré entre les mains de Saül.

Ces versets ont cependant une portée encore plus vaste. Celui qui est délivré de la mort marche sur *le chemin de la vie*, qui n'est pas la simple survie du corps, mais la *joie* et le *bonheur* éternels engendrés par la présence de Dieu. C'est ce que le Nouveau Testament appelle « la vie éternelle », la communion avec Dieu, que la mort physique ne peut interrompre. David ne comprenait certainement pas la pleine signification de tout ce qu'il écrivait, la vie et l'immortalité ne devant être révélées clairement que par Jésus-Christ (2 Tm 1.10) ; ses paroles ne trouvent en effet leur véritablement accomplissement que dans la vie éternelle au-delà de la tombe.

Pierre, en appliquant ces versets à la résurrection de Jésus, alla jusqu'à dire que David n'avait pas pu faire référence à lui-même, puisqu'il est mort et a été enseveli. Il poursuivit : « Mais il était prophète et il savait que Dieu lui avait promis, sous la foi du serment, de faire asseoir sur son trône un de ses descendants. Ainsi il a entrevu par avance la résurrection du Christ, et c'est d'elle qu'il parle en disant que Dieu ne l'abandonnera pas dans le séjour des morts et qu'il ne laissera pas son corps se décomposer » (Ac 2.30, 31).

Ne faisons pas dire à Pierre ce qu'il n'a pas dit. Il a expliqué dans sa première épître (1 P 1.10-12) que les prophètes ne comprenaient pas pleinement à quoi l'Esprit du Christ en eux faisait référence en prédisant les souffrances du Christ et sa gloire à venir. Il serait donc inexact d'affirmer que nous avons là une prophétie délibérée et consciente de David sur la résurrection de Jésus, qu'il aurait parfaitement comprise. Il suffit de dire que l'Esprit de prophétie l'a poussé à parler de la victoire sur la mort et de la plénitude de la vie et de la joie dans la présence de Dieu, qui se réaliseraient, non pas dans sa vie, mais dans celle de son glorieux descendant.

Psaume 19

Dieu se révèle

Selon C.S. Lewis, ce psaume est « le plus beau poème du psautier et l'une des plus merveilleuses œuvres lyriques qui ait jamais été écrites. » Du point de vue chrétien, il présente l'exposé le plus clair qu'on puisse trouver dans tout l'Ancien Testament de la doctrine de la révélation, à savoir que Dieu s'est révélé à toute l'humanité comme le Créateur (v. 2-7), à Israël comme l'auteur de la Loi (v. 8-11) et à l'individu comme le Rédempteur (v. 12-15).

La révélation générale (v. 1-7)

Nul ne peut prétendre ignorer l'existence de Dieu, qui ne cesse de se révéler d'une manière qu'on qualifie de « générale » parce qu'elle s'adresse à tout homme où qu'il soit. Comme l'a dit l'apôtre Paul, « il n'a jamais cessé de leur donner des témoignages de sa bonté (Ac 14.17 ; cf. Ac 17.22-28 et Rm 1.20).

Ce témoignage réside dans la nature, en particulier, comme ici, dans *les cieux*, qui *proclament combien Dieu est glorieux*, car ils sont *l'œuvre de ses mains* (v. 2). À notre époque, grâce aux découvertes de l'astrophysique, les cieux, « leur immensité, leur splendeur, leur ordre et leur mystère », comme l'a dit un commentateur, manifestent encore davantage la gloire et la grandeur de Dieu.

La révélation de Dieu dans les cieux peut se définir de trois manières. Premièrement, elle est continue. *Un jour en informe un autre, une nuit à l'autre nuit...*(v. 3), de manière à offrir un témoignage ininterrompu. Deuxièmement, la révélation est abondante ; le verset 3 parle de connaissance qui se transmet. Troisièmement, enfin, elle est universelle. *Ce ne sont pas des paroles, et ce ne sont pas des discours* (v. 4) et pourtant, on peut en admirer le spectacle jusqu'aux confins de la terre (v. 5). Paul applique même ce dernier verset à la propagation universelle de l'Évangile (Rm 10.18).

Le soleil occupe une place privilégiée dans cette révélation. Dans une envolée lyrique, qui n'est bien entendu qu'une image, l'auteur compare le lever du soleil au jeune époux qui sort de sa chambre, et sa course quotidienne à travers le ciel à celle d'un athlète, sans *rien qui se dérobe à l'ardeur de ses rayons* (v. 7).

La révélation particulière (v. 8-11)

L'auteur change brusquement de sujet, abandonnant la révélation générale de Dieu par sa création, pour considérer sa révélation particulière et surnaturelle par la Torah, « la Loi », un terme qui ne désigne pas seulement la Loi de Moïse, mais tout l'Ancien Testament. La

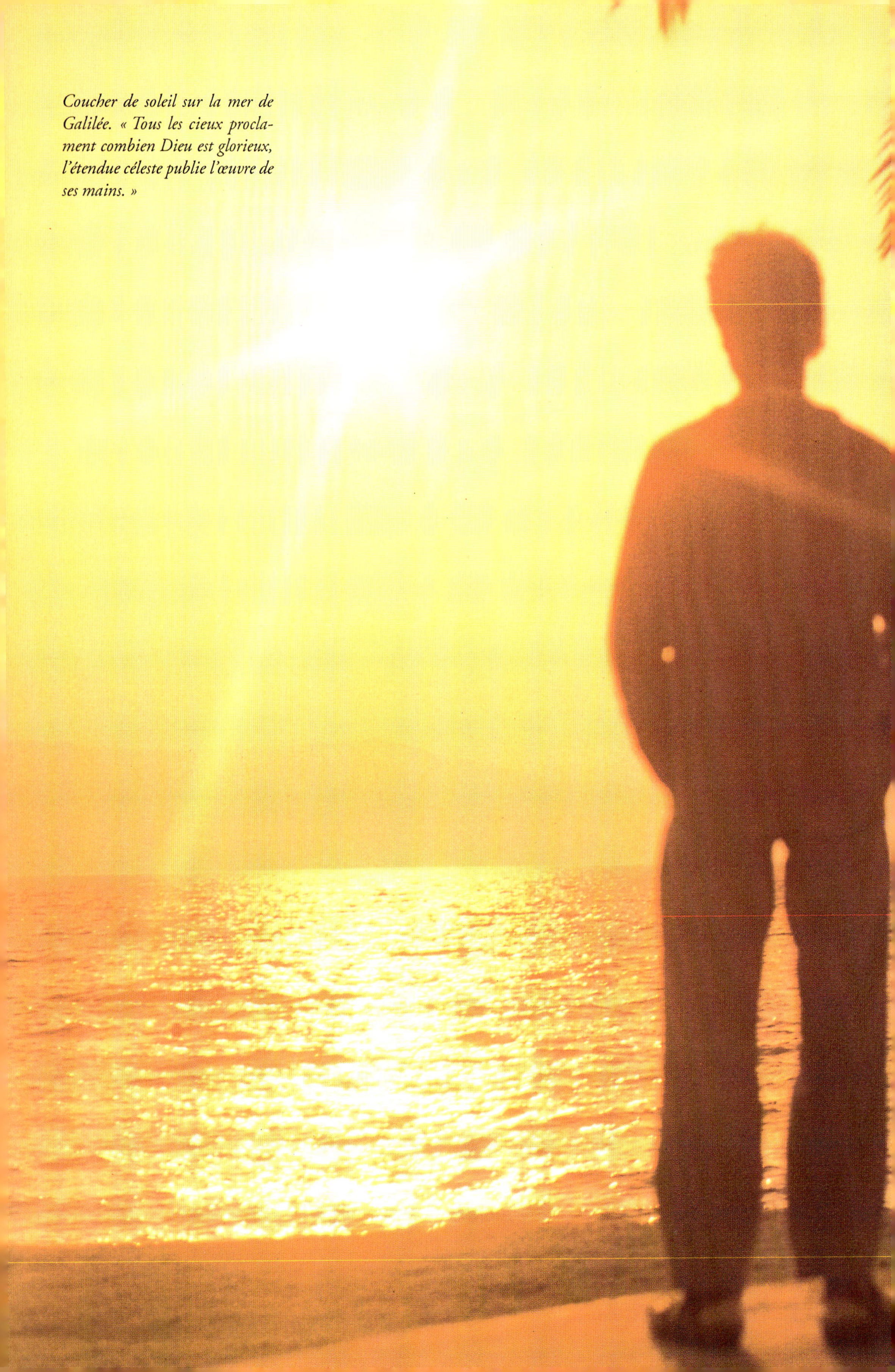

Coucher de soleil sur la mer de Galilée. « Tous les cieux proclament combien Dieu est glorieux, l'étendue céleste publie l'œuvre de ses mains. »

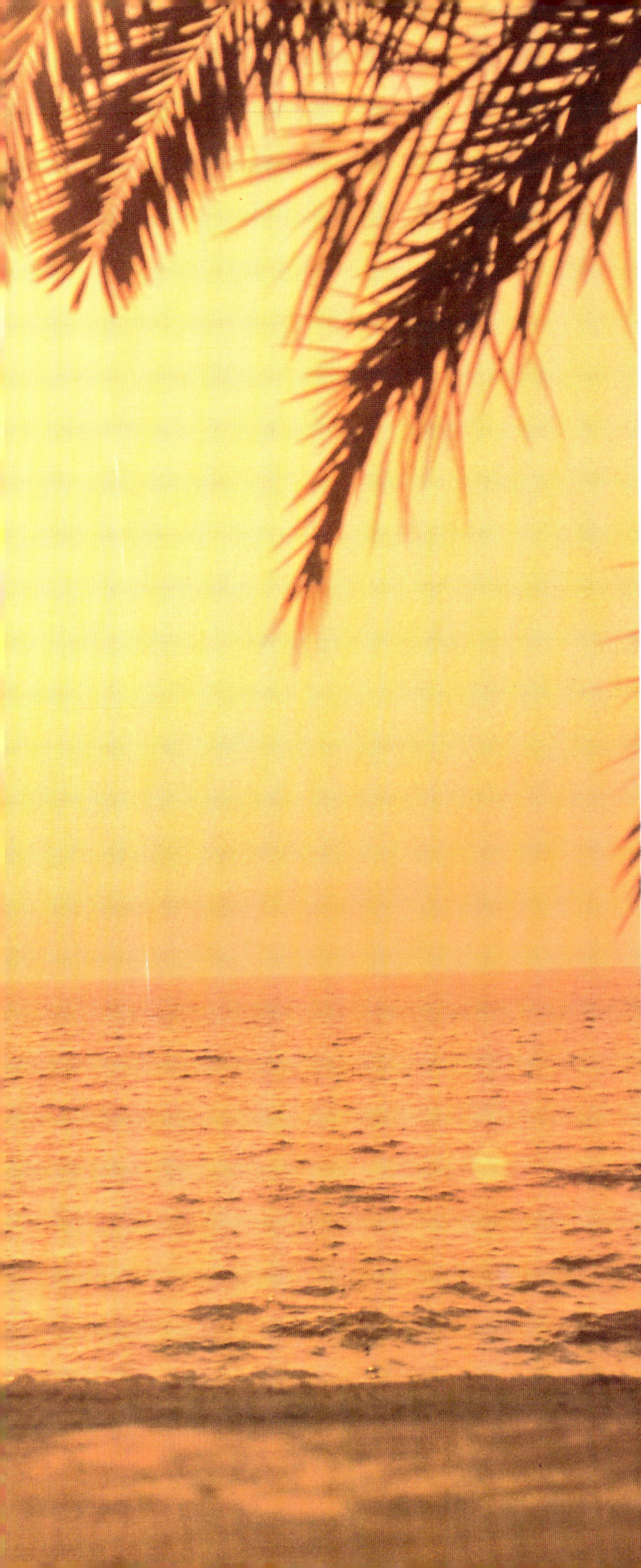

2 Tous les cieux proclament | combien Dieu | est glorieux,
l'étendue céleste | publie l'œuvre de ses mains.
3 Un jour en informe un autre,
une nuit à l'autre nuit | en transmet la connaissance.
4 Ce ne sont pas des paroles, | ce ne sont pas des discours,
ni des voix qu'on peut entendre.
5 Cependant, leur voix parvient | jusqu'aux confins de la terre
et leurs accents dans tout l'univers.
Dieu a dressé dans le ciel | pour le soleil une tente.
6 Comme un jeune époux | qui sort, joyeux, de sa chambre,
comme un champion qui s'avance, | ravi de prendre la course, | surgit le soleil !
7 Tout à l'orient, il se lève,
et son parcours se prolonge | jusqu'au seuil de l'horizon ;
il n'est rien qui se dérobe | à l'ardeur de ses rayons.

8 La Loi de Dieu est parfaite, | elle nous redonne vie.
Toutes ses affirmations | sont dignes de confiance. | Aux gens sans détour | elle donne la sagesse.
9 Justes sont ses exigences, | elles font la joie du cœur ;
et ses ordres, si limpides, | donnent du discernement.
10 Le respect de l'Eternel est pur,
il subsiste à tout jamais ;
les décrets de l'Eternel sont vrais, | ils sont parfaitement justes.
11 Ils sont bien plus désirables | que beaucoup de lingots d'or,
plus savoureux que le miel | le plus doux coulant des ruches.
12 Ton serviteur, Eternel, | en tire instruction :
il y trouve un grand profit.
13 Qui connaît tous ses faux pas ?
Pardonne-moi les péchés | dont je n'ai pas conscience.
14 Garde aussi ton serviteur | des pensées d'orgueil :
qu'elles n'aient sur moi | pas la moindre emprise !
Alors je serai intègre, | innocent de grandes fautes.
15 Veuille agréer mes paroles,
reçois favorablement | ce qu'a médité mon cœur,
ô Eternel, mon Rocher, | mon Libérateur.

transition, quoique abrupte, n'est pas arbitraire. La Loi, tout comme les cieux, permet de connaître Dieu. Peut-être même C.S. Lewis a-t-il raison, qui voit la transition dans la chaleur rayonnante du soleil, « le soleil, pénétrant et purifiant, devenant une image de la Loi, elle aussi pénétrante et purifiante ».

Le changement du sujet entraîne un changement révélateur du nom divin. Celui qui se révèle à tout homme dans la nature est *Dieu*, en hébreu *El* (v. 2), le Dieu de la création, mais c'est *l'Éternel*, Yahvé (le terme est employé quatre fois dans la seconde partie du psaume), le Dieu de l'alliance, qui s'est révélé au travers de sa Loi, à Israël, le peuple de l'alliance. Ce n'est pas ici une révélation de sa gloire, mais de sa volonté, dont les perfections sont admirablement traduites par le rythme des versets 8 à 10.

Dans le texte original, la symétrie de ces versets est telle, que chacun commence par énoncer un aspect de la volonté de Dieu, pour en définir ensuite les caractéristiques et les effets. La *Loi*, ou instruction divine, est donc *parfaite*, elle nous révèle la personne de Dieu au travers de sa volonté et consiste en *affirmations*, en *exigences* et en *ordres*. Ses recommandations, qui sont *dignes de confiance, limpides, pures, vraies, parfaitement justes*, en manifestent la perfection. Elle est aussi appelée *respect de l'Éternel* (v. 10), le but suprême de toute révélation étant de susciter l'adoration humble et respectueuse. Cette révélation de la volonté de Dieu est qualifiée de « pure ».

Mais le psalmiste ne se contente pas de contempler la Loi de l'Éternel pour elle-même. Il dévoile tous les bienfaits de cette Loi qui *redonne vie*, réjouit le cœur et, surtout, *donne la sagesse* (v. 8) et le *discernement* (v. 9) à ceux qui ont assez d'humilité pour les recevoir ou, comme notre Seigneur le dira plus tard, qui possèdent un cœur d'enfant. La nature même des décrets de Dieu et leur action bénéfique les rendent *plus désirables que beaucoup de lingots d'or, plus savoureux que le miel le plus doux coulant des ruches* (v. 11).

Le fait que le psalmiste n'ait pas ressenti cette Loi comme un fardeau peut surprendre ; comme pour C.S. Lewis, l'accent mis sur sa douceur peut nous sembler à première vue « très mystérieux », voire « totalement déroutant ». Certes, ses commandements sont justes et ses promesses dignes de confiance, mais la véritable raison réside dans le fait qu'il s'agit de la révélation de Dieu, du moyen qu'il a choisi tout spécialement pour se faire connaître à son peuple d'Israël.

La révélation personnelle (v. 12-15)

Au verset 10, le psalmiste parle pour la première fois en son nom propre. Après avoir démontré comment la nature manifestait la gloire de Dieu *jusqu'aux confins de la terre* (v. 5) et comment la Loi de Dieu pouvait donner la sagesse *aux gens sans détour* (v. 8), il exprime, dans la deuxième partie du psaume, ses propres aspirations spirituelles en tant que *serviteur* de l'Éternel (v. 12, 14).

Pèlerinage en Terre Sainte.
« Veuille agréer mes paroles, reçois favorablement ce qu'a médité mon cœur, ô Éternel, mon rocher, mon libérateur. »

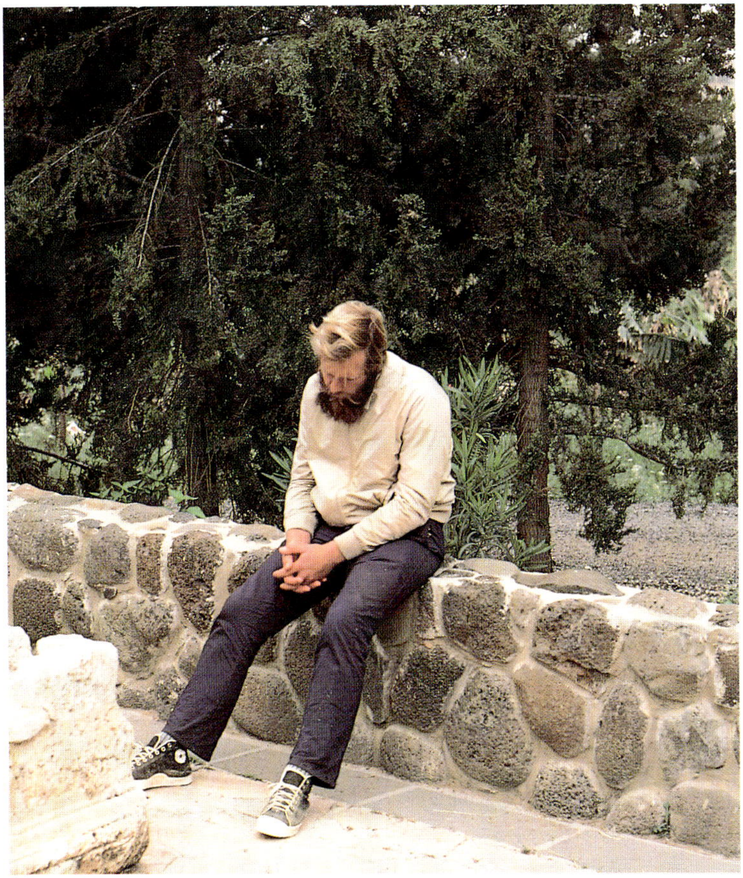

Il a pour sa part tiré instruction de la Loi de Dieu et trouvé un grand profit à s'y conformer (v. 12). Il a probablement expérimenté dans sa propre vie le double rôle de la Loi divine, qui est de révéler le péché (Rm 3.20) et de conduire à la sainteté. Il prie donc pour que Dieu lui pardonne les *péchés dont il n'a pas conscience* (v.13), tout en le préservant des *pensées d'orgueil* (v. 14) qu'il désire éviter, pour ne pas se laisser dominer par elles, mais rester *intègre, innocent de grandes fautes*. Le psalmiste ne fait pas allusion ici à un péché précis particulièrement grave, ni au blasphème contre le Saint-Esprit (comme le pensait ce pauvre John Bunyan), mais à toute faute commise « délibérément », à tout péché volontaire (Nb 15.30, 31).

Le psaume se termine par une prière que les pasteurs aiment à faire leur au début de leur prédication. L'auteur ne se contente plus de prier pour être délivré des péchés, il exprime le désir profond de son cœur que toutes ses paroles, et même ses pensées, soient reçues *favorablement* par l'Éternel, qu'il confesse à présent comme son *Rocher* (sa « force ») et son *Libérateur* (son « Rédempteur »). La rédemption est la délivrance a posteriori du péché ; elle doit être accompagnée d'une vie qui plaise à Dieu (Tt 2.14).

Le vendredi saint, les pèlerins portent une croix le long de la Via Dolorosa à Jérusalem, sur le parcours suivi par Jésus vers le mont Golgotha.

Psaume 22

Les souffrances et la gloire du Christ

C'est le premier des « psaumes de la Passion », qui évoquent la persécution et les souffrances d'une victime innocente, en des termes qui rappellent celles du serviteur souffrant de l'Eternel, dans la deuxième partie d'Ésaïe. Selon certains commentateurs, la victime serait plus symbolique que réelle, peut-être une image de la nation d'Israël exilée au milieu des païens. Cependant, l'évocation des souffrances est émaillée de tant de détails précis, qu'il semble évident que ce texte fait référence à une expérience réelle.

2 Mon Dieu, mon Dieu, | pourquoi m'as-tu abandonné ?
Tu restes loin, | tu ne viens pas me secourir | malgré toutes mes plaintes.
3 Mon Dieu, le jour, j'appelle, | mais tu ne réponds pas.
La nuit, je crie, | sans trouver de repos.
4 Pourtant, tu es le Saint
qui sièges sur ton trône, | au milieu des louanges d'Israël.
5 En toi déjà, | nos pères se confiaient,
oui, ils comptaient sur toi, | et tu les délivrais.
6 Lorsqu'ils criaient à toi, | ils étaient délivrés,
lorsqu'ils comptaient sur toi, | ils n'étaient pas déçus.

7 Mais moi je suis un ver, | je ne suis plus un homme,
tout le monde m'insulte, | le peuple me méprise,
8 ceux qui me voient | se rient de moi.
Tous, ils ricanent. | On fait la moue | en secouant la tête :
9 « Il se confie en l'Eternel ?
Eh bien, que maintenant | l'Eternel le délivre !
Puisqu'il trouve en lui son plaisir, | qu'il le libère donc ! »
10 Oui, c'est bien toi | qui, depuis ma naissance, | m'as protégé.
Tu m'as mis en sécurité | sur le sein de ma mère.
11 Dès mon jeune âge, | j'ai été placé sous ta garde.
Dès avant ma naissance, | tu es mon Dieu.
12 Ne reste pas si loin de moi | car le danger est proche,
et il n'y a personne | qui vienne pour m'aider.

13 De nombreux taureaux m'environnent :
ces fortes bêtes du Basan | sont tout autour de moi.
14 Ils ouvrent largement | leurs gueules contre moi,
ils sont comme un lion | qui rugit et déchire.
15 Je suis comme une eau qui s'écoule
et tous mes os sont disloqués.
Mon cœur est pareil à la cire,
on dirait qu'il se fond en moi.
16 Ma gorge est desséchée | comme un tesson d'argile,
ma langue colle à mon palais,
tu me fais retourner | à la poussière de la mort.
17 Des hordes de chiens m'environnent,
la meute des méchants m'assaille.
Ils ont percé mes mains, mes pieds,
18 je pourrais compter tous mes os ;
ils me regardent, ils me toisent,
19 ils se partagent mes habits
et tirent au sort ma tunique.

20 Mais toi, ô Eternel, | ne reste pas si loin !
O toi, ma force, | viens en hâte à mon aide !
21 Viens me sauver ! | Délivre ma vie de l'épée !
Protège-moi | de la fureur des chiens !
22 Délivre-moi | de la gueule du lion !
Préserve-moi | des cornes des taureaux !

Oui, tu m'as répondu !
23 Je proclamerai à mes frères | quel Dieu tu es,
je te louerai | dans la grande assemblée.
24 Vous qui respectez Dieu, | célébrez-le !
Descendants de Jacob, | glorifiez-le !
Descendants d'Israël, | vénérez-le !
25 Il n'a pas méprisé | le pauvre en son malheur,
il n'a pas détourné | son regard loin de lui.
Non ! il a écouté | l'appel à l'aide | qu'il lui lançait.

26 Grâce à toi, je te loue | dans la grande assemblée,
j'accomplirai mes vœux | en présence de ceux | qui te révèrent.
27 Que les malheureux mangent, | et qu'ils soient rassasiés !
Oui, qu'ils louent l'Eternel, | ceux qui vivent pour lui !
Que votre vie dure toujours !

28 Aux confins de la terre, | tous les peuples du monde | se souviendront de l'Eternel. | Tous, ils se tourneront vers lui,
et toutes les nations | se prosterneront devant lui.
29 Car l'Eternel est roi,
il domine sur les nations.
30 Tous les grands de la terre | mangeront et l'adoreront,
et ceux qui s'en vont vers la tombe,
ceux dont la vie décline, | se prosterneront devant lui.
31 Leur postérité, à son tour, | servira l'Eternel
et parlera de lui | à la génération | qui viendra après elle.
32 Cette postérité | publiera sa justice
et elle annoncera | au peuple qui va naître | ce qu'a fait l'Eternel | pour le salut des siens.

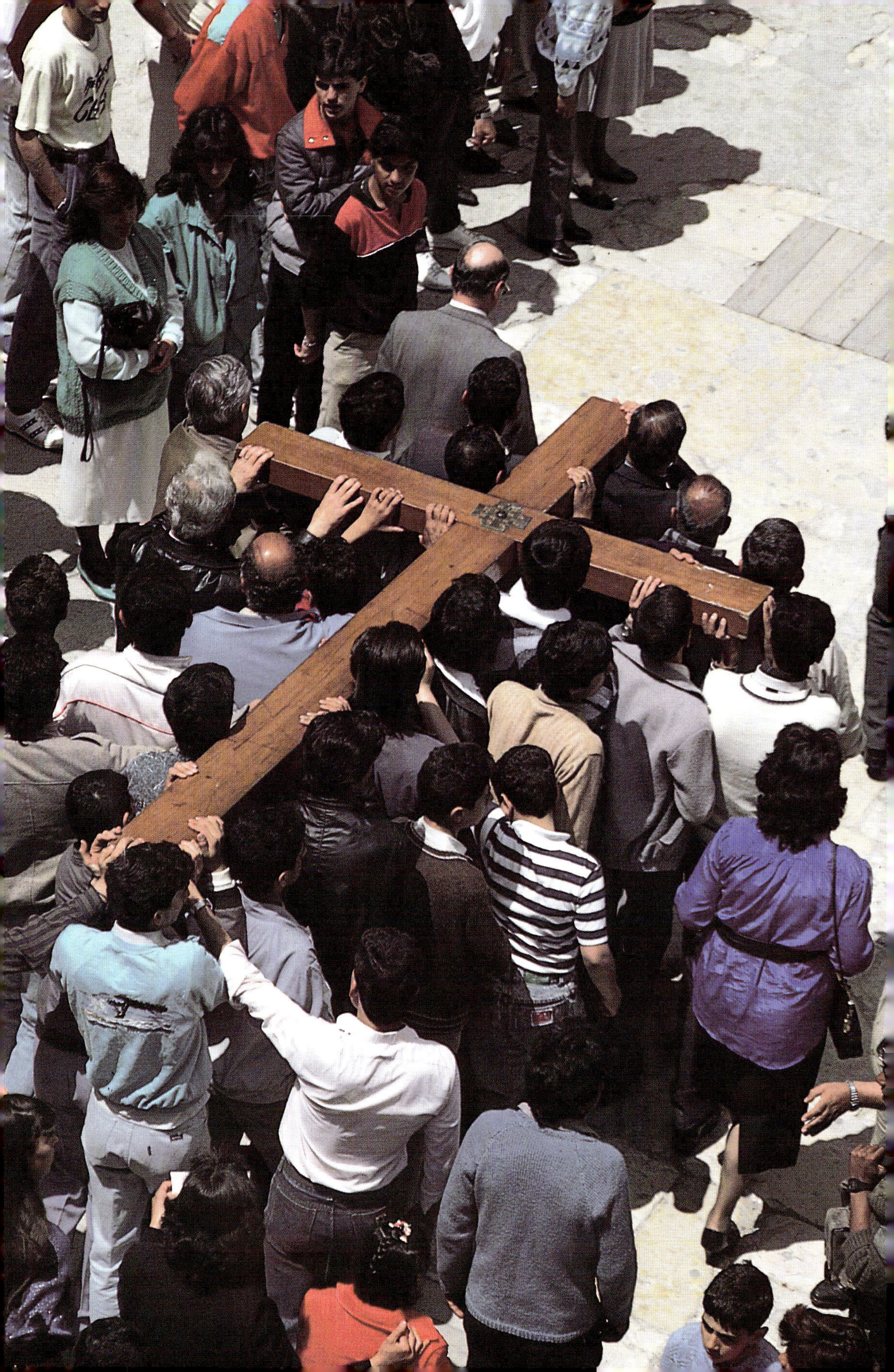

Mais les chrétiens ne peuvent lire ou chanter ce psaume sans l'appliquer aux souffrances du Christ et à sa gloire consécutive. En effet, le premier verset fait partie des sept paroles de Jésus sur la croix (Mt 27.46 ; Mc 15.34) ; la raillerie des versets 8 et 9 a été reprise par les sacrificateurs (Mt 27.39-44 ; Mc 15.31-32 ; Lc 23.35), les soldats se sont partagé ses habits comme annoncé au verset 19 (Jn 19.23, 24) et le verset 23 est appliqué au Christ dans Hébreux 2.11, 12. De plus, le tableau de l'agonie, dressé par les versets 15 à 18 – les os disloqués, la gorge desséchée, les mains et les pieds percés – dépeint remarquablement bien les horreurs de la crucifixion, bien que le Nouveau Testament ne reprenne pas ces versets pour le compte du Christ.

Ce psaume est construit sur un contraste.

Le cri d'angoisse (v. 1-22)

La victime lance un appel angoissé à Dieu : *Pourquoi m'as-tu abandonné ?* Ce n'est pas de la douleur physique, ni des moqueries de ses persécuteurs – il va les évoquer – qu'il souffre le plus, mais du sentiment d'avoir été abandonné par Dieu. Il n'est ni désespéré ni amer, simplement, il ne comprend pas. Ce qui donne un aspect particulièrement poignant à sa situation est que, malgré son sentiment d'abandon et le silence de Dieu, il continue à s'adresser à lui comme *son Dieu.*

Trois constatations semblent aggraver sa situation, en même temps qu'elles renforcent sa foi. Il y a d'abord l'expérience des anciens (v. 4-6). Il sait que Dieu est un Dieu *saint*, inégalable et au-dessus de tout, parce que les pères, qui lui ont fait confiance et ont crié à lui, ont été délivrés et non *déçus*. Il y a ensuite les sarcasmes de ses ennemis (v. 7-9), qui se moquent de lui parce que son expérience n'est pas celle de ses pères : *Il se confie en l'Éternel ? Eh bien, que maintenant, l'Éternel le délivre !* Dieu les laissera-t-il ainsi blasphémer ? Enfin, le psalmiste se souvient de ce qu'il a lui-même vécu avec Dieu dans le passé (v. 10-11). Yahvé a été son Dieu depuis sa naissance, et maintenant, il s'éloigne de lui. Ces trois constats lui arrachent un cri poignant (v. 12), où il supplie Dieu de ne pas rester loin de lui, *car le danger est proche.*

Quelle est exactement la nature de ce danger ? De toute évidence, le psalmiste est très malade, mourant, près de retourner *à la poussière de la mort* (v. 16). Il décrit tous ses symptômes dans les versets 15 et 16.

Mais ses douleurs physiques se trouvent encore aggravées par *la meute des méchants* qui l'environne (v. 17). Il les avait comparé plus haut aux *fortes bêtes* des riches pâturages de Basan et à des lions prêts à le dévorer (v. 13, 14). Il les décrit à présent comme des *chiens* sauvages (v. 17) et plus loin comme des *taureaux* (v. 22), qui attendent pour le mettre en pièces. Ils percent ses mains et ses pieds comme des brutes ; ils le *regardent*, ils le *toisent* (v. 18), ils vont jusqu'à lui arracher les vêtements et se les partager (v. 19), ou se préparent à le faire dès qu'il sera mort. Pour la troisième fois (voir v. 2, 3 et 12), le psalmiste supplie Dieu de s'approcher de lui et de le délivrer (v. 20-22).

Le chant de louange (v. 23-32)

Le ton du psaume change brusquement du tout au tout ; la supplication fait place à la louange et la douleur au triomphe. Nous ignorons comment est intervenue la délivrance divine. Il est dit simplement au verset 25 que Dieu n'a pas *méprisé* son serviteur affligé, comme l'avaient fait les hommes (v. 7), mais qu'il a entendu son cri. Le psalmiste déborde d'adoration et désire que le monde entier participe à sa louange. Le véritable adorateur a toujours un esprit missionnaire ; il ne peut envisager d'être le seul à adorer Dieu. Dans la fin du psaume, le cercle de ceux qui sont appelés à adorer Dieu s'élargit, jusqu'à englober toutes les nations et toutes les générations.

Il commencera par proclamer le nom de Dieu et le louer *dans la grande assemblée* (v. 23, 26). Il désire témoigner publiquement de la délivrance de Dieu auprès de ses frères juifs, les *descendants de Jacob* et le louer devant tous. Il pense ensuite à ceux qui souffrent comme lui a souffert, à ceux qui sont encore *malheureux* (v. 27) comme il l'a été lui-même (v. 25). Il veut les associer à sa joie et désire qu'ils *mangent* et *soient rassasiés*, probablement par le repas offert à l'occasion d'un sacrifice d'actions de grâce. Puis son regard devient prophétique et il évoque la conversion des nations, proclamant que *tous les peuples du monde (...) se tourneront* vers lui, car il *domine sur les nations* (v. 28, 29).

Mais la vision du psalmiste ne s'arrête pas même à cette perspective glorieuse. Le verset 30 n'est pas très clair : il associe dans une prosternation commune soit les orgueilleux et les humbles conscients de leur nature mortelle, soit – simplement – les vivants et les morts. Les versets 31 et 32 font cependant clairement allusion à la *postérité* du psalmiste. *Ce peuple qui va naître* entendra lui aussi parler de l'Éternel et de son salut. La publication de l'Évangile du salut doit donc être à la fois universelle et éternelle et l'issue des souffrances de cet homme pieux préfigure déjà le triomphe final du Crucifié.

Psaume 23

L'Éternel est mon berger

Qui ne connaît pas ce psaume ? C'est même celui que beaucoup d'entre nous préfèrent. Il présente la relation intime entre Dieu et l'un de ses enfants au moyen de deux tableaux éloquents. Le premier est celui du berger et de sa brebis, le second, celui de l'hôte et de son invité.

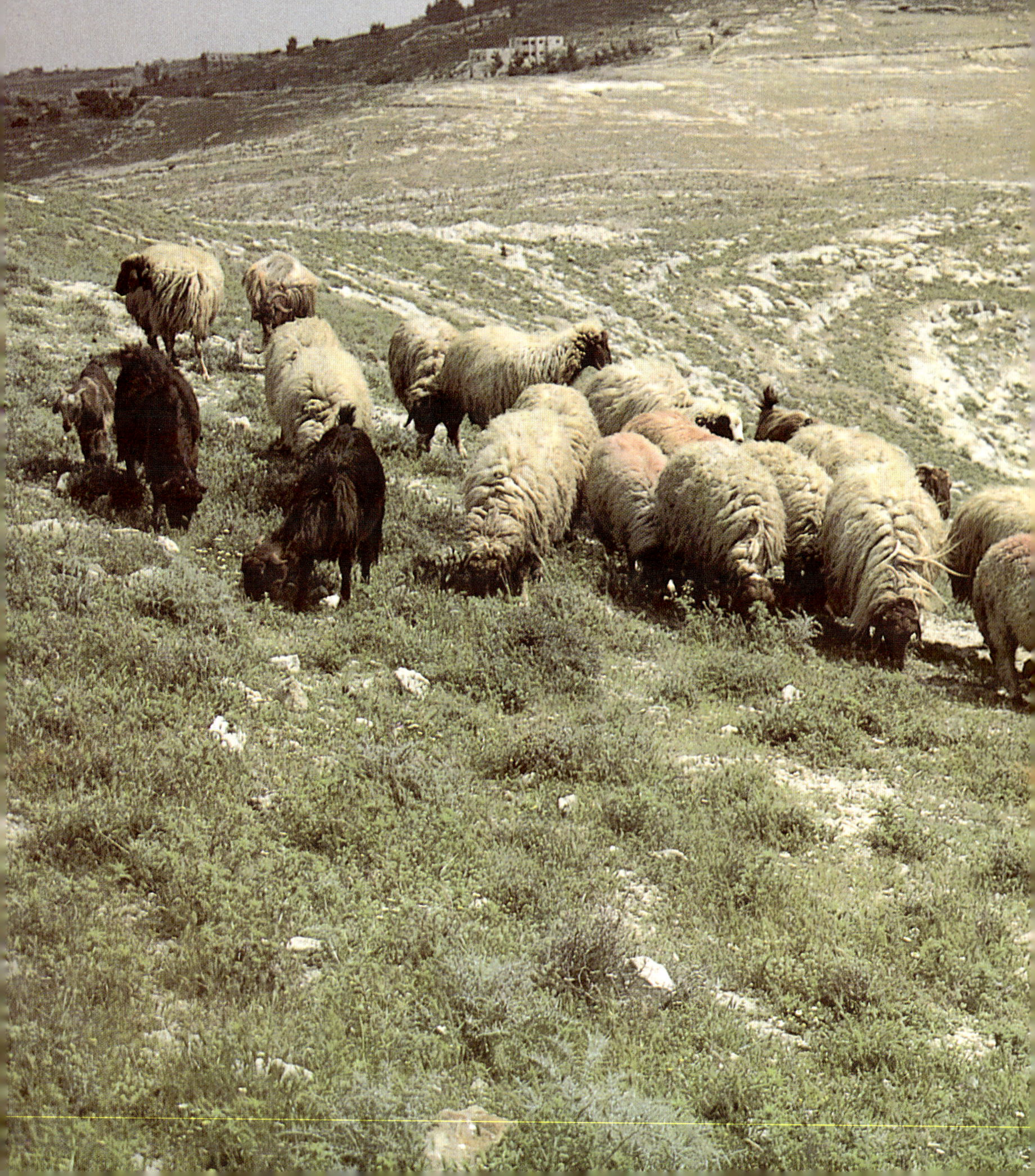

L'Eternel est mon berger.
Je ne manquerai de rien.
2 Grâce à lui, je me repose | dans des prairies verdoyantes,
et c'est lui qui me conduit | au bord des eaux calmes.
3 Il me rend des forces neuves,
et, pour l'honneur de son nom,
il me mène pas à pas | sur le droit chemin.
4 Si je devais traverser | la vallée où règnent | les ténèbres de la mort,
je ne craindrais aucun mal, | car tu es auprès de moi :
ta houlette me conduit | et ton bâton me protège.

5 Pour moi, tu dresses une table
aux yeux de mes ennemis,
tu oins de parfums ma tête,
tu fais déborder ma coupe.
6 Oui, toute ma vie,
ta bonté et ton amour | m'accompagneront
et je pourrai retourner | au temple de l'Eternel
tant que je vivrai.

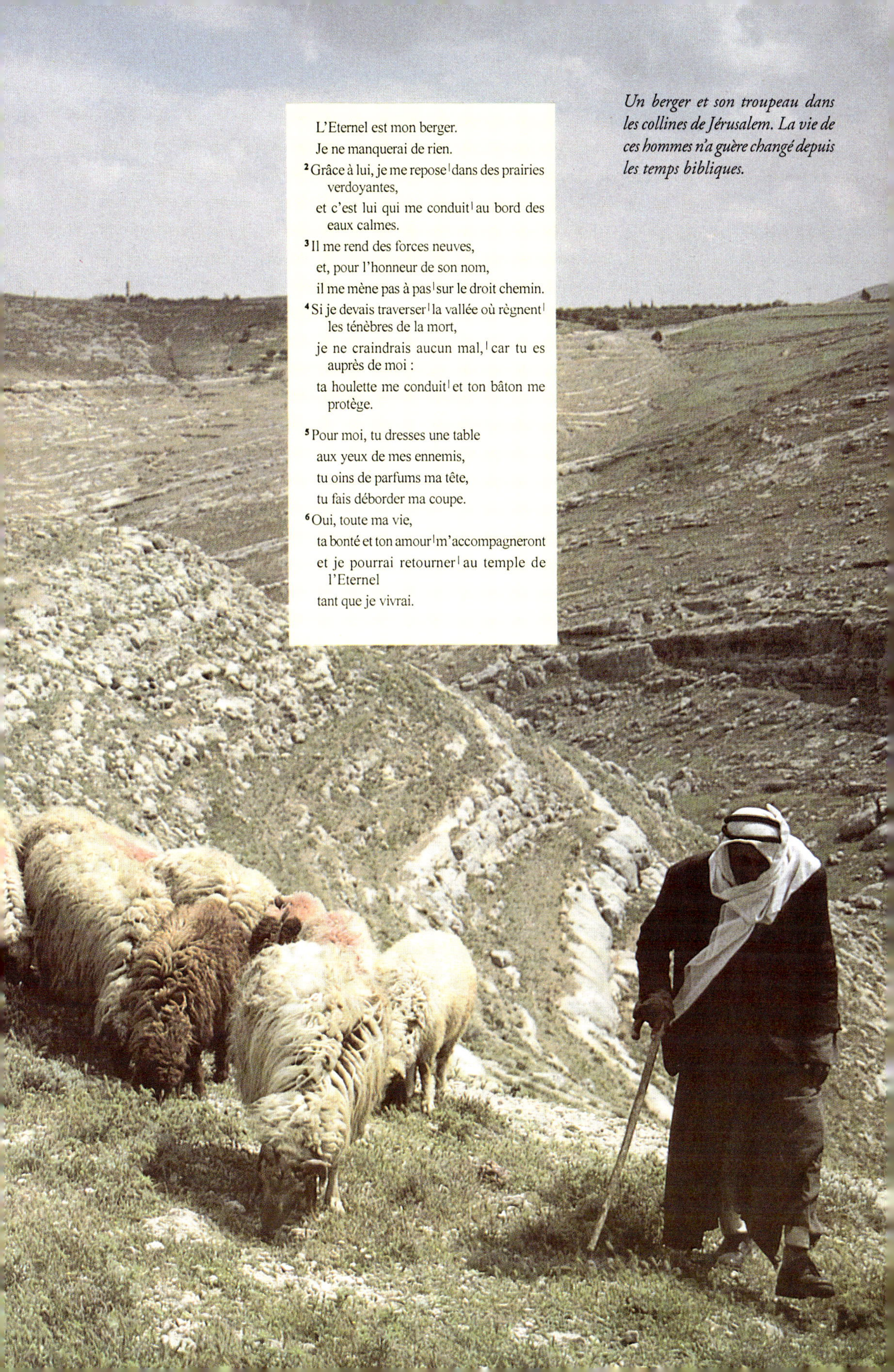

Un berger et son troupeau dans les collines de Jérusalem. La vie de ces hommes n'a guère changé depuis les temps bibliques.

L'Éternel, mon berger (v. 1-4)

Quoi de plus normal pour une communauté pastorale que de penser à l'Éternel comme à son berger, qui, *comme un troupeau (...) fit sortir son peuple et les conduisit dans le désert, tout comme un berger conduit ses brebis* (Ps 78.52 ; voir aussi Ps 80.1 ; Es 40.11). Mais ici, la métaphore est employée sur un plan strictement personnel. *L'Éternel est mon berger*, affirme l'auteur avec assurance, oubliant même les autres brebis du troupeau.

Pour le chrétien, ce psaume évoque tout naturellement Jésus-Christ, qui n'a pas hésité à reprendre à son compte l'image appliquée ici à Yahvé. C'est lui qui est notre « bon berger », « le chef des bergers » et « le grand berger de ses brebis » (Jn 10.11, 14 ; 1 P 5.4 ; He 13.20).

Si mon expérience personnelle me permet de dire que *l'Éternel est mon berger*, alors je peux aussi affirmer que *je ne manquerai de rien*. Le bon berger qui prend soin de ses brebis pourvoit à tous mes besoins. Il me fait reposer dans des *prairies verdoyantes* pour me rassasier et me conduit près des eaux fraîches pour étancher ma soif (v. 2). *Pour l'honneur de son nom*, c'est-à-dire par fidélité envers sa propre personne et ses promesses, il me dirigera *sur le droit chemin*, et ne permettra pas que je m'égare (v. 3).

En effet, même si je traverse *la vallée où règnent d'épaisses ténèbres* (autre traduction possible du verset 4), que ce soient celles de la mort ou d'autres circonstances, je n'aurai rien à craindre et je serai en paix, car mon berger est *auprès de moi*, me conduisant avec sa houlette et me protégeant de son bâton (v. 4). Par conséquent, quelles que soient les circonstances de ma vie – prairies verdoyantes et eaux calmes ou, au contraire, vallées ténébreuses – ce n'est pas en elles que repose ma sécurité, mais dans mon Berger. En sa présence, je ne connais ni le besoin (v. 1), ni la crainte (v. 4).

L'Éternel, mon hôte (v. 5, 6)

Le décor change. Je ne suis plus dehors, mais dans une maison ; je ne suis plus une brebis d'un troupeau, mais un invité à un banquet. Mon hôte divin a dressé *une table... pour moi*. Ce n'est pas une fête secrète, elle se déroule en présence de mes ennemis ; en effet, lorsque l'Éternel comble l'âme, il le fait à la face du monde.

Il fait preuve envers moi d'une générosité sans bornes : une table garnie de nourriture, des huiles parfumées pour oindre ma tête et une coupe débordante (v. 5). Et Dieu ne s'arrête pas là ! Sa *bonté* et son *amour m'accompagneront,* car c'est lui-même qui me *conduit* (v.2, 3). Il me gardera donc par devant et par derrière, *tant que je vivrai*. Enfin, « j'habiterai dans la maison de l'Éternel jusqu'à la fin de mes jours » (Segond), non dans le Tabernacle ou le Temple, ni même en sa présence ici-bas, mais dans cette maison du Père, comportant de nombreuses demeures, où Jésus a promis qu'il préparerait une place pour les siens (Jn 14.1-4).

Psaume 24

Pour gravir le mont de l'Éternel

À l'origine de ce psaume prend place l'épisode triomphal rapporté dans 2 Samuel 6, où le roi David fit transporter l'arche de la maison d'Obed Edom à la tente qu'il avait dressée pour elle à Jérusalem. Il est probable qu'une fête ait été célébrée chaque année, pour commémorer cet événement ou pour se réjouir du choix divin de David et de Jérusalem. On chantait alors ce psaume, en accompagnant l'arche à travers la ville.

Quelle que soit les circonstances exactes, on imagine aisément le cortège gravir la montagne de Sion jusqu'au Temple en chantant ces paroles, les versets 3, 4 et 7 à 10 se répondant tour à tour, comme le font parfois certaines chorales de nos jours.

La terre entière (v. 1, 2)

D'entrée, le psalmiste proclame que la terre entière, avec tous ses habitants, appartient à l'Eternel (v. 1) parce qu'il en est le Créateur (v. 2). *C'est lui qui a fondé la terre sur les mers, qui l'a établie fermement au-dessus des cours d'eau.* Cette évocation de la terre posée sur l'eau relève bien entendu du langage poétique et s'inspire peut-être du récit de la Genèse qui fait apparaître le sec hors de l'eau. Mais cette image peut même se concevoir de nos jours, si l'on sait que les eaux recouvrent environ 70 % de la surface du globe. Lorsque Paul explique aux Corinthiens qu'ils peuvent manger de tout, même des viandes sacrifiées aux idoles, il s'appuie sur le début de ce psaume, qui déclare que la terre et ses richesses appartiennent à l'Eternel.

La terre et ses richesses | appartiennent à l'Eternel.
L'univers est à lui | avec ceux qui l'habitent.
2 C'est lui qui a fondé | la terre sur les mers,
qui l'a établie fermement | au-dessus des cours d'eau.

3 Qui pourra accéder | au mont de l'Eternel ?
Qui pourra se tenir | dans sa demeure sainte ?
4 L'innocent aux mains nettes | et qui a le cœur pur,
qui ne se tourne pas | vers le mensonge,
et qui ne jure pas | pour tromper son prochain.
5 Celui qui vit ainsi | sera béni par l'Eternel,
il obtiendra justice | de son Dieu qui le sauve.
6 O Eternel, tel est le peuple | qui te révère
et qui s'attache à toi, | Dieu de Jacob.

Pause

7 Portes, levez la tête, | ô portes, levez-vous.
Relevez vos frontons, | ô portes, haussez-vous, | vous, portes éternelles,
pour que le Roi de gloire | y fasse son entrée !
8 Qui est ce Roi de gloire ?
C'est l'Eternel, | le Fort et le Vaillant,
oui, l'Eternel, | vaillant dans les combats.
9 Portes, levez la tête, | ô portes, levez-vous.
Relevez vos frontons, | ô portes, haussez-vous, | vous, portes éternelles,
pour que le Roi de gloire | y fasse son entrée !
10 Qui est ce Roi de gloire ?
Le Seigneur des armées célestes,
c'est lui le Roi de gloire.

Pause

Le mont de l'Éternel (v. 3-6)

Bien que toute la terre soit à l'Éternel, il est une certaine montagne qui lui appartient d'une manière toute particulière. C'est la montagne de Sion, appelée le *mont de l'Éternel, sa demeure sainte* (v. 3), où se trouvait l'arche, symbole de sa présence. Mais *qui pourra* y *accéder* et se tenir dans sa sainte présence (v. 3) ? La réponse, qui rappelle le psaume 15, met une fois de plus l'accent sur la relation entre adoration et moralité.

La seule louange que Dieu puisse agréer est celle que lui apportent des hommes *aux mains nettes* et au *cœur pur*, c'est-à-dire saints

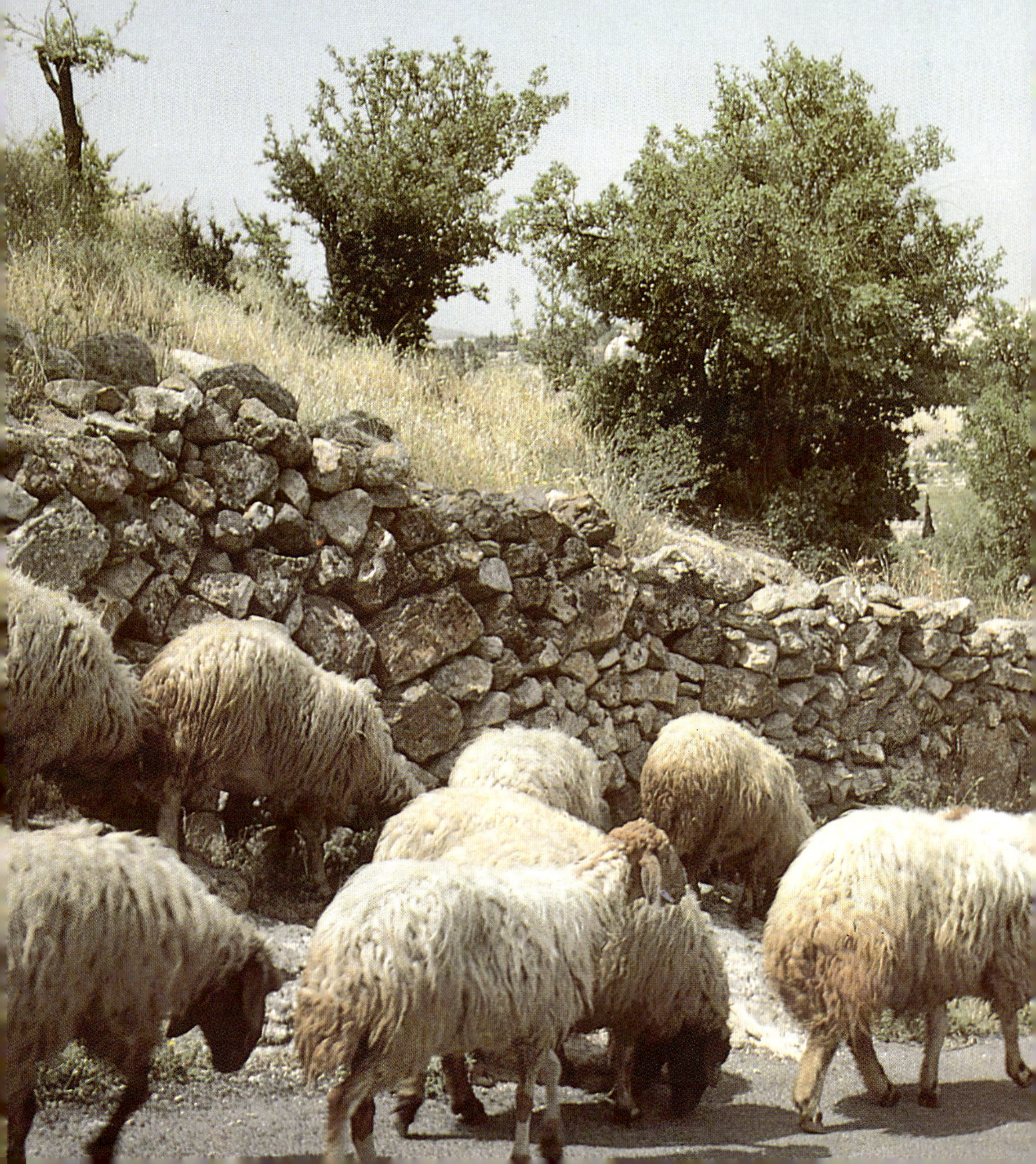

Le Dôme du Rocher et la vieille ville de Jérusalem vus depuis le Mont des Oliviers. Le Dôme du Rocher occupe le site du Temple juif des temps bibliques.

dans leurs pensées, leurs motivations et leurs actes. Qui plus est, cette sainteté transparaît dans leur relation avec Dieu comme avec les autres, car ils ne se tournent pas vers le mensonge (autre traduction : vers les faux dieux) et ne jurent pas pour tromper leur prochain. Ce sont de telles personnes, saintes et justes, que Dieu approuve (v. 5) et bénit ; cette bénédiction est en effet la part de tous ceux qui s'attachent au Dieu de Jacob (v. 6).

Les portes de la ville (v. 7-10)

Le cortège portant l'arche a maintenant atteint les portes de la cité de David et les voix du chœur retentissent : *Portes, levez la tête…pour que le Roi de gloire y fasse son entrée* (v. 7) ! De l'intérieur de la ville, s'élève cette interrogation : *Qui est ce Roi de gloire ?* à laquelle le chœur répond : *C'est l'Éternel, le Fort et le Vaillant, oui, l'Éternel, vaillant dans les combats* (v. 8). Cet échange est repris une deuxième fois mot pour mot (v. 9, 10), le nom de *Seigneur des armées célestes* s'ajoutant alors à celui de *Roi de gloire*. Ce titre, qui apparaît ici pour la première fois dans le Psautier, est le bouquet final de ce psaume.

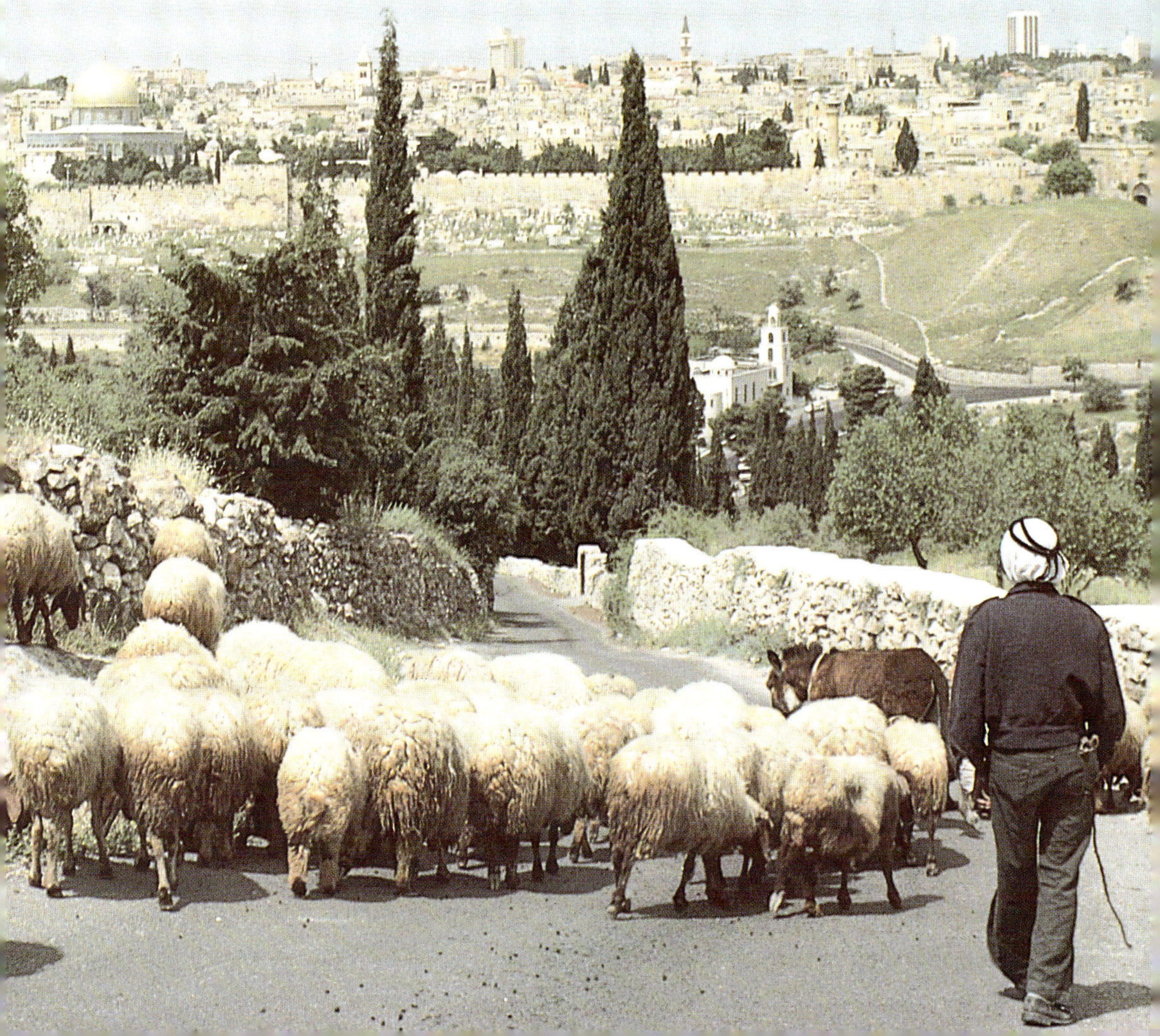

Page suivante : Cascade à En Gedi, sur la rive occidentale de la Mer Morte, un lieu que David connaissait bien. Ce nom signifie en hébreu « chute de la chèvre ».

Psaume 27

L'âme changeante

Les affirmations et les requêtes de ce psaume s'élèvent dans un contexte nettement hostile. Si c'est David qui l'a écrit, (ce qu'il n'y a pas de raison de mettre en doute), il fait référence, soit à sa traque par Saül, soit à sa fuite devant Absalom. Dans un cas comme dans l'autre, les ennemis sont des *méchants* (v. 2) qui le persécutent au nom de la justice et veulent lui nuire par la violence physique et la calomnie (v. 12). Il les compare à des bêtes féroces cherchant à le mettre en pièces (v. 2).

La confiance en Dieu (v. 1-6)

Le début de ce psaume nous livre l'une des plus belles confessions, de tout l'Ancien Testament, proclamant la sécurité dont jouit l'enfant de Dieu. *L'Éternel est ma lumière* pour me guider, *mon Sauveur* pour

Oui, l'Eternel est ma lumière | et mon Sauveur :
de qui aurais-je crainte ?
L'Eternel protège ma vie :
de qui aurais-je peur ?
2 Que des méchants | s'avancent contre moi,
voulant me déchirer,
ce sont mes ennemis, | mes oppresseurs,
qui perdent pied et tombent.
3 Qu'une armée vienne m'assiéger,
mon cœur reste sans crainte.
Que l'on me déclare la guerre,
je suis plein d'assurance.
4 J'ai présenté à l'Eternel | un seul souhait, | mais qui me tient vraiment à cœur :
je voudrais habiter | dans la maison de l'Eternel | tous les jours de ma vie
afin d'admirer l'Eternel | dans sa beauté,
et de chercher à le connaître | dans sa demeure.
5 Car il me cache sous sa tente | dans les jours du malheur.
Au secret de son tabernacle, | il me tient abrité ;
sur un rocher, | il me met hors d'atteinte.
6 Dès à présent, | je peux lever la tête | pour dominer | mes ennemis autour de moi.
J'offrirai dans son tabernacle | des sacrifices | avec des cris de joie,
je célébrerai l'Eternel | par le chant et les instruments.
7 O Eternel, | écoute mon appel | car je t'invoque.
Accorde-moi la grâce | de me répondre.
8 Je pense à toi. | Tu as dit : « Tournez-vous vers moi. »
Oui, c'est vers toi que je me tourne, | ô Eternel,
9 ne te détourne pas de moi
et ne repousse pas | ton serviteur avec colère !
Toi qui m'as secouru,
ne me délaisse pas ! | Ne m'abandonne pas,
ô Dieu, toi qui es mon Sauveur !
10 Si mon père et ma mère | devaient m'abandonner,
l'Eternel me recueillerait.
11 Enseigne-moi la voie | que tu veux que je suive, | ô Eternel,
et conduis-moi | par un sentier égal,
puisque mes ennemis me guettent.
12 Ne m'abandonne pas | aux projets de mes adversaires
lorsque de faux témoins | se dressent contre moi,
respirant la violence.
13 Que deviendrais-je | si je n'avais pas l'assurance | de voir l'amour de l'Eternel
au pays des vivants ?

14 Attends-toi donc à l'Eternel !
Sois fort ! | Affermis ton courage !
Oui, attends-toi à l'Eternel !

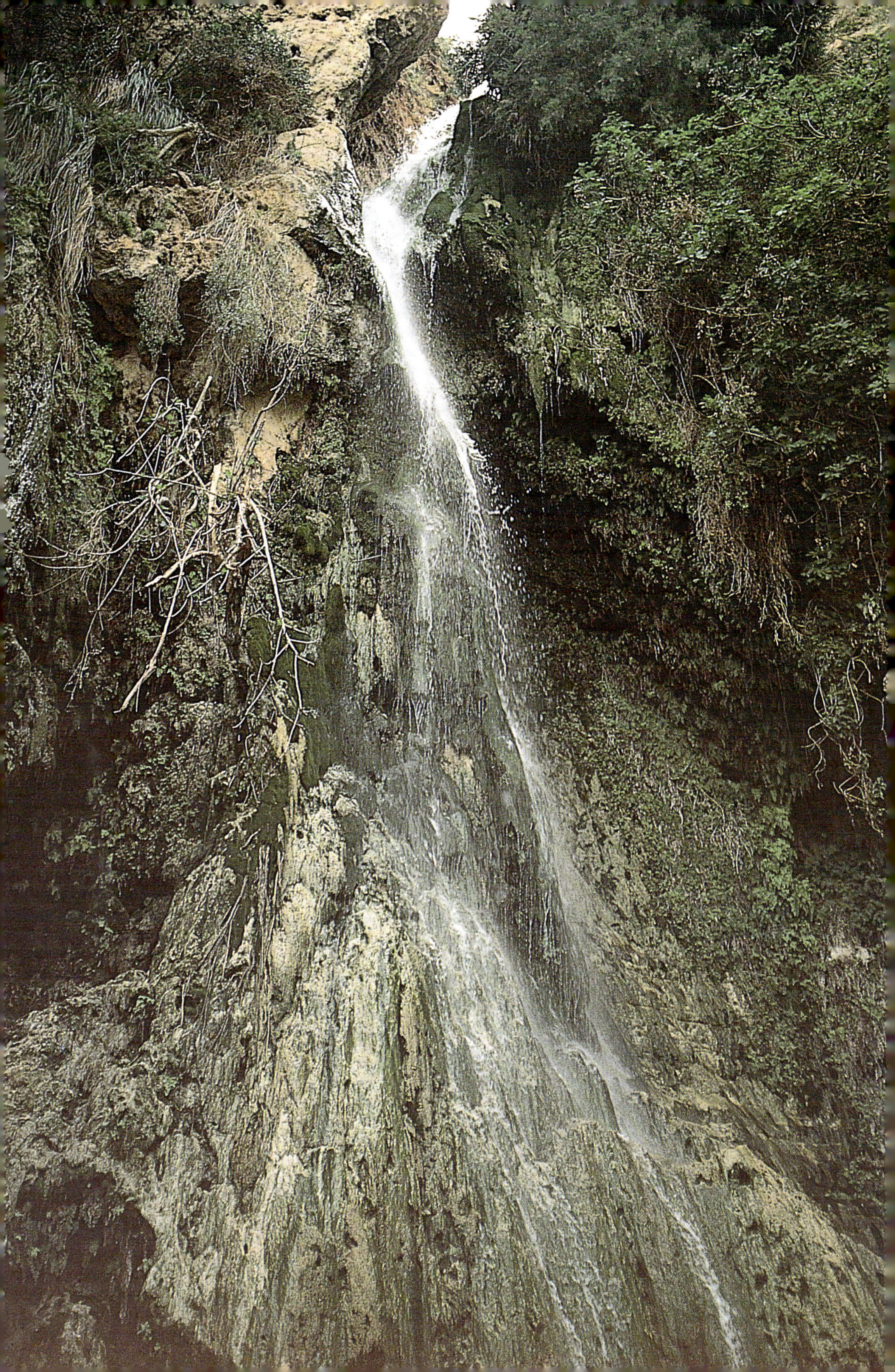

me délivrer et celui qui *protège ma vie*, en qui je trouve refuge. *De qui aurais-je peur ?* Cette question, qui n'attend pas de réponse, rappelle les défis lancés par Paul à la fin de Romains 8. Que les ennemis de David l'attaquent, ils *perdent pied et tombent* (v. 2). Même si toute une armée lui déclarait la guerre (v. 3), il resterait plein d'assurance.

Nombreux sont les chrétiens à avoir été réconfortés par ces paroles, alors que leur situation était désespérée. Parmi eux, James Hannington, premier évêque d'Afrique équatoriale. Il fut capturé et emprisonné en octobre 1885, alors qu'il atteignait le lac Victoria Nyanza. « Brûlant de fièvre, délirant parfois de douleur, dévoré par la vermine, craignant à tout moment pour sa vie, il puisa des forces dans les Psaumes. » Le 28 octobre, à la veille de sa mort en martyr, il écrivit dans son journal : « Je suis brisé et abattu. Réconforté par le psaume 27. »

D'où vient cette assurance inébranlable d'un homme seul contre de nombreux ennemis ? Elle vient, nous explique le psalmiste, de la présence et la protection de Dieu. Il est une chose que David désire par-dessus tout (v. 4), c'est *habiter dans la maison de l'Éternel* toute sa vie, afin de pouvoir *admirer l'Éternel dans sa beauté* ou « dans sa douceur » et *chercher à le connaître dans sa demeure.*

Ce souhait du psalmiste n'est pas à prendre au pied de la lettre. Seuls les prêtres étaient admis à vivre dans l'enceinte de la maison de Dieu, qu'il s'agisse du tabernacle à Siloé ou de la montagne de Sion. De surcroît David, appartenant à la tribu de Juda et non à celle de Lévi, ne pouvait aspirer à la prêtrise. Cette métaphore exprime son aspiration profonde à jouir d'une communion ininterrompue avec Dieu pour l'adorer et discerner sa volonté. Le psaume 23.5, 6 parle de la maison de Dieu dans les mêmes termes.

C'est cette communion intime avec Dieu qui permettait à David de compter sur la délivrance. Dieu le protègerait *dans les jours du malheur*, tout comme une tente abrite le voyageur du soleil, ou comme un rocher élevé le met hors d'atteinte des flots (v. 5, 6). Il louera Dieu dans son tabernacle (au sens propre cette fois-ci) avec des sacrifices et *des cris de joie* (v. 6).

L'appel au secours (v. 7-14)

Soudain tout change. De la troisième personne, on passe à la deuxième, et l'affirmation se transforme en prière. L'état d'âme change aussi. La confiance cède la place à la supplication angoissée.

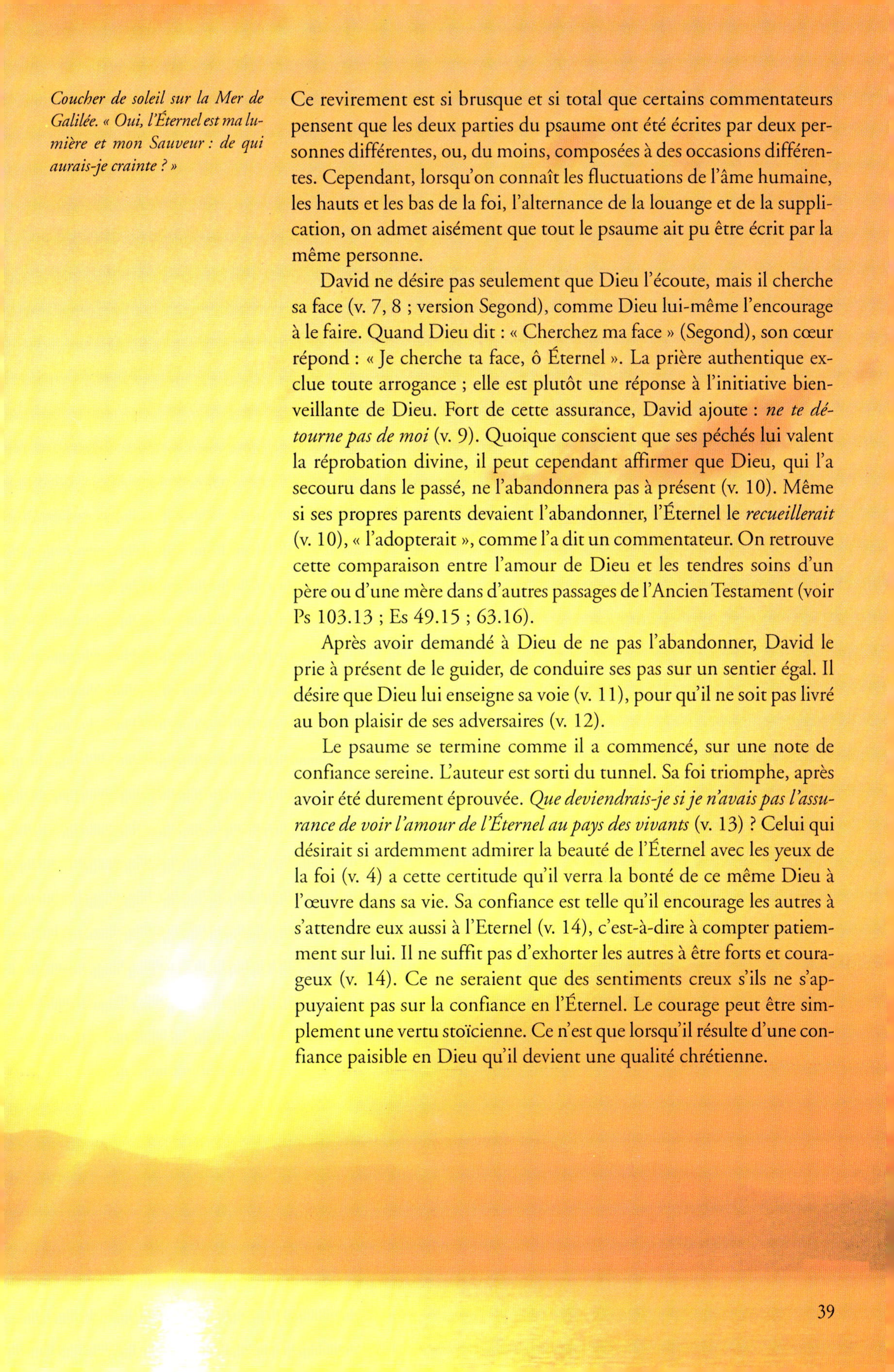

Coucher de soleil sur la Mer de Galilée. « Oui, l'Éternel est ma lumière et mon Sauveur : de qui aurais-je crainte ? »

Ce revirement est si brusque et si total que certains commentateurs pensent que les deux parties du psaume ont été écrites par deux personnes différentes, ou, du moins, composées à des occasions différentes. Cependant, lorsqu'on connaît les fluctuations de l'âme humaine, les hauts et les bas de la foi, l'alternance de la louange et de la supplication, on admet aisément que tout le psaume ait pu être écrit par la même personne.

David ne désire pas seulement que Dieu l'écoute, mais il cherche sa face (v. 7, 8 ; version Segond), comme Dieu lui-même l'encourage à le faire. Quand Dieu dit : « Cherchez ma face » (Segond), son cœur répond : « Je cherche ta face, ô Éternel ». La prière authentique exclue toute arrogance ; elle est plutôt une réponse à l'initiative bienveillante de Dieu. Fort de cette assurance, David ajoute : *ne te détourne pas de moi* (v. 9). Quoique conscient que ses péchés lui valent la réprobation divine, il peut cependant affirmer que Dieu, qui l'a secouru dans le passé, ne l'abandonnera pas à présent (v. 10). Même si ses propres parents devaient l'abandonner, l'Éternel le *recueillerait* (v. 10), « l'adopterait », comme l'a dit un commentateur. On retrouve cette comparaison entre l'amour de Dieu et les tendres soins d'un père ou d'une mère dans d'autres passages de l'Ancien Testament (voir Ps 103.13 ; Es 49.15 ; 63.16).

Après avoir demandé à Dieu de ne pas l'abandonner, David le prie à présent de le guider, de conduire ses pas sur un sentier égal. Il désire que Dieu lui enseigne sa voie (v. 11), pour qu'il ne soit pas livré au bon plaisir de ses adversaires (v. 12).

Le psaume se termine comme il a commencé, sur une note de confiance sereine. L'auteur est sorti du tunnel. Sa foi triomphe, après avoir été durement éprouvée. *Que deviendrais-je si je n'avais pas l'assurance de voir l'amour de l'Éternel au pays des vivants* (v. 13) ? Celui qui désirait si ardemment admirer la beauté de l'Éternel avec les yeux de la foi (v. 4) a cette certitude qu'il verra la bonté de ce même Dieu à l'œuvre dans sa vie. Sa confiance est telle qu'il encourage les autres à s'attendre eux aussi à l'Eternel (v. 14), c'est-à-dire à compter patiemment sur lui. Il ne suffit pas d'exhorter les autres à être forts et courageux (v. 14). Ce ne seraient que des sentiments creux s'ils ne s'appuyaient pas sur la confiance en l'Éternel. Le courage peut être simplement une vertu stoïcienne. Ce n'est que lorsqu'il résulte d'une confiance paisible en Dieu qu'il devient une qualité chrétienne.

Psaume 29

La voix de l'Éternel

Beaucoup de gens craignent les orages violents. Le psalmiste hébreu, lui, y voit plutôt une manifestation de la gloire de Dieu. Il est tellement convaincu que Dieu a le contrôle des éléments, qu'il n'hésite pas à recourir à un anthropomorphisme audacieux, qui dépeint le tonnerre comme *la voix de l'Éternel*. Pas plus que dans d'autres psaumes, où le vent est décrit comme le « souffle » de Dieu, les cieux, comme l'ouvrage de ses « doigts » et où les animaux mangent dans sa « main », il ne faut prendre cette expression au sens propre (voir par ex. Ps 147.18 ; 8.3 et 104.28). Ce sont des effets de style destinés à souligner l'action divine immanente dans le monde.

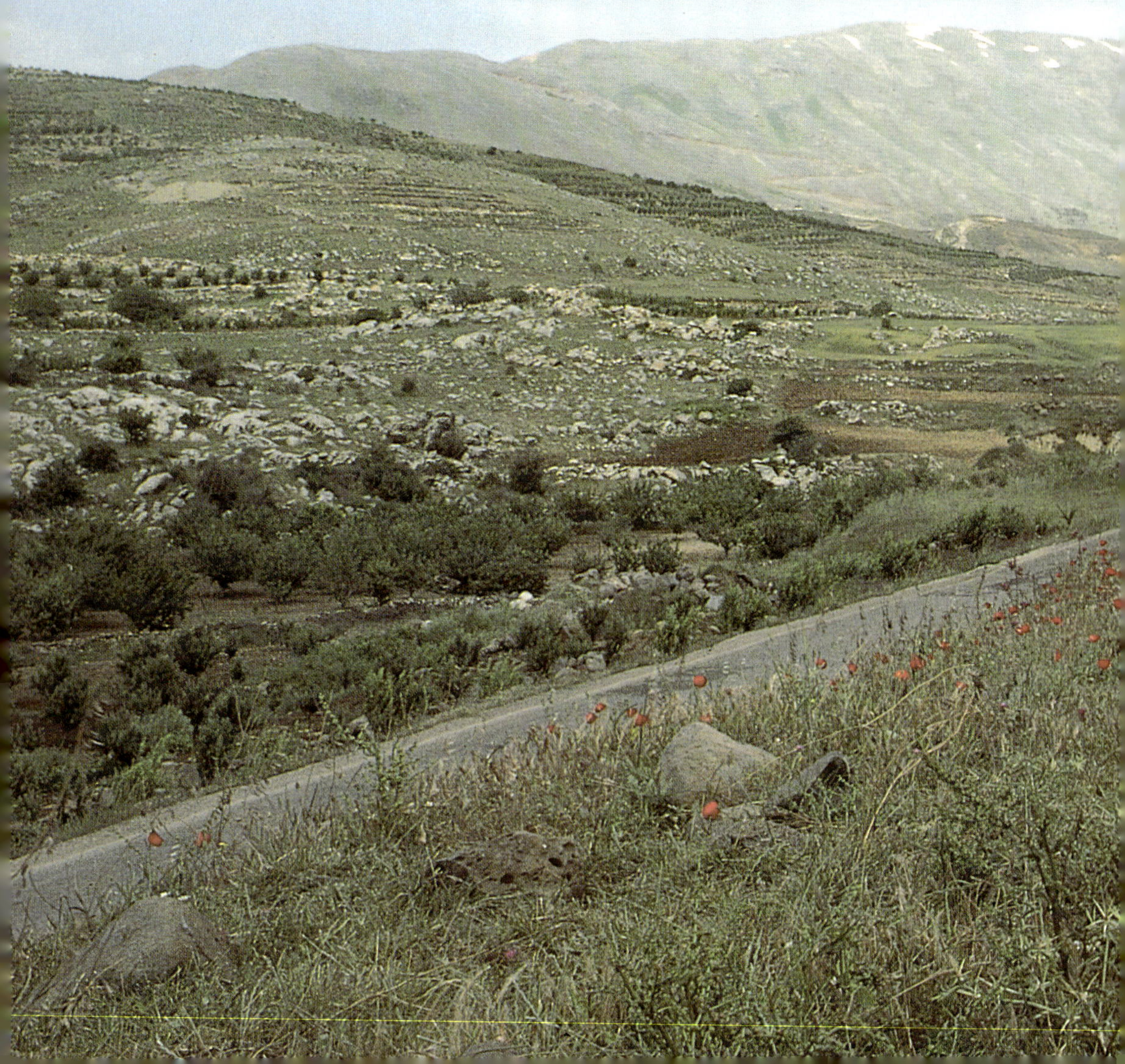

Célébrez l'Eternel, | vous, les anges de Dieu.

Célébrez l'Eternel, | en proclamant | sa gloire et sa puissance !

2 Oui, célébrez la gloire | du nom de l'Eternel,

et prosternez-vous devant lui | parés de sainteté !

3 La voix de l'Eternel | retentit sur les eaux,

Dieu, dans sa gloire, | fait gronder le tonnerre.

La voix de l'Eternel domine | le bruit des grandes eaux.

4 La voix de l'Eternel | retentit avec force,

la voix de l'Eternel résonne | majestueusement.

5 La voix de l'Eternel | foudroie les cèdres,

l'Eternel brise | les cèdres du Liban.

6 Il fait bondir | tout le Liban | comme des veaux

et le Siriôn | comme des buffles.

7 La voix de l'Eternel | fait jaillir des éclairs.

8 La voix de l'Eternel | fait trembler le désert.

L'Eternel fait trembler | le désert de Qadèch.

9 La voix de l'Eternel | fait enfanter les biches

et elle fait tomber les feuilles | des arbres des forêts.

Dans son palais,

tout s'écrie : « Gloire à l'Eternel ! »

10 Lors du déluge, | l'Eternel était roi,

l'Eternel règne | à tout jamais.

11 L'Eternel donnera | la puissance à son peuple.

L'Eternel bénira son peuple | en lui donnant la paix.

Le mont Hermon culmine à 2800 mètres. Son sommet reste enneigé la majeure partie de l'année.

La voix de l'Éternel

Le poète semble suivre le trajet d'un orage qui vient du nord de la Palestine (le Liban et la Syrie, ou le mont Hermon), (v. 5, 6) et passe au-dessus de lui, pour aller se déchaîner plus loin au sud, dans le désert de Qadèch (v. 8). Il est question à huit reprises de *la voix de l'Éternel.* Quelqu'un l'a comparée à « des coups de tonnerre successifs » qui résonnent dans la campagne. On l'entend d'abord *sur les eaux* (v. 3), probablement sur les nuages de pluie, où elle retentit *avec force (...) majestueusement* (v. 4). Puis le tonnerre s'approche et l'orage

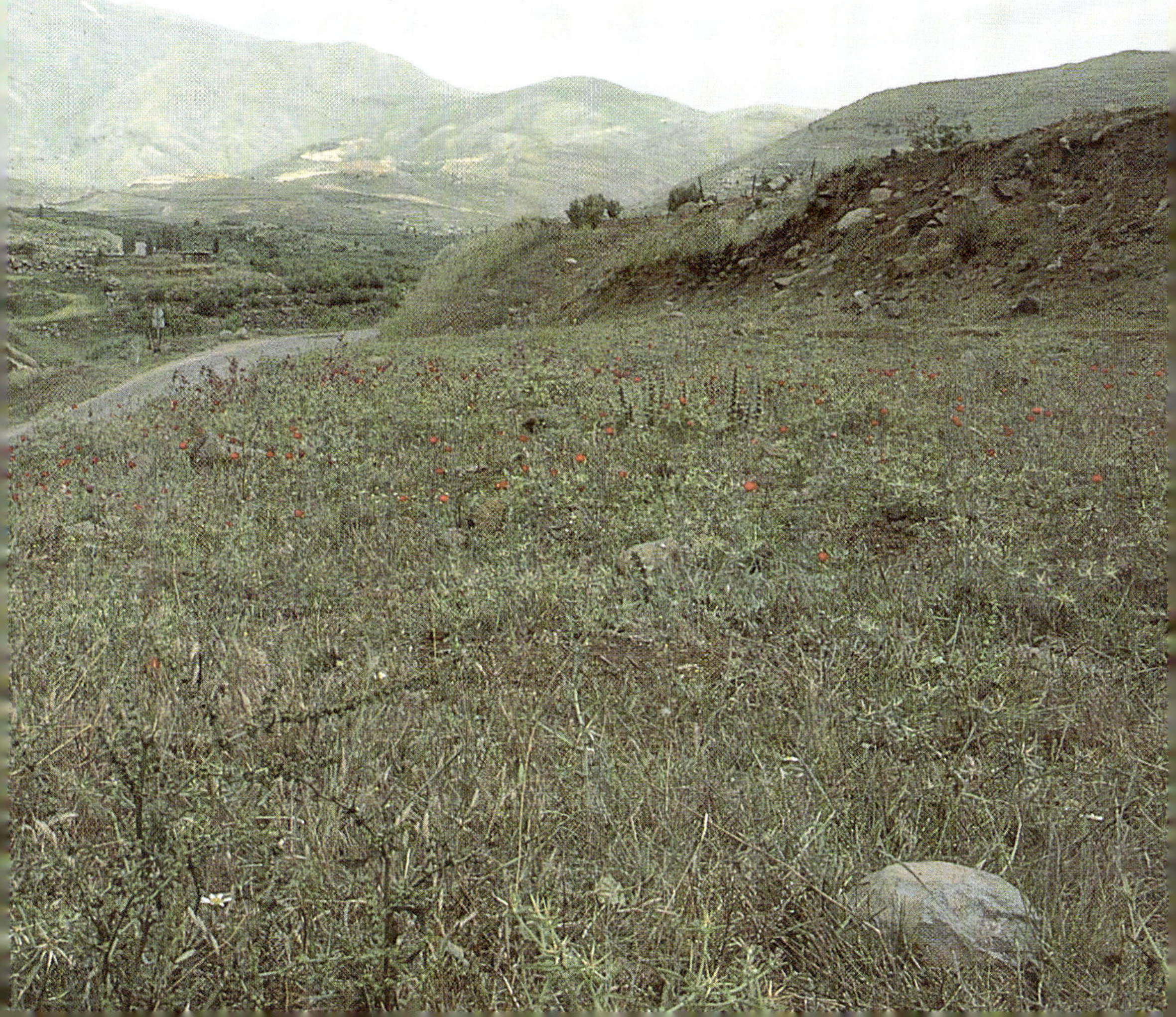

« La voix de l'Éternel retentit sur les eaux... la voix de l'Éternel résonne majestueusement. »

cause des dégâts, foudroyant notamment les puissants *cèdres du Liban* ; la montagne elle-même tremble tellement qu'elle semble *bondir (...) comme des veaux* ou *comme des buffles* (v. 6). Des éclairs arborescents accompagnent les coups de tonnerre (v. 7). Les biches enfantent prématurément (autre traduction : *agite les grands arbres*) et la tempête dépouille les arbres de la forêt (v. 9). La présence de Dieu est tellement tangible que la terre entière semble être *son palais*. Terrassé par sa majesté, tout s'écrie « Gloire ! »

La gloire de l'Éternel

Nous avons là un psaume de la nature, comme le Psautier en comporte plusieurs. Mais ce serait commettre une grave erreur que de croire que le seul but du psalmiste est d'écrire un hymne à la nature. Sa vision du monde est avant tout centrée sur Dieu. Il s'intéresse au soleil et aux étoiles (Ps 8, 19), au tonnerre et aux éclairs (Ps 29), aux oiseaux et aux autres animaux (Ps 104), uniquement dans la mesure où ils lui parlent de la grandeur et de la bonté de Dieu. C'est manifeste du début à la fin du psaume 29.

Ce sont d'abord les anges qui sont invités à reconnaître sa souveraineté (v. 1, 2). Ils célèbrent *la gloire du nom de l'Éternel* (v. 2). Il est « le Dieu de gloire » (version Segond), cette gloire dont la magnificence grandiose d'un orage dévoile un aspect.

Si l'introduction exhorte les anges du ciel à adorer Dieu, la conclusion, elle, formule la prière que ce même Dieu bénisse son peuple sur la terre. Il en a assurément le pouvoir, car il était sur son trône *lors du déluge* et il *règne à tout jamais* (v. 10). Cet enchaînement de l'orage à la bénédiction du peuple est digne d'intérêt dans la mesure où il montre bien que les Juifs ne ressentaient aucune dichotomie entre nature et grâce. Le Dieu du tonnerre était aussi le Dieu d'Israël, souverain dans la nature comme dans les affaires des hommes et des nations. Le sanctuaire ne se trouvait pas seulement à Jérusalem, la forêt et le désert étaient aussi son temple, où on pouvait l'adorer. Un orage n'était pas un phénomène étranger. Yahvé ne s'était-il pas révélé au peuple de son alliance sur le mont Sinaï par le tonnerre et les éclairs (Ex 19.16 ; 20.18) ? Et pourtant, celui qui fait retentir sa voix dans le tonnerre peut aussi apaiser la tempête, et se révéler dans un murmure doux et léger, comme dans un tremblement de terre (1 R 19.11,12). Il est donc à la fois source de puissance et de paix pour son peuple (v. 10).

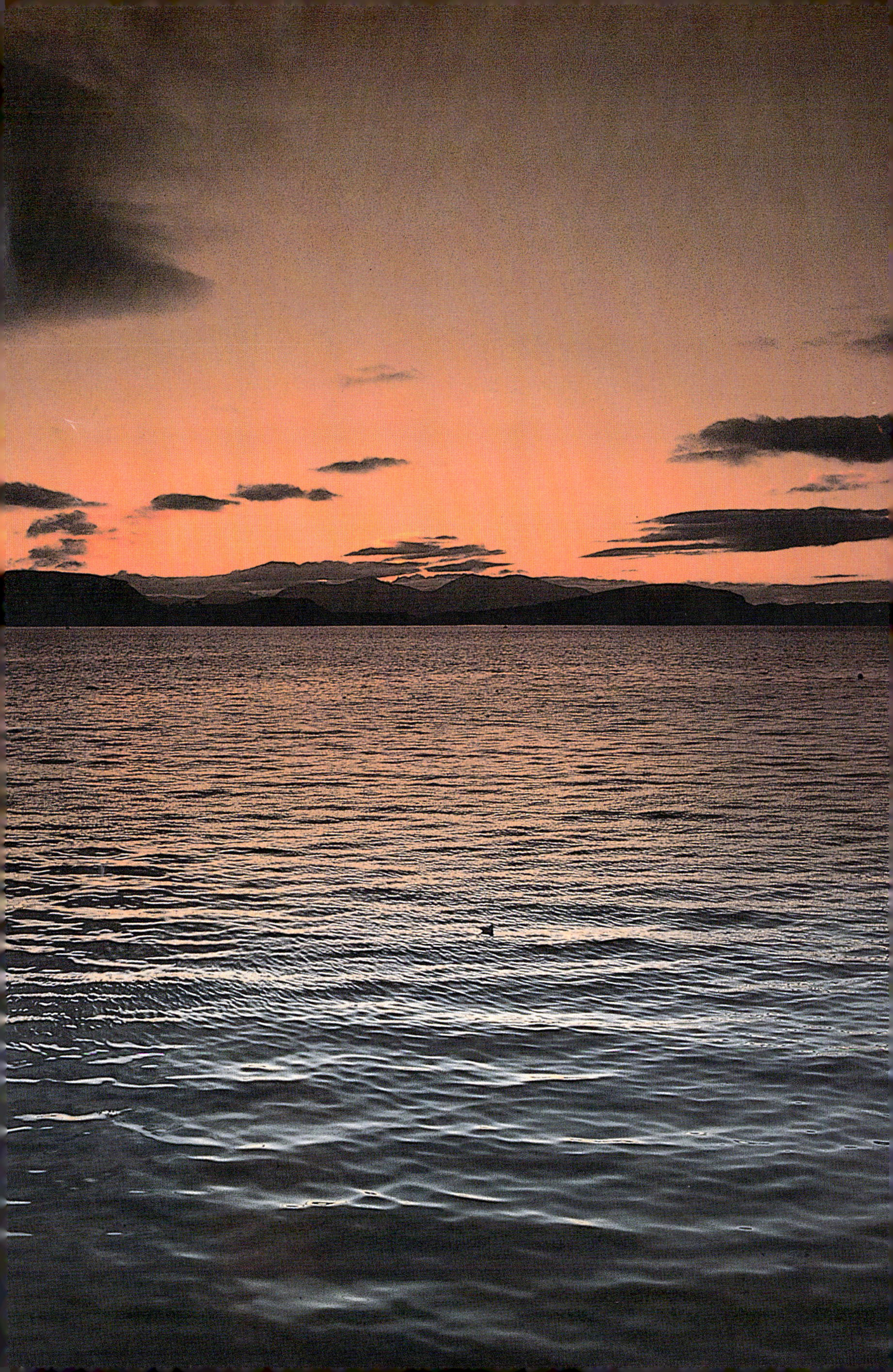

Psaume 32

Le pardon et la direction divines

L'idée générale de ce psaume est donnée par les deux derniers versets. On y retrouve l'opposition biblique classique entre les *méchants* et les *justes*, entre les croyants et les incroyants. La différence entre eux réside ici dans le fait que les justes peuvent se réjouir, mettre leur *joie en l'Éternel,* tandis que *les tourments qui attendent les méchants* sont nombreux. Si les croyants sont dans la joie, est-il dit plus loin, c'est parce qu'ils sont *comblés par son amour*. Dieu manifeste cet amour, qui réjouit le cœur de l'homme, en ce qu'il pardonne au pécheur et dirige sa vie, comme l'explique la suite du psaume.

Le pardon de Dieu pour le passé (v. 1-7)

Les deux béatitudes de l'Ancien Testament énoncées ici ne concernent pas l'homme qui aime la Loi de Dieu, mais celui dont les péchés sont pardonnés (v. 1, 2). Trois termes symétriques sont employés pour désigner respectivement le péché et le pardon. Le mal est une *faute* par excès, une violation, le franchissement d'une limite connue, tandis que le *péché* est un manquement par défaut, une négligence, l'incapacité à atteindre un idéal ; enfin, « l'iniquité » (version Segond) représente la dépravation morale, la corruption de la nature humaine, ce qu'on appelle « le péché originel ».

Le pardon, quant à lui, présente également trois aspects. Le terme hébreu traduit par *effacé* (v. 1) semble évoquer ce qui est supprimé, enlevé. Le péché est aussi *pardonné* (« couvert », dans la version Darby),

Heureux l'homme | dont la faute est effacée,
et le péché pardonné !
2 Heureux l'homme | au compte de qui | l'Eternel | ne porte pas le péché
et qui est exempt | de mauvaise foi !
3 Tant que je taisais ma faute,
je m'épuisais à gémir | sans cesse, à longueur de jour.
4 Sur moi, le jour et la nuit, | ta main s'appesantissait,
ma vigueur m'abandonnait | comme l'herbe se dessèche | lors des ardeurs de l'été.
Pause
5 Je t'ai avoué ma faute,
je n'ai plus caché mes torts,
j'ai dit : « Je reconnaîtrai | devant l'Eternel | les péchés que j'ai commis. »
Alors tu m'as déchargé | du poids de ma faute.
Pause
6 Ainsi, que tout homme pieux | te prie au temps opportun.
Si les grandes eaux déferlent,
leurs flots ne l'atteignent pas.
7 Tu es un abri pour moi, | tu me gardes du danger.
Autour de moi retentissent | les chants de la délivrance.
Pause
8 Tu as dit : « Je vais t'instruire | et t'indiquer le chemin | que tu devras emprunter,
je serai ton conseiller, | mes yeux veilleront sur toi.
9 Ne soyez donc pas stupides | comme un cheval, un mulet | dépourvus d'intelligence
dont il faut dompter la fougue | par la bride et par le mors
pour qu'ils t'obéissent ! »

10 Ils sont nombreux les tourments | qui attendent les méchants,
mais les hommes qui ont mis | leur confiance en l'Eternel | sont comblés par son amour.
11 Justes, réjouissez-vous ! | Mettez votre joie en l'Eternel
et poussez des cris de joie, | vous qui êtes droits de cœur !

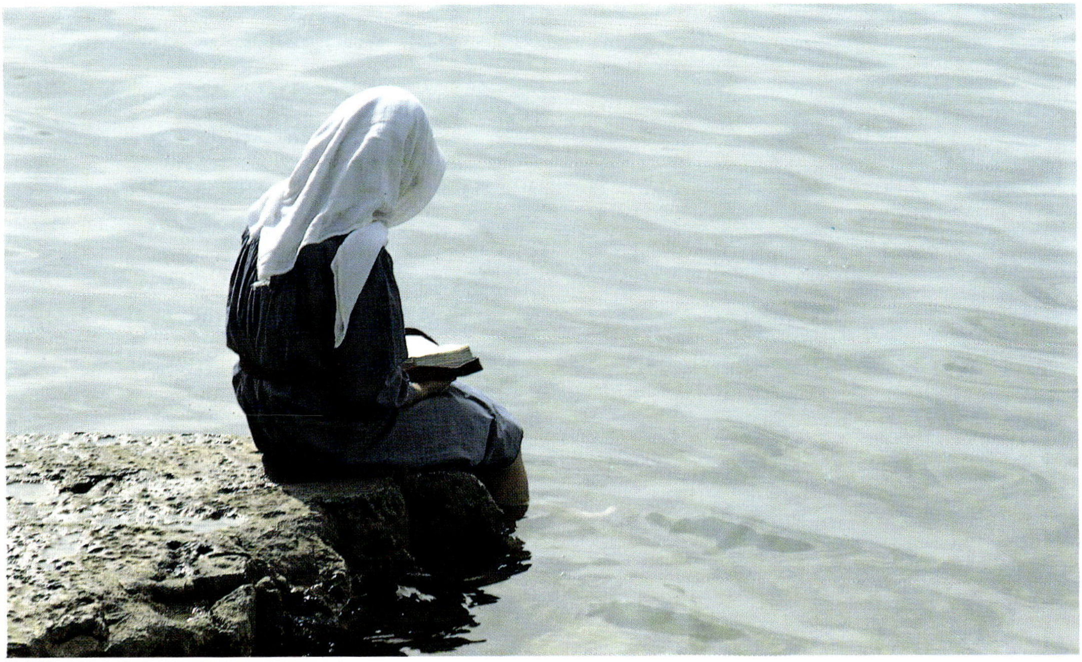

Le lac de Galilée invite à la méditation. Des milliers de chrétiens viennent chaque année se ressourcer sur ses rivages agréables.

c'est-à-dire ôté de la vue de l'Éternel, qui ne peut plus l'imputer au pécheur. Le pardon est donc vu comme le retrait d'un fardeau, la suppression d'un spectacle hideux et la remise d'une dette. Ce sont ces mêmes versets que l'apôtre Paul cite dans Romains 4.6-8 pour affirmer que le pécheur de l'Ancien Testament était justifié par la grâce de Dieu au moyen de la foi, indépendamment des œuvres.

À ce bonheur de se savoir pardonné, David oppose à présent son expérience personnelle de la détresse de celui qui refuse de confesser son péché. D'un côté l'homme *qui est exempt de mauvaise foi* (v. 2), de l'autre, la mauvaise foi avec ses conséquences douloureuses.

Il évoque probablement ici sa relation coupable avec Bath-Chéba. En effet, près d'une année s'était écoulée depuis son adultère et le meurtre du mari de Bath-Chéba, avant que le prophète Nathan ne l'amène à la repentance (2 S 11). Durant toute cette période, où il cherchait à tromper Dieu et à se tromper lui-même, il ne put trouver la paix. Bien avant la reconnaissance des maladies psychosomatiques, David apprit comment le remords et la culpabilité pouvaient produire des symptômes physiques graves (v. 3, 4). Il finit néanmoins par céder et reconnaître son péché devant Dieu, dont le pardon lui redonna la paix (v. 5).

Heureux d'avoir obtenu le pardon suite à la confession de son péché et à sa repentance, David exhorte les autres à faire de même, pour être bénis comme il l'a été lui-même. Une prière humble adressée à Dieu au temps convenable apporte toujours la délivrance (v. 5b). Qui plus est, David décide d'agir ainsi toute sa vie (v. 6). La leçon a porté, il ne commettra pas deux fois la même erreur.

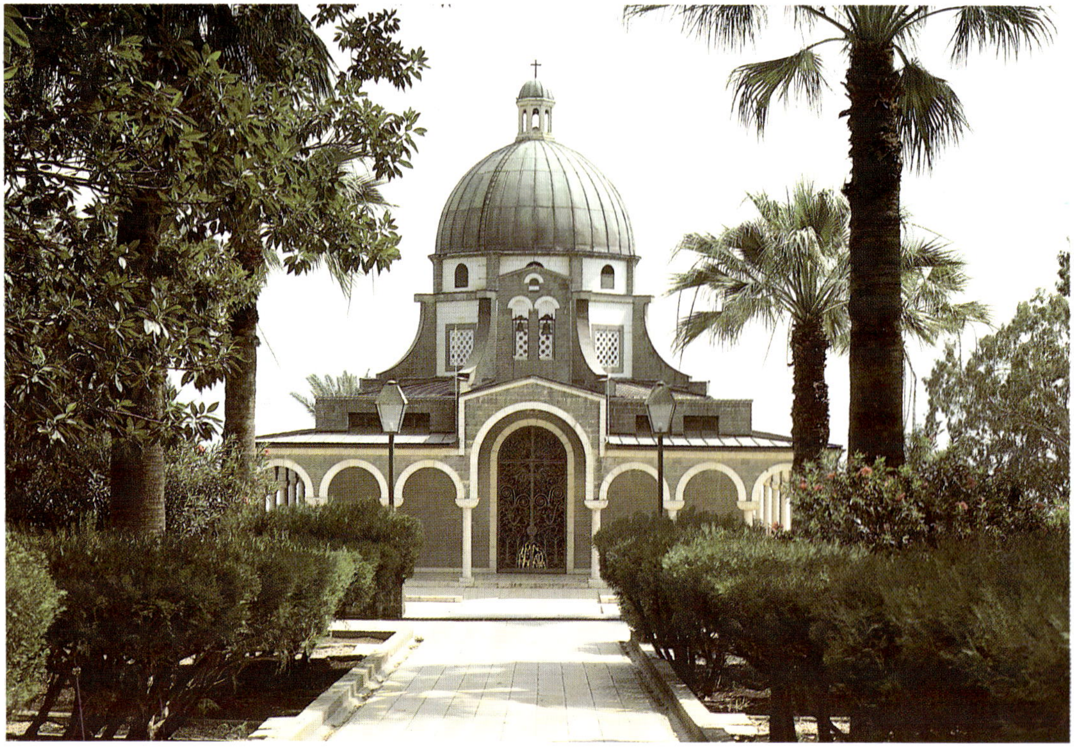

L'église des Béatitudes, sur la rive nord du lac de Galilée, est érigée sur le site du Sermon sur la montagne.

La direction de Dieu pour l'avenir (v. 8, 9)

La réponse de Dieu à la confiance que David a placée en lui ne se fait pas attendre (v. 8). Il lui promet de diriger sa vie, car, dans son grand amour, il désire non seulement lui pardonner le passé, mais également le conduire à l'avenir. Tout comme le pardon, la direction divine est explicitée par plusieurs termes : *Je vais t'instruire et t'indiquer le chemin que tu devras emprunter, je serai ton conseiller, mes yeux veilleront sur toi* (v. 8). L'image est celle d'une mère qui apprend à marcher à son enfant ; elle ne le quitte pas des yeux. C'est ainsi que notre Dieu entoure et aime ses enfants.

Il convient néanmoins de noter que la promesse du verset 8 est immédiatement suivie de la recommandation du verset 9. Ce n'est pas parce que Dieu dirige nos pas que nous pouvons faire l'économie de notre intelligence. Elle est donc assortie de l'avertissement : *Ne soyez donc pas stupides comme un cheval, un mulet dépourvus d'intelligence dont il faut dompter la fougue par la bride et par le mors.* Le cheval et le mulet, qui sont des animaux nerveux et têtus, doivent être domptés par la pression, voire la force, car ils sont dépourvus de raison. Pour nous, qui avons une intelligence, Dieu ne va pas utiliser la bride et le mors. Il va nous traiter en êtres humains, non en mulets.

Heureux en vérité ceux qui sont environnés par l'amour inébranlable de Dieu, qui pardonne leurs péchés lorsqu'ils les lui confessent et qui guide leurs pas lorsqu'ils s'appuient sur ses promesses et font preuve d'intelligence, comme il le leur demande.

Psaume 34

L'Éternel, sujet de ma fierté

Dans ce psaume, adoration et témoignage vont de pair. Dieu a entendu le cri du psalmiste et l'a délivré d'un grand danger. Débordant de reconnaissance, David tour à tour loue Dieu et exhorte les autres à goûter et à constater dans leur propre vie la bonté de l'Éternel. L'Éternel est son *sujet de fierté,* dit-il (v. 3). Il proclame en effet publiquement que c'est Dieu qui l'a sauvé, incitant par là même ceux qui l'entendent à lui rendre gloire eux aussi. De l'avis du grand prédicateur baptiste C.H. Spurgeon, « les onze premiers versets de ce psaume sont un hymne et les douze derniers, un sermon. »

Une expérience personnelle (v. 2-11)

Le psalmiste désire offrir une louange à la fois ininterrompue (v. 2) et communautaire (v. 3, 4). Il sait que *les humbles* (« les malheureux » dans la version Segond) l'entendront et se réjouiront, car l'Éternel est le seul sujet de fierté auquel ils soient sensibles. Il les invite donc à glorifier l'Éternel avec lui (v. 4) et à regarder à lui pour être eux aussi rayonnants de joie (v. 6).

C'est l'intervention de Dieu à un moment précis de sa vie, où il a été délivré de toutes ses *frayeurs* (v. 5) et *de toutes ses détresses* (v. 7), qui a mis dans son cœur ce désir de louer Dieu et d'encourager les autres

2 Oui, en tout temps, | je remercierai l'Eternel
et à jamais, | mes lèvres le loueront.
3 Mon sujet de fierté, | c'est l'Eternel !
Que les humbles l'entendent | et qu'ils se réjouissent !
4 Venez proclamer avec moi | que l'Eternel est grand !
Exaltons-le ensemble | pour ce qu'il est !

5 Moi, je me suis tourné | vers l'Eternel | et il m'a répondu.
Oui, il m'a délivré | de toutes mes frayeurs.
6 Qui regarde vers lui | est rayonnant de joie,
et jamais son visage | ne rougira de honte.
7 Un malheureux a appelé, | et l'Eternel a entendu,
car il l'a délivré | de toutes ses détresses.
8 L'ange de l'Eternel | monte la garde | autour de ceux qui le révèrent ;
c'est lui qui les libère.
9 Goûtez et constatez | que l'Eternel est bon !
Oui, heureux l'homme | qui trouve son refuge en lui.
10 Vous qui appartenez | à l'Eternel, | révérez-le !
Car rien ne manque | à ceux qui le révèrent.
11 Le lion peut connaître | la disette et la faim,
mais ceux qui se tournent vers l'Eternel | ne manquent d'aucun bien.

12 Venez, mes fils, écoutez-moi,
et je vous apprendrai | comment vivre en révérant l'Eternel.
13 Qui désire une longue vie ?
Qui voudrait être heureux ?
14 Qu'il veille sur sa langue | pour ne faire aucun mal,
qu'aucun propos menteur | ne passe sur ses lèvres.
15 Détourne-toi du mal, | et fais ce qui est bien,
cherche la paix avec ténacité.

16 Les yeux de l'Eternel | se tournent vers les justes,
son oreille est tendue | pour écouter leurs cris.
17 Mais l'Eternel s'oppose | à ceux qui font le mal,
pour ôter de la terre | jusqu'à leur souvenir.
18 Lorsque les hommes justes | lancent leurs cris vers lui, | l'Eternel les entend ;
aussi, il les arrache | à toutes leurs détresses.
19 Car l'Eternel est proche | de ceux qui ont le cœur brisé.
Il sauve ceux | qui ont un esprit abattu.

20 Le juste doit passer | par beaucoup de souffrances
mais l'Eternel | l'en délivre toujours.
21 Il veille sur ses os :
aucun d'eux n'est brisé.
22 Le malheur tuera le méchant,
les ennemis du juste | auront leur châtiment,
23 mais l'Eternel | sauve la vie | de tous ses serviteurs,
et ceux dont il est le refuge | ne seront jamais condamnés.

à le faire. C'est lui le malheureux du verset 7. Nous n'avons aucun détail sur la nature de son malheur.

Quelle que soit la détresse dont il a été secouru, le psalmiste sait que Dieu peut faire pour d'autres ce qu'il a fait pour lui. *L'ange de l'Éternel* (cette expression revient fréquemment dans l'Ancien Testament pour désigner Dieu lui-même) entoure ceux qui le craignent, tout comme une armée campe autour d'une ville pour la protéger et la délivrer (v. 8). Fort de son assurance, le psalmiste exhorte les autres : *goûtez et constatez (...) révérez-le,* car rien ne manque *à ceux qui le révèrent* (v. 9, 10). Même *le lion,* connu pour être le plus féroce des animaux et un prédateur redoutable, peut éprouver la faim, mais ceux qui s'attendent à Dieu *ne manquent d'aucun bien* (v. 11).

Notez ici l'emploi répété du terme « craindre » (version Segond). Ceux qui craignent l'Éternel (v. 8, 10) seront délivrés de leurs craintes (v. 5).

La crainte de Dieu n'est pas la peur, mais, comme le montre le contexte, le fait de « se tourner vers lui » (v. 5), de « l'appeler » (v. 7) et de « trouver son refuge en lui » (v. 9). C'est l'attitude de l'homme conscient de sa faiblesse et s'attendant à lui pour la délivrance (cf. Lc 1.50).

Un enseignement général (v. 12-23)

De cette expérience personnelle, le psalmiste va tirer un enseignement général. Tout comme le sage du début du livre des Proverbes, il invite ses élèves à se rassembler autour de lui et à écouter ce qu'il a à leur dire (v. 12). Celui qui veut *être heureux* (v. 13) doit manifester sa crainte de Dieu, non pas simplement par la foi, mais en actes, c'est-à-dire par une conduite appropriée. Que nul ne dise qu'il craint Dieu s'il ne se détourne pas du mal (cf. Jb 1.1 ; Pr 16.6) par ses paroles (v. 14) comme par ses actes (v. 15). Encore ne suffit-il pas d'éviter le mal ; nous devons faire *ce qui est bien* et rechercher *la paix* avec persévérance (v. 15).

Les versets 16 à 19 présentent les bénédictions réservées aux justes, c'est-à-dire à ceux qui craignent Dieu, évitent le mal et font le bien. C'est vers eux que l'Éternel se tourne. Par contre, il se détourne des méchants (v. 16, 17). Il entend les justes et les délivre, s'approche *de ceux qui ont le cœur brisé* et *sauve ceux qui ont un esprit abattu* (v. 19).

Il n'est pas dit que les justes seraient préservés de tous les problèmes. Au contraire, *le juste doit passer par beaucoup de souffrances* (v. 20), mais Dieu en limite à la fois la durée et l'intensité. Il les délivre de leurs épreuves (v. 20) et quelle que soit l'étendue de leurs blessures, qui souvent sont graves, il ne permettra pas qu'un seul de leurs os ne soit brisé (v. 21), ce qui est certainement une image pour désigner l'anéantissement total (voir aussi Mi 3.3). Paul dira : « Nous sommes accablés par toutes sortes de détresses et cependant jamais écrasés » (2 Co 4.8).

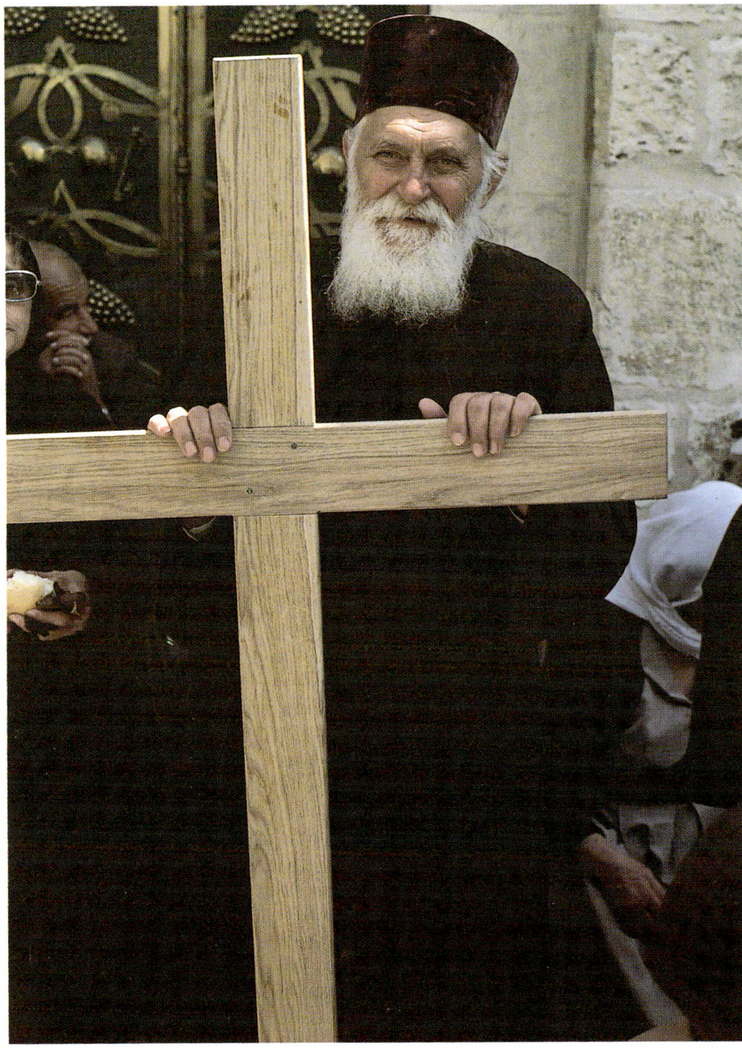

Le vendredi saint, des chrétiens de toutes les dénominations empruntent le trajet suivi par Jésus dans les rues de Jérusalem jusqu'au mont Golgotha.

L'incroyant ne manquera pas d'objecter que les faits contredisent cette affirmation ; la seule chose que nous pouvons dire, c'est que le principe de la protection divine est vrai. De plus, au jour du jugement de Dieu, la différence de destinée entre les méchants et les justes sera pleinement manifestée, et ce pour l'éternité. Les méchants *auront leur châtiment*, mais *ceux dont il est le refuge ne seront jamais condamnés* (v. 22, 23).

Psaume 40

Tiré de la fosse de la destruction

Ce qui fortifie le chrétien dans ses épreuves, c'est le souvenir des bénédictions antérieures. L'expérience de la fidélité de Dieu dans le passé justifie notre confiance pour aujourd'hui. C'est là le thème de ce psaume, où le récit détaillé de la délivrance est suivi d'un appel pressant à une miséricorde renouvelée.

Le souvenir d'une délivrance antérieure (v. 1-11)

Le psalmiste se trouvait plongé au fond du *puits de destruction*, plein de *boue.* Cette image n'est pas à prendre au sens propre, au contraire de Jérémie, que ses ennemis avaient fait descendre par des cordes dans une citerne, jusqu'à ce qu'il s'enfonçât dans la vase (Jr 38.1-13). Le puits et la boue représentent ici l'expérience pénible du péché, de la dépression ou de la maladie. Dans sa faiblesse, incapable de s'en sortir tout seul, il a mis *tout* son *espoir en l'Éternel.* Les versets qui suivent décrivent comment l'Éternel l'a délivré, étape après étape. Il a d'abord prêté l'oreille à son cri, puis s'est penché vers lui, l'a fait

2 J'ai mis tout mon espoir | en l'Eternel.
Il s'est penché vers moi, | il a prêté l'oreille | à ma supplication.
3 Il m'a fait remonter | du puits de destruction
et du fond de la boue.
Il m'a remis debout, | les pieds sur un rocher,
et il a affermi mes pas.
4 Il a mis dans ma bouche | un cantique nouveau,
un hymne de louanges | pour chanter notre Dieu.
Quand ils verront ce qu'il a fait, | beaucoup voudront | révérer l'Eternel
et lui faire confiance.

5 Bienheureux l'homme | qui fait confiance à l'Eternel
et ne se tourne pas | vers les gens orgueilleux
perdus dans le mensonge.
6 O Eternel, mon Dieu,
que d'œuvres merveilleuses | tu as faites pour nous, | et combien de projets !
Nul n'est semblable à toi.
Je voudrais publier, | redire tes merveilles,
mais leur nombre est trop grand.
7 Tu n'as voulu | ni offrande ni sacrifice.
Tu m'as ouvert l'oreille,
car tu n'as demandé | ni holocaustes | ni sacrifices | pour expier le péché.
8 Alors j'ai dit : Voici, je viens,
dans le rouleau du livre, | il est question de moi.
9 Je prends plaisir à faire | ta volonté, mon Dieu,
et ta Loi est gravée | tout au fond de mon cœur.
10 Dans la grande assemblée, | j'annonce la bonne nouvelle | de ton salut.
Je ne la tairai pas,
Eternel, tu le sais.
11 Je ne garde pas dans mon cœur | comme un secret la délivrance | que tu m'as accordée.
Je proclame bien haut | combien tu es fidèle | et que tu m'as sauvé.
Non, je ne cache pas | ton amour, ta fidélité
dans la grande assemblée.

12 Et toi, ô Eternel, | tu ne retiendras pas | loin de moi ta tendresse :
ton amour, ta fidélité | sans cesse me protégeront.
13 De malheurs innombrables | je suis environné,
mes transgressions m'accablent :
je n'en supporte pas la vue :
elles dépassent, par leur nombre, | les cheveux de ma tête ;
je n'ai plus de courage.
14 Veuille, Eternel, me délivrer !
Eternel, viens vite à mon aide !

15 Qu'ils soient couverts de honte, | remplis de confusion,
ceux qui en veulent à ma vie !
Qu'ils battent en retraite, | qu'ils soient déshonorés,
ceux qui se réjouissent | de mon malheur !
16 Qu'ils soient paralysés | sous le poids de la honte,
ceux qui ricanent | à mon sujet.
17 Mais que tous ceux | qui te sont attachés
soient débordants de joie, | et qu'ils s'égaient en toi.
Et que tous ceux qui aiment ton salut
redisent constamment : | « Que l'Eternel est grand ! »
18 Moi, je suis pauvre et malheureux,
mais le Seigneur prend soin de moi.
Toi qui es mon secours | et mon libérateur,
ô mon Dieu, hâte-toi !

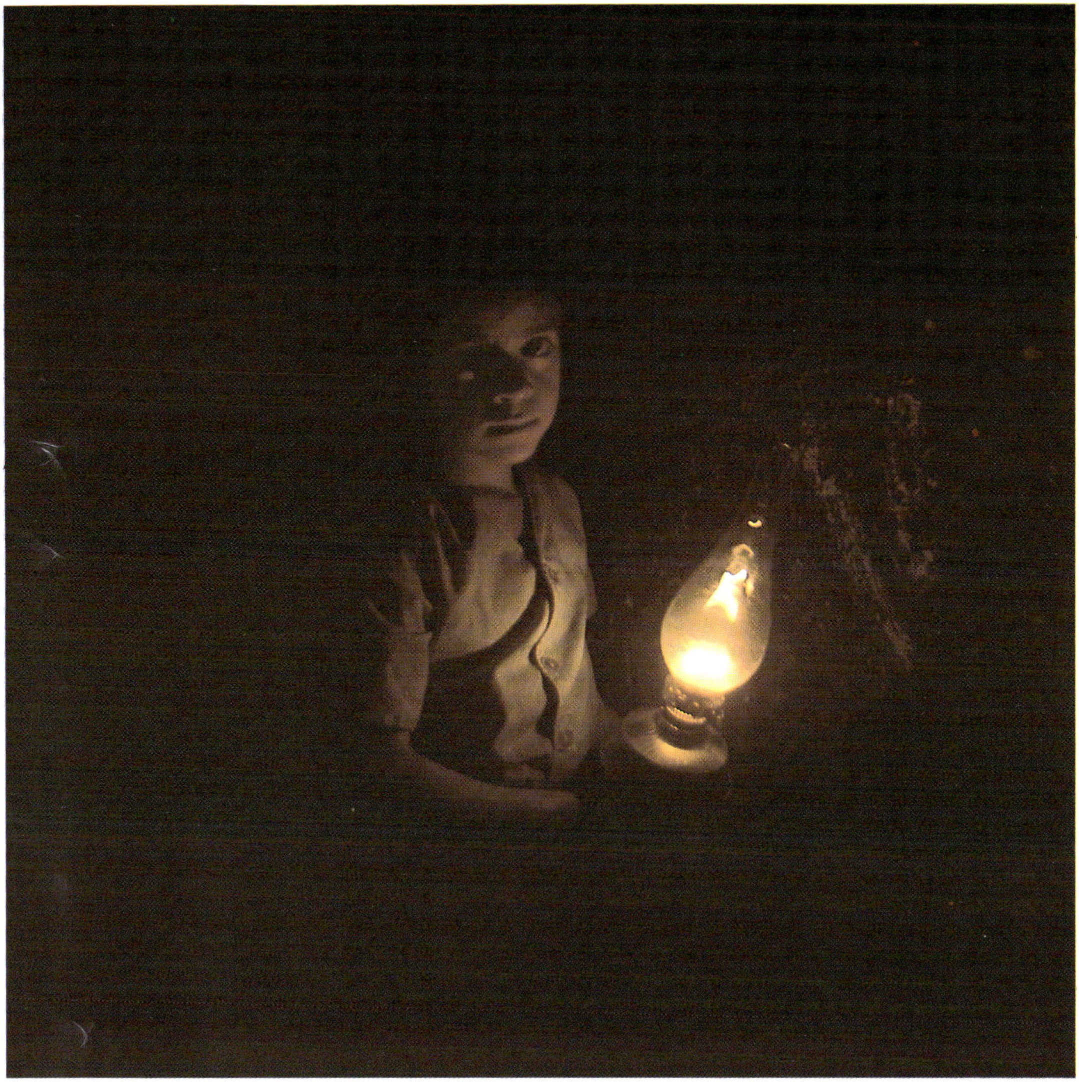

Un jeune arabe dans le tombeau des prophètes, situé sur le mont des Oliviers, à Jérusalem.

remonter du puits de destruction, a posé ses pieds sur un rocher et, enfin, a mis dans sa bouche un cantique nouveau, qui servira de témoignage pour beaucoup (v. 2-4).

L'expérience d'un tel salut porte des fruits d'adoration (v. 5-7), d'obéissance (v. 8-10) et de témoignage (v. 11-13). Le psalmiste exprime son adoration, à la fois en proclamant le bonheur du croyant (v. 5) et en exaltant les œuvres et les pensées sans nombre de Dieu (v. 6). Mais la véritable adoration ne s'arrête pas aux mots. Pas même aux sacrifices. Elle implique le don de soi et l'obéissance. (Pour la primauté de l'obéissance sur les sacrifices, voir 1 S 15.22 ; Es 1.10-17 ; Jr 7.21-26 ; Os 6.6 ; Mi 6.6-8). C'est *le rouleau du livre*, c'est-à-dire la Loi, qui réclame cette obéissance. Cette dernière commence par notre *oreille*, que Dieu a *ouverte* (v. 7), littéralement « creusée », pour que nous puissions entendre et comprendre sa volonté.

Dieu, dans sa grâce, va encore plus loin. Il ne se contente pas d'écrire sa Loi dans un livre pour que nous puissions la lire, de la souffler à notre oreille pour que nous puissions la comprendre, il veut aussi l'écrire dans notre cœur, pour que nous y prenions *plaisir* (v. 9). Si tous les enfants de Dieu connaissent, aiment et accomplissent partiellement sa volonté, seul son Fils fait homme, auquel ces versets sont appliqués dans Hébreux 10.5-9, s'en est parfaitement acquitté.

Cependant, si le salut suscite en nous un élan d'adoration et d'obéissance, il nous enseigne également à prendre soin de notre prochain, pour lui permettre de connaître lui aussi la grâce de Dieu. Le psalmiste répète à plusieurs reprises qu'il ne cache pas l'*amour* et la *fidélité* de Dieu dans la grande assemblée, mais qu'il *les proclame bien haut* (v. 10-11). Lorsque Dieu affermit nos pieds sur le rocher et qu'il inscrit sa Loi dans nos oreilles et notre cœur, il nous faut ouvrir nos bouches pour proclamer sa bonté.

Un appel au secours (v. 12-18)

À l'instar du psaume 27, le ton change brusquement. Si, dans la première partie, le psalmiste pouvait proclamer avec assurance l'*amour* et la *fidélité* de Dieu, il en est réduit à présent à l'implorer, à le supplier d'intervenir. À nouveau, il se trouve dans une situation angoissante, environné *de malheurs innombrables*, dont il nous dévoile cette fois la nature : *mes transgressions m'accablent : je n'en supporte pas la vue.* Leur force et leur nombre l'écrasent. Il a perdu courage (v. 13) et, en proie au désespoir, supplie Dieu de le délivrer (v. 14).

Les derniers versets du psaume opposent deux types de personnes, à savoir *ceux qui en veulent à sa vie* et *ceux qui sont (...) attachés* à l'Éternel (« ceux qui cherchent à m'ôter la vie », et « ceux qui te recherchent », selon la version synodale), autrement dit les incroyants et les croyants. Les premiers se plaisent à persécuter les seconds et le psalmiste prie à trois reprises pour leur anéantissement (v. 15, 16). Toute autre est sa prière pour ceux qui cherchent Dieu et qui aiment son salut, desquels il fait partie. Il désire en effet que leur expérience personnelle les amène à répéter sans cesse : *Que l'Éternel est grand !* (v. 17). Il sait qu'en lui-même il est *pauvre et malheureux*, mais l'Éternel, qui l'a sauvé, continue à prendre soin de loin et le délivrera encore (v. 18).

Psaumes 42, 43

La dépression spirituelle, ses causes et ses remèdes

Ce psaume (car il ne fait aucun doute que les psaumes 42 et 43 n'en forment qu'en seul) traite de la dépression spirituelle, de ses causes et de ses remèdes. L'âme du psalmiste *est abattue* et *gémit* (v. 6). C'est là une chose qui arrive fréquemment, même à des croyants, comme en témoignent de nombreuses biographies d'hommes de Dieu. Du reste, il est presque certain que notre Seigneur lui-même pensait à ce texte lorsqu'il disait : « À présent, je suis troublé » et « Je suis accablé de tristesse, à en mourir » (Jn 12.27 ; Mc 14.34).

Toutefois, et c'est ce qui donne un aspect particulièrement pathétique à ce texte, le psalmiste se refuse à accepter cet état et, à trois reprises, qui reviennent comme un refrain, il s'interroge sur les causes de son abattement et s'exhorte à faire confiance à Dieu (42.6, 12 ; 43.5).

Psaume 42

2 Comme un cerf qui soupire | après l'eau des ruisseaux,
de même je soupire | après toi, ô mon Dieu.
3 J'ai soif de Dieu, | du Dieu vivant !
Quand pourrai-je venir | et me présenter devant Dieu ?
4 Mes larmes sont le pain | de mes jours comme de mes nuits.
Sans cesse, on me répète :
« Ton Dieu, où est-il donc ? »
5 Avec quelle émotion | je me souviens du temps
où, avec le cortège, | je m'avançais,
en marchant à sa tête | vers le temple de Dieu,
au milieu de la joie | et des cris de reconnaissance
de tout un peuple en fête.
6 Pourquoi donc, ô mon âme, | es-tu si abattue
et gémis-tu sur moi ?
Mets ton espoir en Dieu ! | je le louerai encore,
car il est mon Sauveur.
7 Mon Dieu, mon âme est abattue,
Voilà pourquoi, je pense à toi | du pays du Jourdain,
des cimes de l'Hermon | et du mont Mitséar.
8 Un abîme en appelle un autre : | tu fais gronder tes chutes ;
tous tes flots et tes lames | ont déferlé sur moi.
9 Que, le jour, l'Eternel | me montre son amour :
je passerai la nuit | à chanter ses louanges
et j'adresserai ma prière | au Dieu qui me fait vivre.
10 Car je veux dire à Dieu, | lui qui est mon rocher :
« Pourquoi m'ignores-tu ?
Pourquoi donc me faut-il | vivre dans la tristesse,
pressé par l'ennemi ? »
11 Mes membres sont meurtris, | mes ennemis m'insultent,
sans cesse, ils me demandent : |
« Ton Dieu, où est-il donc ? »
12 Pourquoi donc, ô mon âme, | es-tu si abattue, | et gémis-tu sur moi ?
Mets ton espoir en Dieu ! | Je le louerai encore,
mon Sauveur et mon Dieu.

Psaume 43

1 Fais-moi justice, ô Dieu,
et prends en main ma cause | contre un peuple infidèle !
Sauve-moi de ces gens | menteurs et criminels !
2 O Dieu, tu es ma forteresse, | pourquoi donc me rejettes-tu,
et pourquoi me faut-il | vivre dans la tristesse,
pressé par l'ennemi ?
3 Fais-moi voir ta lumière, | avec ta vérité
pour qu'elles m'accompagnent
et qu'elles soient mes guides | vers ta montagne sainte | jusque dans ta demeure.
4 Alors j'avancerai | jusqu'à l'autel de Dieu,
vers toi, Dieu de ma joie | et de mon allégresse.
Alors je te louerai | en m'accompagnant de la lyre. | O Dieu : tu es mon Dieu !
5 Pourquoi donc, ô mon âme, | es-tu si abattue | et gémis-tu sur moi ?
Mets ton espoir en Dieu ! | Je le louerai encore,
mon Sauveur et mon Dieu.

Dans chacune des trois strophes de ce psaume, l'auteur commence par exprimer sa douleur, à Dieu ou au lecteur, pour terminer par le refrain, dans lequel il s'interpelle lui-même.

Les causes de la dépression spirituelle

Le psalmiste se présente, non pas comme un homme abattu, mais comme quelqu'un qui a soif. Il a soif de Dieu, comme a soif un *cerf* poursuivi par des chasseurs ou incapable de trouver une source. C.S. Lewis a écrit qu'il avait « un vif appétit de Dieu ». C'est là une chose normale et bonne, que connaît, ou que devrait connaître, chaque croyant. En effet, quoique Dieu « désaltère les assoiffés et comble de

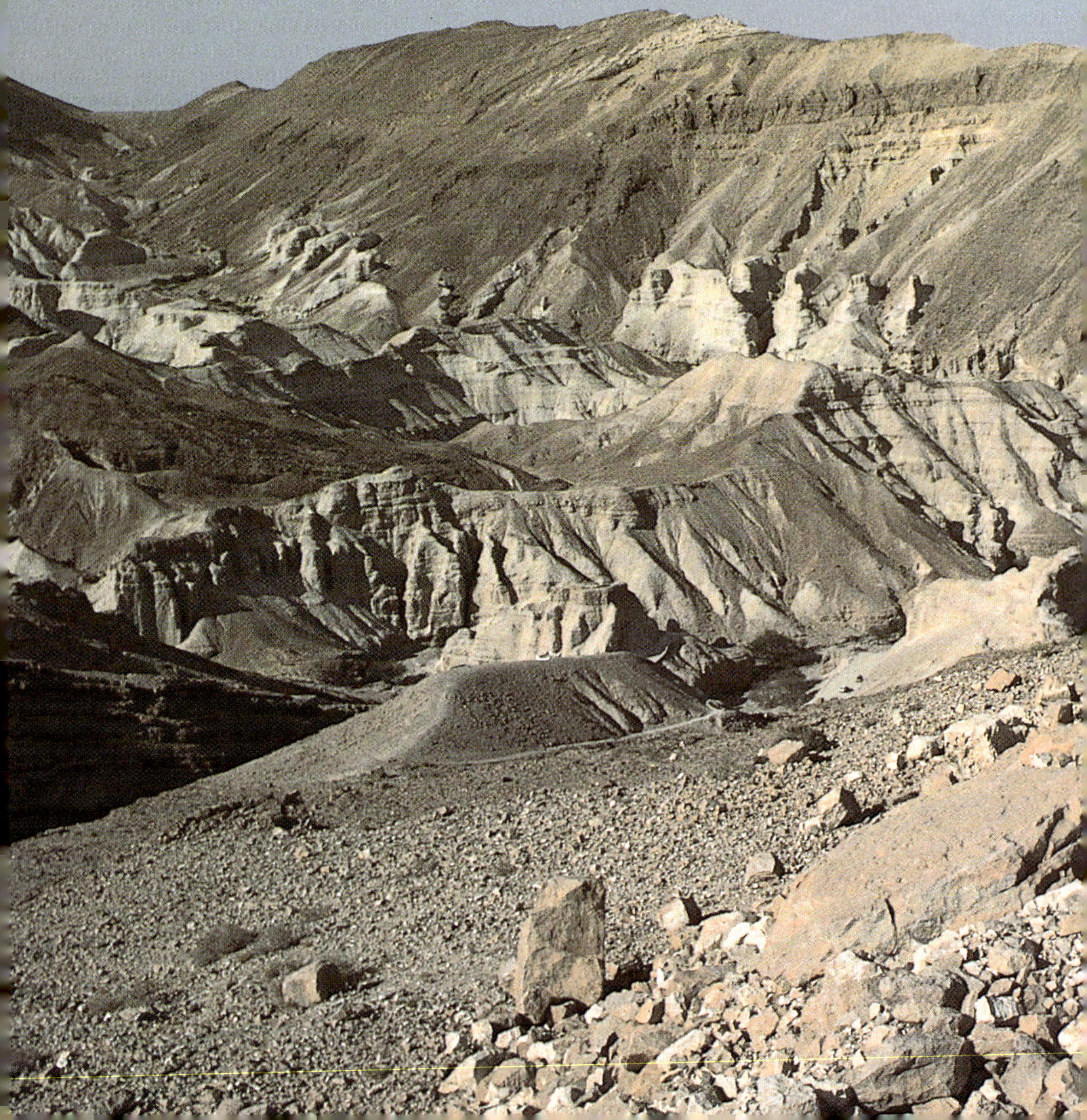

Le désert aride des montagnes de Judée avec, à l'horizon, la Mer Morte .

biens les affamés » (Ps 107.7, cf. Ps 36.9, 10), notre faim et notre soif de lui, même satisfaites, reviennent sans cesse, de plus en plus pressantes (cf. Ps 63.2)

Dans le cas de l'auteur, cependant, deux épreuves exacerbent encore sa soif. La première transparaît dans sa question, *Quand pourrai-je venir et me présenter devant Dieu* (v. 3) ? Il fait allusion à l'obligation qu'avait tout Israélite de monter trois fois par an à Jérusalem pour les principales fêtes (Ex 23.17), ce que le psalmiste ne pouvait manifestement pas faire à ce moment-là. Par ailleurs, les moqueries de ceux qui lui demandent sans cesse *« Ton Dieu, où est-il donc ? »* le font cruellement souffrir et les larmes sont sa nourriture quotidienne (v. 4). Voilà donc définies les raisons de sa dépression, à savoir l'absence de Dieu et les moqueries des hommes. Ces deux thèmes reviennent dans chaque strophe.

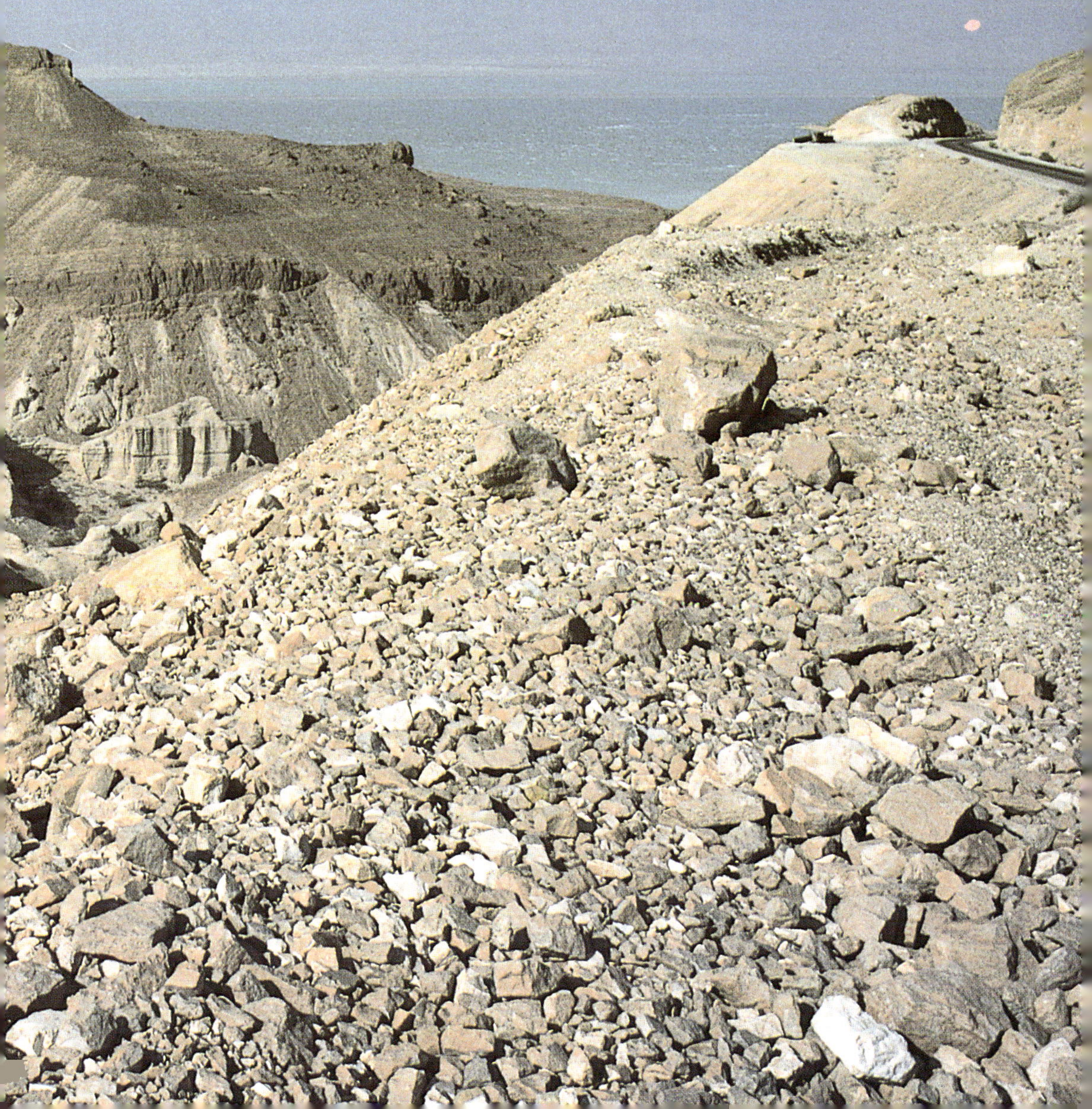

Au moment où il écrit, le psalmiste se trouve dans le Nord de la Palestine, loin du Temple et de son culte, ce qui explique son sentiment d'éloignement. Le mont Mitséar, qui n'a pu être localisé, fait certainement partie de la chaîne de l'Hermon. De cette colline lointaine ses pensées se dirigent vers la *montagne sainte* de Dieu (43.3), où il aspire à retourner. Il évoque avec nostalgie les jours passés où il adorait Dieu dans la joie (42.5).

L'intitulé du psaume 42, *Méditation des Qoréites,* a fait dire à certains que l'auteur était peut-être un des descendants de Qoré (l'arrière-petit-fils de Lévi), qui occupaient les fonctions de portiers, gardiens et musiciens dans le Temple (1 Ch 6.22-48 ; 9.17-32 ; 2 Ch 20.19). Certes, il parle ici de louer l'Éternel avec sa voix et sa lyre (42.12 ; 43.4), mais son exil l'en empêche. Au lieu de la musique du Temple, il n'entend que le fracas assourdissant des cascades et des torrents de montagne en crue, dont les versants se renvoient l'écho, *un abîme* en appelant *un autre,* qui semblent symboliser ses malheurs : ce sont les *flots* et les *lames* de Dieu qui *ont déferlé* sur lui (v. 8). Tout son être aspire à retourner dans le Temple pour louer Dieu jour et nuit (v.9).

Dans la troisième strophe, il prie donc Dieu de ne pas lui refuser sa lumière et sa vérité, qui le guideront à travers le désert jusqu'à la montagne de l'Éternel, sa demeure et son autel, où il pourra à nouveau rencontrer et adorer le Dieu de sa joie et de son allégresse (43.3, 4). Cela ne signifie pas que pour le psalmiste le Temple était le seul endroit où l'âme pouvait rencontrer Dieu, le psaume lui-même ayant été composé en période d'exil. Ce qu'il désire ardemment, c'est retrouver cette communion privilégiée avec Dieu qu'il avait connue pendant les cultes d'adoration, en présence de tout le peuple.

La deuxième cause de sa dépression est l'attitude des païens qui ne cessent de se moquer de lui en lui demandant *« Ton Dieu, où est-il donc ? »* C'étaient en effet des idolâtres qui servaient des dieux qu'ils pouvaient voir et toucher, alors que le Dieu vivant était invisible (v. 2 ; cf. Ps 115.2) ; par ailleurs, ce Dieu semblait aussi absent qu'invisible, et ne volait pas au secours de son peuple lorsque ce dernier était oppressé par des ennemis (cf. Ps 79.10). Le psalmiste se sent oublié, ignoré (v.10). Son esprit est devenu si vulnérable qu'il ressent la douleur des sarcasmes comme une blessure physique (v. 11). Il appelle de ses prières la justice et la délivrance (43.1).

Confronté à la fois aux moqueries des autres et à l'indifférence et l'éloignement apparents du Dieu vivant, le psalmiste a donc plongé dans la dépression, voire le désespoir.

Le remède à la dépression spirituelle

C'est à chaque fois par le même refrain digne d'admiration que le psalmiste met un terme au récit de ses souffrances (42.6, 12 ; 43.5). Il convient de noter avec quel courage il s'interpelle lui-même, refu-

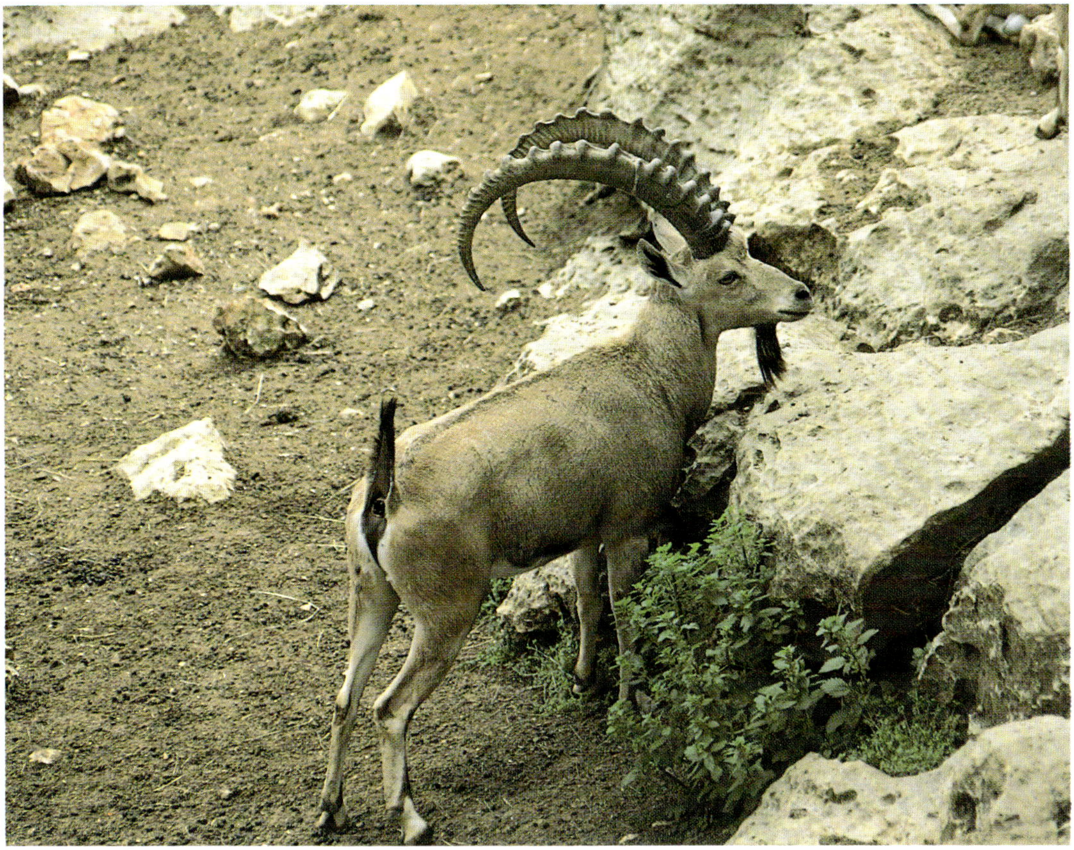

« Comme un cerf qui soupire après l'eau des ruisseaux, de même je soupire après toi, ô mon Dieu. »

sant de céder à ses états d'âme. Il se prend en main et se reproche sa dépression. Il reconnaît que son âme est accablée par un fardeau écrasant et secouée intérieurement comme une mer agitée (Ps 46.3). Mais pourquoi ? se demande-t-il. Cette question répétée contient un reproche implicite. Au lieu d'y répondre ou de se justifier, il propose aussitôt le remède : la confiance, ou l'*espoir en Dieu*. Il faut qu'il arrête de se livrer à l'introspection et de s'apitoyer sur son sort ; le temps n'est plus aux souvenirs nostalgiques ni à la rancœur.

Ni le chagrin au fond de nous, ni le passé derrière nous, ni les problèmes autour de nous ne nous aideront à sortir de notre dépression. Regardons plutôt vers le haut, au Dieu vivant. Il est notre aide et notre Dieu et, si nous lui faisons confiance, nous ne tarderons pas à retrouver des raisons de le louer. Comme l'a si bien résumé quelqu'un, « la foi emporte le découragement et l'espoir triomphe du désespoir. »

Mais quel chagrin te dévore ?
Mon âme, rassure-toi
Espère en Dieu car encore
Il sera loué de moi.
(Th. de Bèze, 1552)

Page suivante : « Nous avons pour citadelle le Dieu de Jacob. » La Citadelle, à Jérusalem, est une forteresse turque, érigée sur le site du palais d'Hérode.

Psaume 46

Emmanuel, Dieu avec nous

Le nom de Martin Luther restera à jamais associé à ce psaume, grâce à son adaptation célèbre « Ein' feste Burg ist unser Gott », qu'il chantait probablement avec Philippe Melanchthon dans leurs moments de découragement intense. Ruben Saillens, par sa traduction « C'est un rempart que notre Dieu » l'a rendu accessible aux chrétiens francophones. C'est une expression sublime de la confiance tranquille dans la souveraineté de Dieu au milieu des tumultes de la nature et de l'histoire.

À l'origine de ce psaume, une libération mémorable de Jérusalem d'entre les mains d'envahisseurs païens. *La cité de David* (v. 5) a fait l'objet de plusieurs libérations, mais le contexte et une analogie de style et de vocabulaire avec certaines prophéties d'Ésaïe donnent à penser qu'il s'agit ici du renversement de l'armée de Sennachérib en 701 avant Jésus-Christ.

Bien que roi de Juda, Ézéchias était le vassal de Sennachérib, à qui il devait payer un tribut. Lorsqu'il tenta de se révolter, la puissante armée assyrienne se déploya à l'ouest et au sud, comme les flots impérieux de la mer. Jérusalem fut rapidement encerclée. Sennachérib se vanta de ce qu'il avait enfermé Ezéchias « comme un oiseau dans sa cage » et lui demanda de se rendre.

La situation était critique. Vingt ans auparavant, le prédécesseur de Sennachérib avait pris d'assaut Samarie, la capitale du nord et déporté la population. Tout indiquait que Juda allait subir le même sort. Ézéchias consulta le prophète Ésaïe, qui lui dit de la part de l'Éternel : « Ne te laisse pas effrayer (...) Je protègerai cette ville et je la sauverai. » L'intervention de Dieu fut soudaine et spectaculaire, comme en a témoigné l'historien séculier Hérodote. « Cette nuit-là,

2 Dieu est pour nous un rempart,| il est un refuge,
un secours toujours offert| lorsque survient la détresse.
3 Aussi, nous ne craignons rien| quand la terre est secouée,
quand les montagnes s'effondrent,| basculant au fond des mers,
4 quand, grondants et bouillonnants,| les flots des mers se soulèvent
et ébranlent les montagnes.
Pause

5 Il est un cours d'eau| dont les bras réjouissent| la cité de Dieu
qui est la plus sainte| des demeures du Très-Haut.
6 Dieu réside au milieu d'elle,| elle n'est pas ébranlée,
car Dieu vient à son secours| dès le point du jour.
7 Des nations s'agitent| et des royaumes s'effondrent :
la voix de Dieu retentit,| et la terre se dissout.
8 Avec nous est l'Eternel| des armées célestes ;
nous avons pour citadelle| le Dieu de Jacob.
Pause

9 Venez, contemplez| tout ce que l'Eternel fait,
les ravages| qu'il opère sur la terre.
10 Il fait cesser les combats| jusqu'aux confins de la terre,
l'arc, il l'a brisé| et il a rompu la lance,
il a consumé au feu| tous les chars de guerre.
11 « Arrêtez ! dit-il,| reconnaissez-moi pour Dieu.
Je triomphe des nations,| je triomphe sur la terre. »
12 Avec nous est l'Eternel| des armées célestes.
Nous avons pour citadelle| le Dieu de Jacob.
Pause

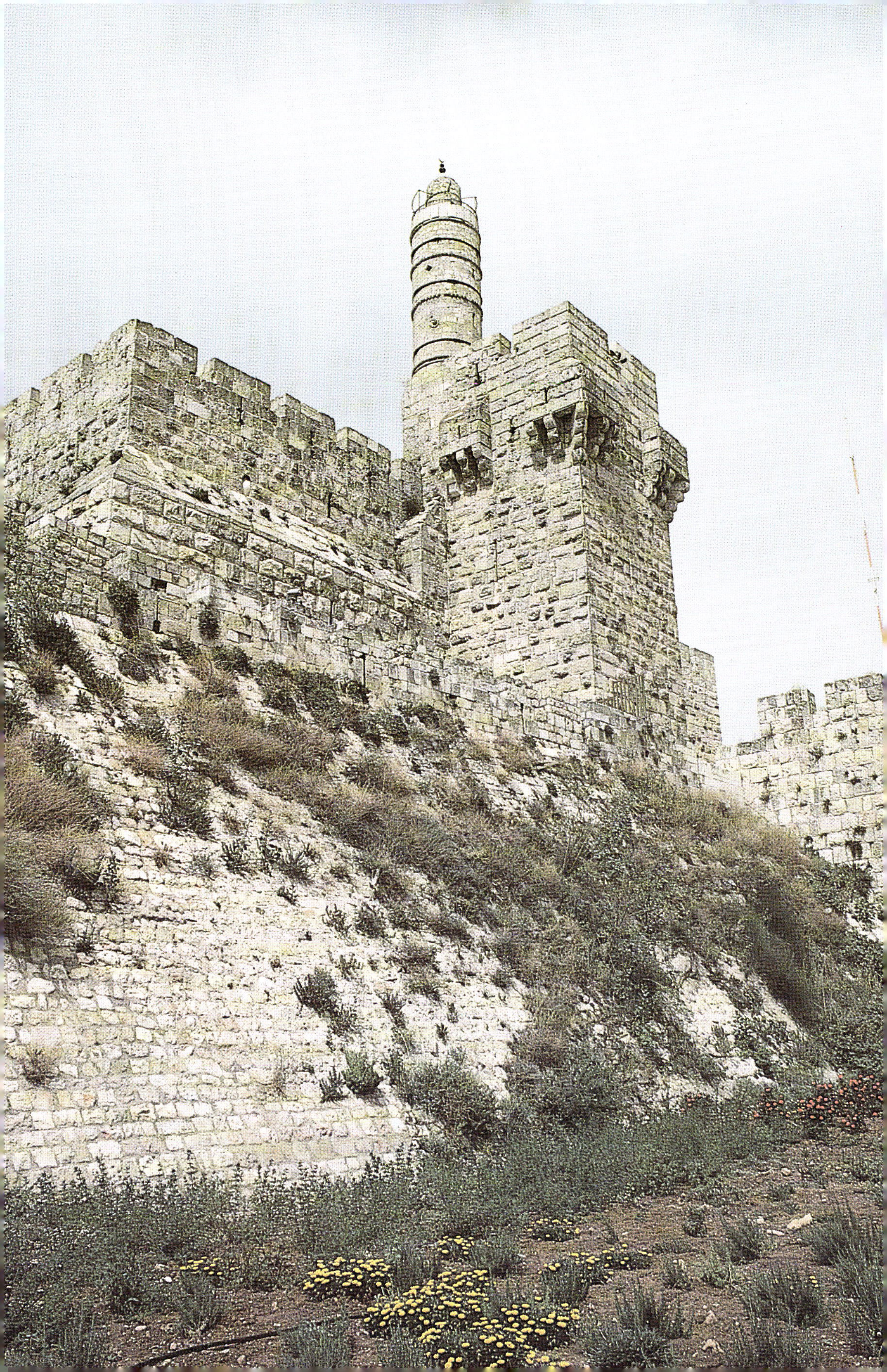

l'ange de l'Éternel intervint dans le camp assyrien et y fit périr 185 000 hommes. Le lendemain matin au réveil, le camp était rempli de tous ces cadavres. » Et Sennachérib se retira. Voir 2 Rois 18.18.

Ce psaume est composé de trois parties. Après avoir exprimé sa confiance dans la puissance et le secours de Dieu en général, le psalmiste évoque le cas précis de la libération de la ville, pour proclamer enfin sa certitude que Dieu établira son royaume universel de paix. Les deuxième et troisième strophes se terminant par le refrain : *Avec nous est l'Éternel des armées célestes ; nous avons pour citadelle le Dieu de Jacob* (v. 8, 12), les règles de symétrie permettent de penser qu'il figurait aussi en fin de la première. Au-delà de la simple affirmation de la protection divine, ce refrain confesse que Celui qui est notre rempart est à la fois l'*Éternel des armées célestes,* Tout-Puissant, et *le Dieu de Jacob*, le Dieu fidèle, qui a conclu avec son peuple une alliance solennelle.

La confiance en général (v. 1-4)

Le psalmiste affirme que *Dieu est pour nous un rempart (...) un refuge, un secours toujours offert lorsque survient la détresse.* Cette confiance lui permet d'ajouter, presque avec défi : *aussi nous ne craignons rien.* Même les pires bouleversements de la nature, tels que séismes, ouragans et tempêtes, qui remplissent de terreur les personnes sans protection, ne nous feront pas peur (v. 3-4).

Une expérience précise (v. 5-8)

Aux flots *grondants et bouillonnants* de la mer (v. 4), le psalmiste oppose les eaux calmes du *cours d'eau dont les bras réjouissent la cité de Dieu* (v. 5). Il fait probablement allusion aux eaux de Siloé, dont Ésaïe compare le cours paisible à l'action douce et bienfaisante de Dieu (Es 8.6). On retrouve cette même image dans les visions d'Ézéchiel (Ez 47.1-12) et de Jean (Ap 22.1-5).

Le gouvernement bienfaisant de Dieu « réjouit » sa cité (v. 5), qui *n'est pas ébranlée,* car Dieu, qui est *au milieu d'elle,* la protège et vient à son secours (v. 6). Les nations peuvent bien « s'agiter » comme la mer et « s'effondrer » comme des montagnes (les termes du texte original sont les mêmes que dans les versets 3 et 4), mais Dieu dit un seul mot *et la terre se dissout.* La voix de l'Éternel n'a-t-elle pas dispersé l'armée assyrienne ?

Une assurance ultime (v. 9-12)

L'auteur exhorte à présent le peuple à considérer comment Dieu a protégé Jérusalem et opéré des *ravages* parmi ses ennemis. Cette délivrance divine est un gage et un avant-goût du jour où Dieu renversera tous les bellicistes et établira son royaume de paix. *L'arc, il l'a brisé et il a rompu la lance, il a consumé au feu tous les chars de guerre* (v. 10). Cette vision rappelle les prophéties d'Ésaïe, où les épées se-

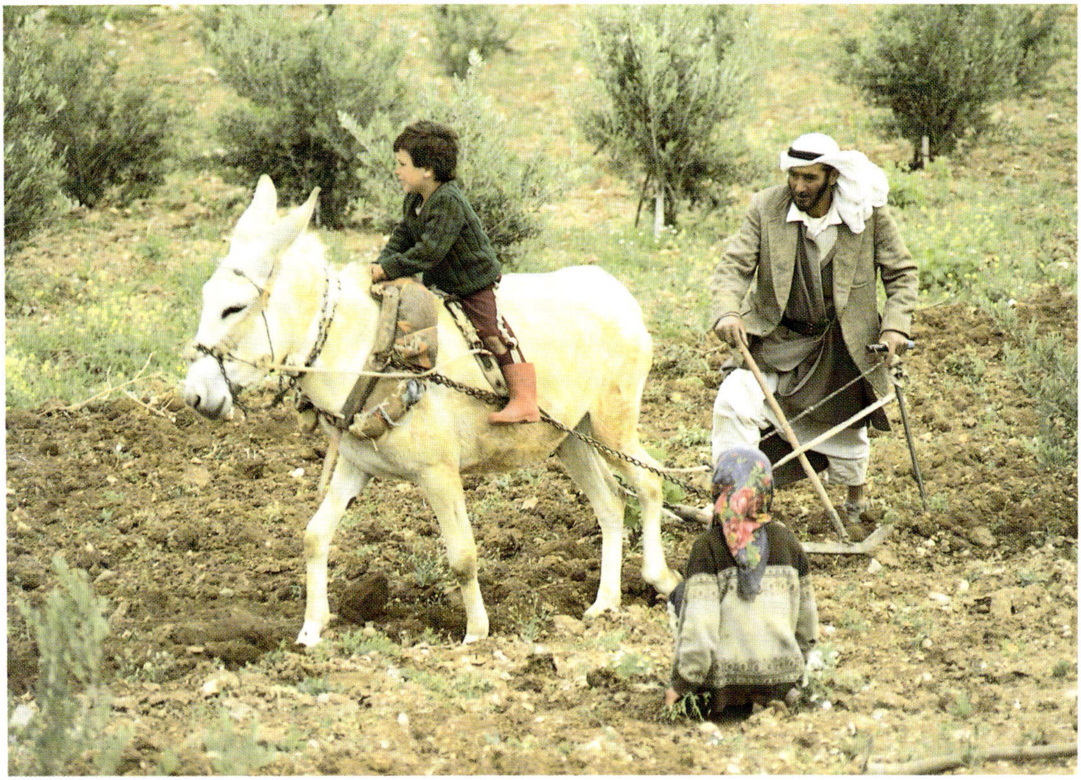

Une famille arabe laboure son petit lopin de terre rocailleux près de Bethléhem. Ces paysans ont conservé les méthodes de leurs ancêtres.

ront transformées en socs pour les charrues, les lances en faucilles, et où les chaussures des guerriers et les vêtements pleins de sang alimenteront le feu (Es 2.4 ; 9.4).

La voix de Dieu, le garant de cette promesse, s'élève alors : *Arrêtez ! (…) reconnaissez-moi pour Dieu.* C'est sa voix qui a renversé les Assyriens (v. 7), et c'est sa voix qui établit la paix pour son peuple. Il est Dieu éternel, qui triomphe dès à présent sur la terre (v. 11). *Avec nous est l'Éternel des armées célestes,* répond le peuple à cette affirmation solennelle. Ces paroles rappellent une nouvelle fois Ésaïe, dans sa prophétie bien connue sur Emmanuel, *Dieu avec nous* (Es 7.14 ; 8.8, 10).

Nous vivons, nous aussi, dans une période de crise. L'ancien ordre a disparu. La révolution sociale commencée il y a 150 ans se poursuit et s'accélère. Nous entendons parler de guerres et de bruits de guerres, les hommes sont terrorisés. Pouvons-nous affirmer : « Nous ne craignons rien » ? Oui, à condition d'accepter aussi les autres exigences et affirmations de ce psaume : *Reconnaissez-moi pour Dieu* et *Avec nous est l'Éternel des armées célestes.* Comme l'a dit John Wesley au moment de son dernier souffle : « Le meilleur de tout, c'est que Dieu est avec nous. »

Psaume 51

La miséricorde de Dieu envers celui qui se repent

Le Dieu souverain du psaume 46 est aussi un Dieu de miséricorde, comme le souligne celui-ci, le quatrième des sept « psaumes de pénitence ». Le Dieu qui « triomphe des nations » (Ps 46.11) ne dédaigne pas le cœur brisé et contrit qui se repent (51.18).

L'intitulé fait référence au péché bien connu de David. Un après-midi de printemps, alors qu'il se promenait sur le toit de son palais, il vit une femme très belle nommée Bath-Chéba. Il la désira et commit adultère avec elle. Puis il fit envoyer son mari, Urie le Hittite, en première ligne du combat contre les Ammonites, où il savait qu'il serait probablement tué. C'est ce qui arriva et David prit Bath-Chéba pour femme. Ce ne fut que lorsque Dieu lui envoya le prophète Nathan pour le reprendre, que David reconnut son péché, le confessa et implora la miséricorde divine. Les quelques mots qu'il prononça alors, « J'ai péché contre l'Éternel » (2 S 12.13), sont développés dans ce psaume en une prière de repentir que les pénitents de toutes les époques ont prononcée pour implorer la purification et le renouvellement divins.

3 Aie pitié de moi, ô Dieu, | toi qui es si bon !
Efface mes torts, | tu es si compatissant !
4 Lave-moi de mon péché !
Purifie-moi de ma faute !
5 Car je reconnais mes torts :
la pensée de mon péché | me poursuit sans cesse.
6 Contre toi, contre toi seul, | j'ai péché,
j'ai commis | ce qui est mal à tes yeux.
Voilà pourquoi tu es juste | quand tu émets ta sentence,
et tu es irréprochable | quand tu rends ton jugement.
7 Je suis, depuis ma naissance, | marqué du péché ;
depuis qu'en ma mère | j'ai été conçu, le péché est attaché à moi.
8 Mais tu veux que la droiture | demeure au fond de mon être.
Tu m'enseignes la sagesse | au plus profond de moi-même.
9 Purifie-moi du péché | avec un rameau d'hysope, | et je serai pur !
Lave-moi et je serai | plus blanc même que la neige.
10 Fais que j'entende à nouveau | les cris de la joie | et de l'allégresse !
Les os que tu as broyés | se remettront à danser.
11 Ne regarde plus mes fautes !
Tous mes torts, efface-les !
12 O Dieu, crée en moi | un cœur pur !
Fais renaître en moi | un esprit bien disposé !
13 Ne me renvoie pas | loin de ta présence,
et ne me retire pas | l'Esprit Saint | qui vient de toi !
14 Rends-moi la joie du salut,
et affermis-moi | par ton Esprit généreux !
15 Alors je pourrai montrer | à qui est coupable | le chemin que tu prescris
pour que les pécheurs | reviennent à toi.
16 O Dieu, toi le Dieu qui me libères, | viens me délivrer | du poids de mon crime,
alors, par mes chants, | je proclamerai | ton salut.
17 Eternel, ouvre mes lèvres
et je te louerai.
18 Car tu ne désires pas | que je t'offre un sacrifice.
Je t'aurais offert des holocaustes,
mais tu n'y prends pas plaisir.
19 Le seul sacrifice | qui convienne à Dieu, | c'est un esprit humilié.
O Dieu, tu n'écartes pas | un cœur brisé et contrit.

20 Dans ta bonté, fais du bien | à la ville de Sion,
et bâtis les murs | de Jérusalem !
21 Alors tu prendras plaisir | à des sacrifices | qui sont conformes à la Loi :
holocaustes et offrandes totales,
et l'on offrira | des taureaux sur ton autel.

Le besoin de la miséricorde divine

Pour prendre conscience de notre besoin de miséricorde, il nous faut d'abord comprendre la gravité de notre péché. Tout comme dans le psaume 32, trois termes différents sont utilisés en hébreu dans les versets 3 et 4, pour définir le crime de David, à savoir le *tort* ou la « transgression » (Segond), pour désigner le franchissement d'une limite, le *péché*, qui est un manquement, et l'« iniquité » (Segond), c'est-à-dire la perversité de la nature humaine. L'explication de ces termes donne lieu à une analyse approfondie de l'essence et de l'origine du péché.

L'essence du péché est la révolte contre Dieu : *Contre toi, contre toi seul, j'ai péché, en commettant ce qui est mal à tes yeux. Voilà pourquoi tu es juste quand tu émets ta sentence, et tu es irréprochable quand tu rends ton jugement* (v. 6). S'il est vrai que David a péché contre Bath-Chéba et Urie, il a d'abord et avant tout bafoué l'amour de Dieu et enfreint sa Loi. En convoitant, volant, commettant un adultère et tuant, il a transgressé quatre des cinq derniers commandements, tombant sous la juste sentence de Dieu. Dans Romains 3.4, Paul reprend ce verset pour affirmer la justice inébranlable de Dieu envers les hommes. C'est parce que nous tombons sous le jugement de Dieu que nous avons besoin de sa miséricorde.

Si l'essence du péché est la rébellion, il trouve son origine dans notre nature déchue. *Je suis, depuis ma naissance, marqué du péché ; depuis qu'en ma mère j'ai été conçu, le péché est attaché à moi* (v. 7). Cela ne veut évidemment pas dire que le processus merveilleux de la conception et de la naissance soit péché, mais plutôt que notre nature humaine a été contaminée par le péché dès le départ, entachée de l'égocentrisme hérité de nos parents. C'est le « péché originel », que David a reconnu dans les passions coupables qui l'ont dominé et vaincu, à savoir l'envie, la jalousie, la cruauté et l'avarice.

Lorsque nous nous voyons tels que nous sommes, c'est-à-dire, d'une part rebelles contre Dieu et sous le coup de son jugement, et d'autre part prisonniers de notre nature corrompue, alors, comme David, nous en venons à désespérer de nous-mêmes et à implorer la miséricorde de Dieu.

L'expression de la miséricorde divine

La miséricorde est la réponse de Dieu au besoin de pureté et de pardon du pécheur.

David a recours à deux métaphores pour implorer le pardon. Il demande d'abord à Dieu d'« effacer » ses torts (v. 3, 11). Ce verbe évoque l'action d'enlever une inscription d'un livre (voir par ex. Ex 32.32). Il considère ses péchés comme une liste de fautes à son actif, ou un relevé de dettes qu'il ne peut payer. Il prie que cette écriture soit annulée.

Il reconnaît ensuite que ses péchés l'ont souillé et supplie Dieu de le laver et de le purifier (v. 4), jusqu'à ce que ses taches noires aient

Page suivante : Vendredi saint à Jérusalem. « Aie pitié de moi, ô Dieu, toi qui es si bon ! Efface mes torts, tu es si compatissant ! »

disparu et qu'il devienne *plus blanc même que la neige* (v. 9). L'hysope est ici le symbole de la purification ; selon les rites de l'ancienne alliance, on pratiquait en effet l'aspersion de purification avec une branche d'hysope préalablement trempée dans le sang ou l'eau.

Mais David sait qu'il a autant besoin de pureté que de pardon. Dieu désire *que la droiture demeure au fond de* l'*être* (v. 8), alors que sa nature entière est corrompue (v. 7). Seule la puissance créatrice de Dieu peut faire de lui un homme nouveau, c'est pourquoi il prie : « *Ô Dieu, crée en moi un cœur pur ! Fais renaître en moi un esprit bien disposé !* » (v. 12). Il semble qu'il ait compris, avant même la révélation complète du Nouveau Testament, que seul le Saint-Esprit pouvait opérer cette transformation en lui (v. 14).

Si Dieu, dans sa miséricorde, daigne purifier à la fois sa conscience et son cœur, alors le tourment de son péché se transformera en *joie* et en *allégresse* (v. 10 ; cf. v.14).

Les conséquences de la miséricorde divine

La miséricorde purificatrice et créatrice de Dieu ne reste pas sans conséquences, comme le montre la fin du psaume (v. 15-21). David décide de changer d'attitude, à la fois envers les autres et envers Dieu.

Il accepte d'abord d'assumer sa responsabilité envers les hommes. Il a péché contre eux, mais il va désormais les servir d'une manière nouvelle. Quand il aura obtenu le pardon pour ses péchés, il s'attachera à *montrer à qui est coupable* quelle est la voie de Dieu, pour que le pécheur revienne à lui (v.15). Il prie pour être délivré *du poids de* son *crime* (v. 16). Il faut certainement comprendre par là que, s'il se reconnaît coupable du meurtre d'Urie, il ne veut pas toutefois que Dieu lui demande compte de la mort des pécheurs qu'il n'aurait pas avertis (cf. Ez 3.16-27 et 33.1-20).

Il a également une responsabilité envers Dieu. Sa bouche servira à la louange et au témoignage. *Éternel, ouvre mes lèvres et je te louerai* (v. 17). C'est là ce que Dieu désire, plutôt qu'un *sacrifice* ou des *holocaustes*. Non que Dieu n'aime aucun sacrifice, mais ce qu'il attend avant tout, surtout de la part d'un pécheur comme David, c'est *un cœur brisé et contrit*. Alors, lorsque son cœur aura été purifié, il pourra offrir un sacrifice de louange et d'actions de grâce (v. 17 ; cf. Ps 50.14, 23).

Beaucoup de commentateurs hésitent à rattacher les deux derniers versets à ce psaume. Il semble que le verset 20 fasse allusion à la reconstruction des murs de Jérusalem, à moins que cette phrase ne soit à prendre au sens figuré. De plus, le verset 21 (*alors tu prendras plaisir à des (...) holocaustes*) semble contredire le verset 18 (*je t'aurais offert des holocaustes, mais tu n'y prends pas plaisir*). Cette contradiction n'est toutefois qu'apparente et l'enseignement est en accord avec le message des Psaumes et des prophètes. Ce ne sont pas les sacrifices en tant que tels que Dieu refuse, mais il ne les agrée que lorsqu'ils sont l'expression d'un cœur contrit, d'un esprit d'adoration et d'une volonté soumise.

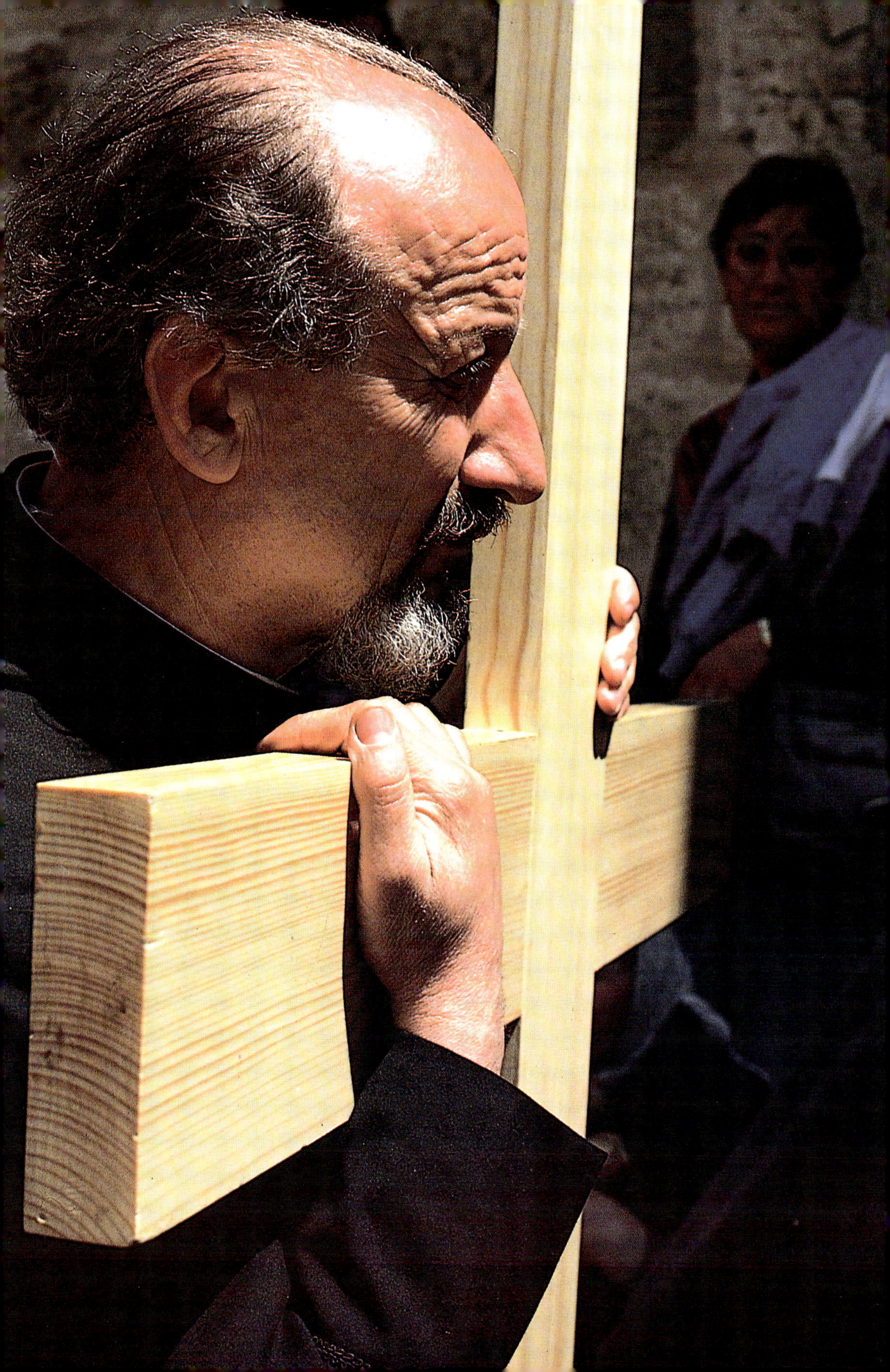

Sur la rive occidentale, une femme arabe coupe le blé avec la faucille de ses ancêtres. « La terre a produit sa récolte, Dieu, notre Dieu, nous a bénis. »

Psaume 67

La bénédiction des nations

Le thème de la bénédiction de Dieu, qui revient par trois fois dans les huit versets de ce psaume, soit sous forme de prière, soit sous forme d'affirmation, semble être ici la préoccupation principale du psalmiste.

C'est ce qui nous rend ce psaume sympathique, proche, car la bénédiction de Dieu est un sujet que nous évoquons fréquemment, nous aussi. « Que Dieu vous bénisse », ajoutons-nous à la fin d'une conversation, ou au bas d'une lettre. Les Anglais le disent même quand quelqu'un éternue ! Nous semblons tellement désireux que nos amis jouissent de la bénédiction divine, que nous ne manquons aucune occasion de l'invoquer sur eux.

Que voulons-nous dire au juste ? Le langage de ce psaume s'inspire de la bénédiction du grand prêtre, dictée par Dieu lui-même à Moïse, afin qu'Aaron et ses fils l'emploient pour le service du tabernacle. Elle est rapportée dans Nombres 6.24-26 : « Que l'Éternel te bénisse et te protège ! Que l'Éternel te regarde avec bonté ! Et qu'il te fasse grâce ! Que l'Éternel veille sur toi et t'accorde la paix ! » Cette bénédiction sera utilisée régulièrement lors des services liturgiques du Temple et reste très appréciée dans nos cultes chrétiens. D'autres psaumes en reprennent des extraits (par ex. Ps 4.7 ; 29.11 ; 31.17 ; 80.4, 8). Ce psaume, de toute évidence un psaume liturgique, s'articule donc autour de l'ancienne bénédiction d'Aaron.

Lu dans son ensemble, il nous enseigne qu'il est légitime de prier pour nous-même, et donne deux raisons, l'une pour un résultat immédiat, l'autre à plus long terme, pour lesquelles il convient de demander la bénédiction de Dieu sur nous.

2 Que Dieu nous fasse grâce ! | Qu'il nous bénisse !
Qu'il nous regarde | avec bonté,
Pause
3 afin que sur la terre | on reconnaisse | comment tu interviens,
et que dans toutes les nations | on voie comment tu sauves !
4 Que les peuples te louent, | ô Dieu,
que tous les peuples | t'adressent leurs louanges !
5 Que les nations jubilent | et qu'elles chantent | dans l'allégresse,
car c'est avec justice | que tu juges le monde,
et c'est avec droiture | que tu juges les peuples.
Pause
6 Que les peuples te louent, | ô Dieu,
que tous les peuples | t'adressent leurs louanges !
7 La terre a produit sa récolte,
Dieu, notre Dieu, nous a bénis.
8 Oui, que Dieu nous bénisse
et qu'il soit révéré | jusqu'aux confins du monde !

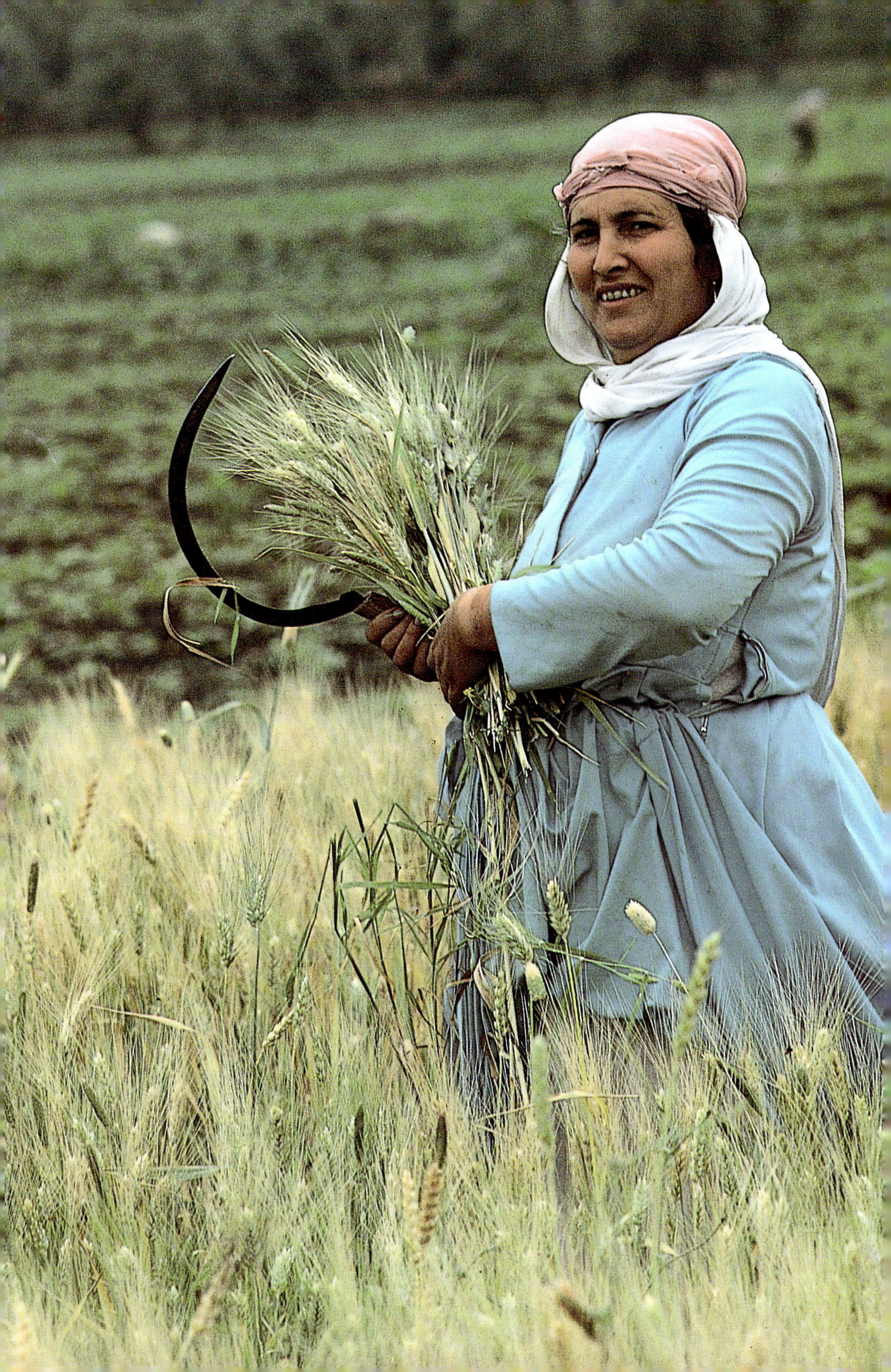

La connaissance de Dieu

Si Dieu nous bénit, toute l'humanité aura, par notre intermédiaire, connaissance de son salut (v. 2, 3). La prière d'Israël n'avait rien d'égoïste. Le peuple d'Israël a demandé à Dieu de le bénir, non pas pour sa jouissance personnelle, mais pour qu'au travers de lui cette bénédiction puisse en atteindre d'autres. Par la miséricorde que Dieu témoignera à son peuple, les nations seront touchées et pourront elles aussi connaître ses voies et goûter à ses bienfaits.

Souvenons-nous des allégations audacieuses du peuple d'Israël concernant son statut et son Dieu. Il affirmait être le peuple élu, avec lequel Dieu avait conclu une alliance éternelle. Il méprisait les idoles muettes et sans vie des nations et proclamait que Dieu était le seul Dieu vivant, agissant et vrai. Ces affirmations lui attiraient la curiosité, tantôt moqueuse, tantôt incrédule, des nations païennes, qui voulaient voir des preuves de ce qu'Israël prétendait. « Ton Dieu, où est-il donc ? » demandaient-elles. Elles voulaient savoir ce que Dieu était capable de faire pour son peuple, s'il avait quelque chose qu'elles n'avaient pas, si les prétentions d'Israël étaient justifiées.

Voilà pourquoi Israël priait *Que Dieu nous fasse grâce ! Qu'il nous bénisse !* Si seulement la bénédiction d'Aaron se réalisait ! Si seulement Dieu leur accordait sa miséricorde et les bénissait tout particulièrement, les regardant toujours avec bonté ! Alors peut-être les nations comprendraient-elles ! Elles auraient la preuve tangible de l'existence, de l'intervention et de la grâce de Dieu. Les peuples connaîtraient ses voies et son salut et verraient que Dieu est un juste juge et un bon berger (v. 5).

Ce principe reste vrai de nos jours. Les non-chrétiens nous regardent vivre. Nous prétendons connaître, aimer et suivre Jésus-Christ, nous disons qu'il est notre Seigneur, notre Maître et notre Ami. « Qu'est-ce que ça change dans leur vie ? » s'interroge le monde, curieux. « Leur Dieu, où est-il ? » On peut affirmer que, paradoxalement, le principal obstacle à l'évangélisation de nos jours est la difficulté dans laquelle se trouve l'Église de témoigner, dans sa vie et dans ses actes, de la puissance salvatrice de Dieu. Nous faisons bien de demander sur nous la bénédiction de Dieu, sa miséricorde et son appui, non pas pour monopoliser sa grâce et jouir égoïstement de sa faveur, mais pour que les autres, témoins des bienfaits et de la beauté de Dieu en nous, soient attirés vers lui.

L'adoration rendue à Dieu

Les versets 4 à 6 font figure de refrain. Nous y trouvons la deuxième raison de rechercher la bénédiction de Dieu. Que d'autres gens parviennent à la connaissance de Dieu n'est pas suffisant. Car pourquoi voulons-nous qu'ils connaissent Dieu ? Juste pour eux-mêmes ? Juste pour qu'ils reçoivent son salut ? Voudrions-nous que les autres fassent ce que nous nous refusons à faire nous-mêmes ? Si nous ne recherchons pas la bénédiction de Dieu pour satisfaire nos besoins égoïstes, accepterions-nous que d'autres le fassent ? Ce n'est pas très logique !

Il nous faut considérer le but ultime du salut des nations, qui est de les amener à louer et à adorer Dieu. Si nous désirons leur salut, ce n'est pas seulement afin qu'elles le connaissent pour ce qu'il leur apporte, mais aussi qu'elles le louent pour ce qu'il est. Le but suprême de toute évangélisation, ce n'est pas le besoin de l'être humain, mais la gloire de Dieu ; non pour que l'homme reçoive le salut, mais pour qu'il rende à Dieu l'honneur dû à son nom, qu'il le reconnaisse pour Dieu et l'adore à jamais. Notre tâche ne sera pas achevée tant que nous n'aurons pas fait de chaque converti un adorateur.

Un moine balaie les jardins de l'église située au bord du lac de Galilée, où Jésus ressuscité apparut aux apôtres et confia sa mission à Pierre : « Pais mes brebis. »

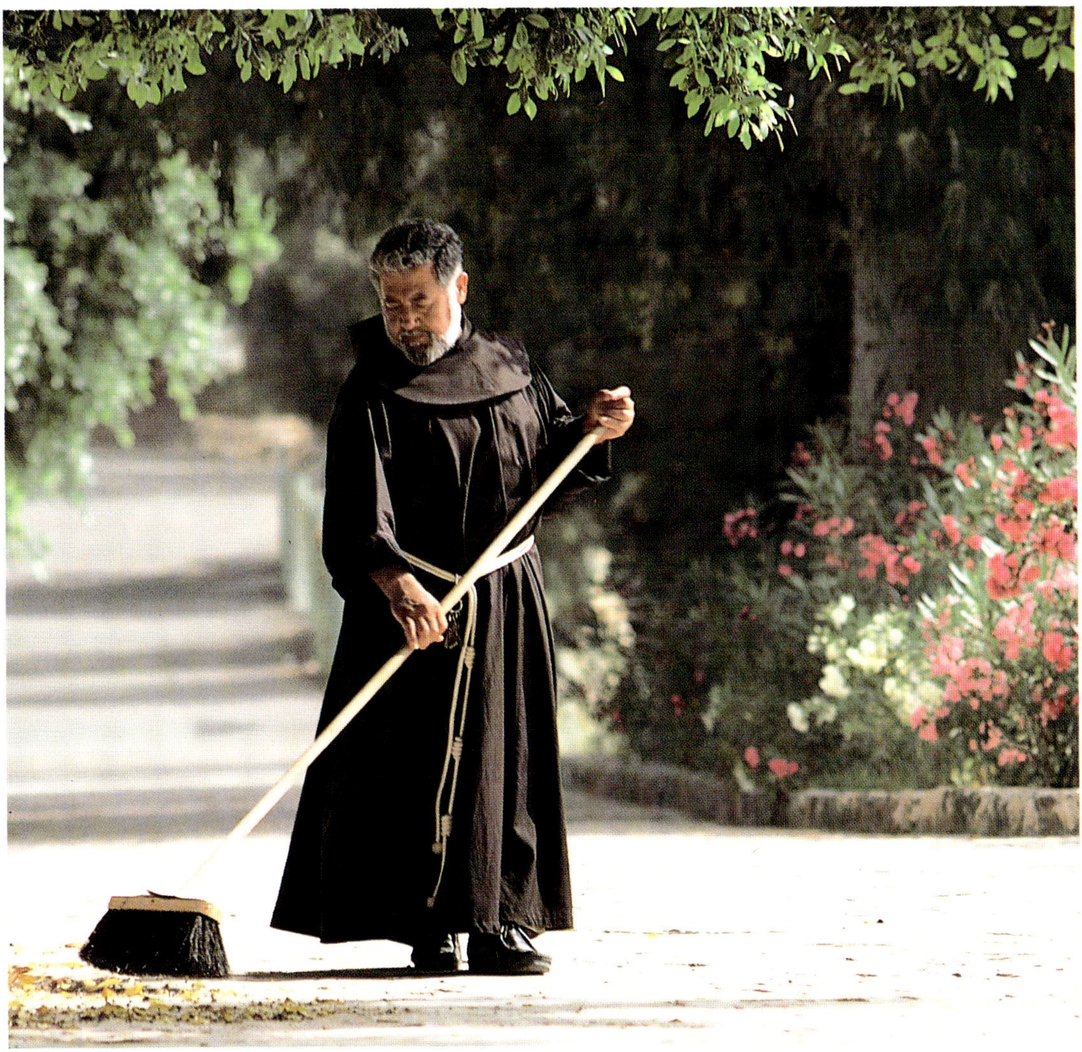

Psaume 73

La réussite des méchants

Les hommes de tous les temps se sont interrogés sur la providence de Dieu, sa façon de diriger le monde. Le livre de Job, de même que les psaumes 37, 49 et 73, y sont entièrement consacrés. L'énoncé du problème est simple. Dieu s'est révélé comme un Dieu bon et juste, qui punit la méchanceté et récompense la bonté. Pourquoi alors, s'il est tout-puissant et fondamentalement bon, ne met-il pas fin à l'injustice qui sévit sur terre ? Au lieu d'avoir ce que méritent leurs actes, les méchants croissent « comme un cèdre vert » (Ps 37.35). Non seulement leur méchanceté n'est pas punie, mais, de surcroît, ils semblent dispensés des ennuis qui sont le lot des autres. Autrement dit, l'honnêteté ne paie pas. Cela ne sert à rien d'être bon. Ce sont les méchants qui prospèrent, alors que le malheur s'acharne sur les justes. Voilà les grandes lignes de ce psaume.

L'énoncé du problème (v. 1-15)

Le psalmiste commence par énoncer la conviction qui est celle de tout homme pieux, quelles que soient les circonstances : *Oui, Dieu est bon (...) pour tous ceux qui ont le cœur pur* (v. 1). C'est là une vérité de base inéluctable de la religion révélée. *Pourtant,* ajoute-t-il aussitôt, *il s'en fallut de peu que mes pieds ne trébuchent, un rien de plus, et je tombais. J'étais jaloux des arrogants en voyant la prospérité des gens méchants* (v. 2, 3). Les sujets de mécontentement ne manquent pas. Non seulement les maladies et les malheurs ne semblent pas atteindre les méchants (v. 4, 5), mais, de plus, ils sont arrogants (v. 6-9). Tout en eux, leurs yeux et leur cœur, leurs paroles et leurs regards, trahit leur suffisance (v. 7, 8). Comme si ce n'était pas assez que *leur langue* sévisse *sur la terre, leur bouche s'en prend au ciel même* (v. 9). Sans parler du succès qu'ils ont auprès de tout le monde (v. 10, 11). On se demande pourquoi Dieu, si du moins il voit ce qu'ils font, ne les punit pas (v. 11).

Le psalmiste conclut son portrait des méchants en ces termes : *toujours tranquilles, ils accumulent les richesses* (v. 12), avant d'ajouter avec amertume : *Alors, c'est donc en vain que je suis resté pur* (v. 13). En effet, tandis qu'eux prospèrent, *tous les jours je subis des coups* (v. 14). Si la réussite est pour les méchants, alors il ne sert à rien d'être juste. La droiture ne paie pas ; ce sont les méchants qui empochent les gros dividendes.

Oui, Dieu est bon pour Israël,
pour tous ceux qui ont le cœur pur.
2 Pourtant, il s'en fallut de peu | que mes pieds ne trébuchent,
un rien de plus, et je tombais.
3 J'étais jaloux des arrogants
en voyant la prospérité | des gens méchants.
4 Car ils sont exempts de souffrance ; | jusqu'à leur mort,
ils ont santé et embonpoint.
5 Ils passent à côté des peines | qui sont le lot commun des hommes.
Ils ne subissent pas les maux | qui frappent les humains.
6 Aussi s'ornent-ils d'arrogance | comme on porte un collier,
et la violence est leur parure,
7 leurs yeux sont pétillants | dans leur visage plein de graisse,
les mauvais désirs de leur cœur | débordent sans mesure.
8 Ils sont moqueurs, | ils parlent méchamment
et, sur un ton hautain, | menacent d'opprimer.
9 Leur bouche s'en prend au ciel même,
leur langue sévit sur la terre.
10 Aussi le peuple les suit-il,
buvant à longs traits leurs paroles,
11 tout en disant : « Dieu ? Que sait-il ?
Celui qui est là-haut | comment connaîtrait-il ? »
12 Voilà comment sont les méchants :
toujours tranquilles, | ils accumulent les richesses.
13 Alors, c'est donc en vain | que je suis resté pur,
que j'ai lavé mes mains | en signe d'innocence !
14 Tous les jours, je subis des coups,
je suis châtié chaque matin !
15 Si je disais : « Parlons comme eux »,
alors je trahirais tes fils.

16 Je me suis mis à réfléchir : | j'ai cherché à comprendre,
je trouvais tout cela | bien trop injuste
17 jusqu'au jour où je suis entré | dans la maison de Dieu
et où j'ai réfléchi | au sort qui les attend.
18 Car, en fait, tu les mets | sur un terrain glissant,
tu les entraînes vers la ruine.
19 Et soudain, c'est la catastrophe : | en un instant, ils sont perdus,
ils sont détruits, | et l'épouvante les saisit.
20 Comme les images du rêve | s'évanouissent, après le réveil,
ô Eternel, quand tu interviendras, | tu les feras tous disparaître.

21 Oui, quand j'avais le cœur amer
et tant que je me tourmentais,
22 j'étais un sot, un ignorant,
je me comportais avec toi | comme une bête sans raison.
23 Mais je suis toujours avec toi,
et tu m'as saisi la main droite,
24 selon ton plan, tu me conduis,
puis tu me prendras dans la gloire.
25 Qui ai-je au ciel, si ce n'est toi ?
Et ici-bas que désirer, | car je suis avec toi ?
26 Mon corps peut s'épuiser | et mon cœur défaillir,
Dieu reste mon rocher, | et mon bien précieux pour toujours.
27 Qui t'abandonne se perdra,
et tu anéantiras | tous ceux qui te sont infidèles.
28 Tandis que mon bonheur à moi, | c'est d'être toujours près de Dieu.
Oui, j'ai placé dans le Seigneur, | dans l'Eternel, | mon sûr refuge,
et je raconterai ses œuvres.

La bonne manière d'aborder le problème (v. 16,17)

Si le psalmiste a eu cette réaction, c'est que son approche du problème était mauvaise. Il a commis au moins trois erreurs. Premièrement, il était *jaloux* des méchants (v. 3). Il ne faut jamais envier la liberté du pécheur. « N'envie pas le sort de ceux qui font le mal, mais en tout temps révère l'Éternel » (Pr 23.17). Deuxièmement, il en a voulu à Dieu, comme il le confessera par la suite (v. 21, 22). C'est se comporter comme un animal ignorant, et non comme un être humain raisonnable, que de vouloir donner des leçons à Dieu. Troisièmement, enfin, il a été tenté de baisser les bras. Il avait beau chercher à comprendre, il trouvait *tout cela bien trop injuste* (v. 16). Devant l'absence de solution, il a failli céder au désespoir.

Jusqu'au jour où il est *entré dans la maison de Dieu* (v. 17). À ceux qui cherchent humblement sa face, Dieu accorde le discernement. C'est une leçon que le chrétien du vingtième siècle a besoin d'apprendre. Si l'attitude de Dieu nous paraît incompréhensible, la solution n'est pas d'envier les méchants, ni de nous apitoyer sur notre sort avec amertume. Gardons-nous de même du fatalisme et du désespoir, mais tombons plutôt à genoux pour regarder à Dieu. Alors, « depuis la demeure secrète du Très-Haut, nous voyons les choses comme lui les voit » (Campbell Morgan).

La solution (v. 17-26)

Notre problème, c'est que notre esprit est limité et notre vue faussée. C'est une question de perspective. Une montagne qui paraît impressionnante à celui qui se tient à sa base, devient insignifiante vue de loin ou d'avion. De même, la question de la providence divine ne peut se résoudre dans le contexte limité de la vie sur cette terre et ne trouvera sa solution que dans l'éternité. Il y aura toujours beaucoup d'injustice en ce monde, mais le jugement final redressera les torts, vengera le mal et reconnaîtra le bien. C'est pourquoi nous devons continuer à entrer *dans la maison de Dieu*, où la perspective se trouve corrigée et notre vision éclaircie.

Ce que le psalmiste a compris *dans la maison de Dieu*, c'est le *sort qui attend* les méchants (v. 17). S'il est vrai qu'ils prospèrent pour l'instant, Dieu les place cependant *sur un terrain glissant*. Jésus dira qu'il sont « sur le chemin large qui mène à la perdition. » La mort finira par les réclamer et ils seront *détruits*. On ne se souviendra plus d'eux, *comme les images du rêve s'évanouissent, après le réveil* (v. 18-20).

Les justes, par contre, ont un tout autre destin : *je suis toujours avec toi* (v. 23). En effet, si les méchants prospèrent maintenant, pour périr ensuite, les hommes pieux, par contre, bénéficient constamment de la présence de Dieu, dès à présent et à jamais (v. 24). Même si la misère et la persécution sont parfois la part de ceux appartiennent à Dieu, leur richesse réside en Dieu. Le psalmiste poursuit : *Qui ai-je au ciel, si ce n'est toi ? Et ici-bas, que désirer, car je suis avec toi ?* (v. 25), nous offrant là l'une des plus belles formulations de la piété personnelle, de tout l'Ancien Testament. Au ciel comme sur la terre, dans le temps comme dans l'éternité, le Dieu vivant est son *bien précieux pour toujours* (v. 26). Cette communion avec Dieu est la vie éternelle, que la mort ne peut ni ébranler ni détruire.

La conclusion résume ce que le psalmiste a compris dans la maison de Dieu, à savoir la différence de destinée entre les justes et les infidèles (v. 27-28). *Qui t'abandonne se perdra (...) Tandis que mon bonheur à moi, c'est d'être toujours près de Dieu.* Il ne fait aucun doute que pour le matérialiste, la communion avec Dieu n'est pas synonyme de « bonheur », puisqu'elle peut impliquer des soucis et des souffrances. Mais ceux qui apprécient les vraies richesses savent que le « bonheur » véritable et éternel est en Dieu.

Psaume 84

Les parvis de l'Éternel

Il n'existait pas pour un Juif d'endroit plus sacré sur terre que le Temple de Jérusalem, car c'était là, dans le Saint des Saints, que se trouvait la *Chékina*, la manifestation visible de la gloire de Dieu. Les Israélites pieux savaient, bien entendu, que Dieu n'habitait pas *sur la terre* et que *le ciel dans toute son immensité ne saurait le contenir*, selon ce qu'avait dit Salomon (1 R 8.27). L'Éternel a néanmoins choisi d'« établir son nom » à Jérusalem et de faire apparaître le symbole de sa présence au-dessus du propitiatoire, derrière le voile du Temple. Par conséquent, tout Israélite aimait le Temple et ne manquait aucune occasion de s'y rendre, surtout à l'occasion des trois fêtes annuelles. Il pouvait chanter de tout son cœur : *Oh ! que j'aime tes demeures, Éternel, Seigneur des armées célestes !* (v. 1). On retrouve ce même amour du Temple dans les psaumes 42 et 43, ainsi que dans certains psaumes de pèlerinage (120-134).

Le bonheur de certains (v. 1-8)

Le psalmiste commence par dire son amour pour les demeures de l'Éternel. Son être entier aspire à s'y trouver. Il *languit* et *soupire*, parce qu'entrer dans les *parvis* de l'Éternel équivaut à entrer dans la présence du *Dieu vivant*. Pour une raison qui nous est inconnue, le psalmiste est empêché d'accomplir les désirs de son cœur, et il envie tous ceux, oiseaux et hommes, qui en ont, eux, la possibilité.

Il évoque le moineau, l'oiseau le plus répandu et le plus ordinaire qui soit, qui construit son nid dans tous les coins et recoins du Temple.

2 Oh ! que j'aime tes demeures, | Eternel, | Seigneur des armées célestes !

3 Je languis et je soupire, | Eternel, après tes parvis,

mon être entier crie sa joie | vers le Dieu vivant.

4 Le moineau découvre un gîte,

l'hirondelle trouve un nid | où déposer ses petits,

près de tes autels, | Eternel, | Seigneur des armées célestes,

mon Roi et mon Dieu !

5 Bienheureux ceux qui habitent | ta maison,

car ils pourront te louer toujours.
Pause

6 Bienheureux les hommes | dont tu es la force :

dans leur cœur, ils trouvent | des chemins tracés.

7 Car lorsqu'ils traversent | la vallée des Larmes,

ils en font une oasis,

et la pluie d'automne | vient la recouvrir | de bénédictions.

8 D'étape en étape, | leur vigueur s'accroît

et ils se présentent | à Dieu en Sion.

9 Eternel, | ô Dieu des armées célestes, | entends ma prière !

Veuille m'écouter, | ô Dieu de Jacob !
Pause

10 Toi, ô Dieu, qui nous protèges, | veuille regarder

celui que, par ton onction, | tu as établi : | fais-lui bon accueil !

11 Car un jour dans tes parvis | vaut bien mieux que mille ailleurs.

Plutôt rester sur le seuil | de la maison de mon Dieu,

que de demeurer | sous les tentes des méchants.

12 Car l'Eternel Dieu | est pour nous comme un soleil, | il est comme un bouclier.

L'Eternel accorde | bienveillance et gloire,

il ne refuse aucun bien

à ceux qui cheminent | dans l'intégrité.

13 Eternel, | Seigneur des armées célestes,

bienheureux est l'homme | qui met sa confiance en toi.

Page suivante : Le Dôme du Rocher est érigé sur l'emplacement du Temple de Jérusalem, qui représente pour les Juifs l'endroit le plus sacré sur terre.

Ce qu'il appelle *hirondelle* est probablement le martinet. Les martinets sont nombreux encore aujourd'hui à passer par la Palestine pendant la migration et à nicher dans la cour de la mosquée d'Omar à Jérusalem. Combien il les envie ! Ils ont le droit d'habiter à proximité immédiate des autels de Dieu. Les pépiements des moineaux et les cris des martinets se mêlent aux louanges de son peuple. C'est à lui que l'auteur pense à présent, aux prêtres qui, habitant la maison de Dieu, peuvent le louer sans cesse (v. 4) et aux pèlerins qui s'y rendent de temps en temps. Ils sont tous *bienheureux* (v. 5, 6).

Le psalmiste porte son attention sur les pèlerins (v. 6-8), dont il aimerait tellement faire partie, et décrit leur périple jusqu'à Jérusalem. Ils « ont à cœur ce pèlerinage » (version en Français Courant) et trouvent dans leur détermination la vigueur nécessaire à ce voyage long et pénible. Il les voit traversant une vallée aride (la vallée des Larmes). Même ces régions inhospitalières n'ont pas raison de leur courage, ils y trouvent au contraire *une oasis, et la pluie d'automne vient la recouvrir de bénédictions* (ou : d'étangs). Autrement dit, « l'espoir soutient chacun de leurs pas » (Perowne). *D'étape en étape, leur vigueur s'accroît* à la pensée de se présenter devant Dieu en Sion (v. 8).

Une prière personnelle (v. 9- 13)

Éternel, ô Dieu des armées célestes, entends ma prière (v. 9). C'est la prière que formule le psalmiste en pensant au bonheur des moineaux et des martinets, des pèlerins et des prêtres, au nombre desquels il aimerait tellement se trouver. Elle est suivie d'une autre prière pour celui qui est l'oint de Dieu, probablement le roi (v. 10). Si cette demande apparaît dans ce contexte, c'est peut-être parce que le roi est garant du bonheur de la nation.

L'auteur explique alors, à la fois en termes de temps et d'espace, pourquoi il désire se rendre au Temple (v. 11). Un jour dans les parvis de l'Éternel, dit-il, *vaut bien mieux que mille ailleurs,* et il préférerait *rester sur le seuil* de la maison de l'Éternel que *demeurer sous les tentes des méchants.* Rien qu'un jour. Rien que le seuil. Peu importe si c'est peu et si c'est de loin ; ce serait suffisant, car Dieu, qui est un *soleil* et un *bouclier,* nous inonde de lumière et nous protège du mal. Mieux encore, il *accorde bienveillance et gloire* et *ne refuse aucun bien à ceux qui cheminent dans l'intégrité* (v. 12).

Avec les prêtres qui habitent dans le Temple (v. 5) et les pèlerins qui y montent de temps en temps (v. 6), *bienheureux* sont aussi tous ceux qui mettent leur confiance en Dieu (v. 13), qu'ils puissent ou non se rendre à Jérusalem. C'est ce que le psalmiste affirme en conclusion.

Ce psaume peut aisément s'appliquer aux chrétiens et le Nouveau Testament parle de ce Temple que nous devons « aimer » et appeler de nos vœux. Il s'agit dans un premier temps de l'Église, non seulement universelle (Ep 2.21), mais locale (1 Co 3.16 ; 2 Co 6.16),

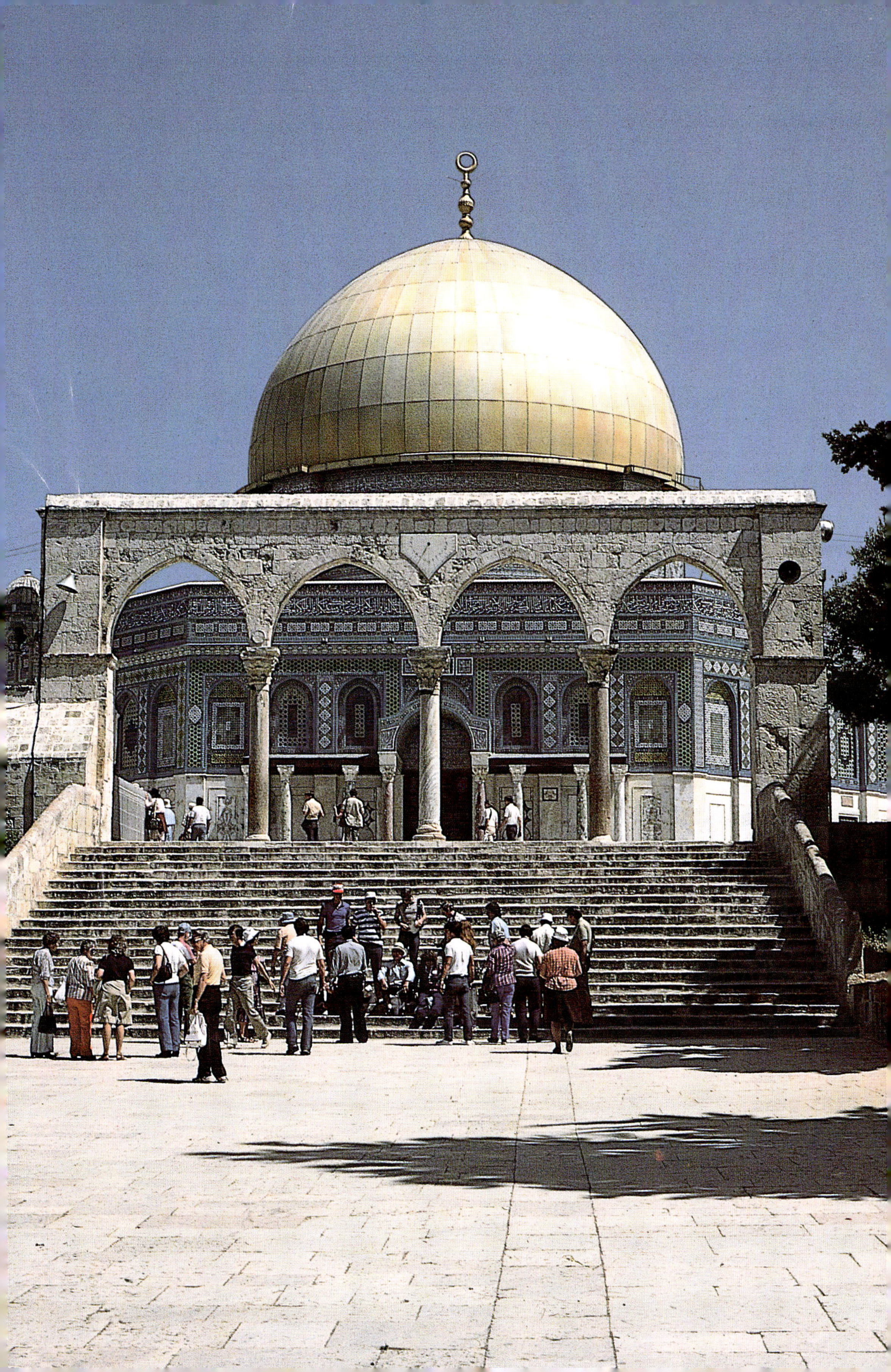

c'est-à-dire de toute assemblée de croyants. Dieu n'habite pas dans des temples construits par des mains humaines (Ac 7.48), mais au milieu de son peuple. Nul n'est besoin de se rendre à Jérusalem pour le rencontrer. Lorsque nous nous réunissons, même à deux ou trois, dans le nom du Christ, il est là, au milieu de nous (Mt 18.20), et c'est pourquoi nous aimons nous retrouver pour l'adorer ensemble.

Cependant, la raison d'être du Temple ne trouvera sa pleine réalisation qu'au ciel, dans la nouvelle Jérusalem, dont il est écrit : « Je ne vis aucun temple dans la ville : son Temple, c'est le Seigneur, le Dieu Tout-Puissant, ainsi que l'Agneau » et « Voici la Tente de Dieu avec les hommes. Il habitera avec eux ; ils seront ses peuples et lui, Dieu avec eux, sera leur Dieu » (Ap 21.22, 3). C'est dans cette perspective que l'aspiration des chrétiens rejoint celle du psalmiste. Nous avons soif de Dieu et notre espérance chrétienne nous soutient tout au long de notre pèlerinage difficile vers le ciel.

Psaume 90

Le rêve éphémère de la vie

Ce psaume souligne la brièveté de l'existence humaine à la lumière de l'éternité de Dieu. L'auteur pense à une période particulièrement difficile de l'histoire (v. 15), en même temps qu'à la fragilité et au péché de l'homme en général. On ne discerne pourtant chez lui aucune trace de désespoir ni d'apitoiement, mais une attitude de soumission humble et confiante.

L'éternité de Dieu (v. 1-6)

Dieu, de par son caractère éternel, a été le *refuge* de son peuple à travers les générations. Telle est la magnifique confession du psalmiste. Notre seule sécurité au milieu des hauts et des bas de l'existence, est en Celui qui, avant même la naissance des montagnes et la création de la terre, *de toute éternité et pour l'éternité*, est Dieu.

Devant lui, les êtres humains ne sont que poussière. Dieu est celui qui leur ordonne de retourner à la poussière (v. 3), écrit le psalmiste, faisant clairement référence au texte de Genèse 3.19. Telle est la réalité de la mort, « la terre à la terre, les cendres aux cendres, la poussière à la poussière. » Nous sommes mortels et, de surcroît, notre vie est extrêmement courte. Pour Dieu, mille ans apparaissent comme un jour (cf. 2 P 3.8) ou même comme *une seule veille* de la nuit (v. 4). À la lumière

O Seigneur, d'âge en âge
tu as été notre refuge.
2 Avant que soient nées les montagnes,
et que tu aies créé | la terre et l'univers,
de toute éternité | et pour l'éternité, | toi, tu es Dieu.
3 Tu fais retourner l'homme | à la poussière,
et tu dis aux humains : | « Retournez-y ! »
4 Car mille ans, à tes yeux,
sont comme le jour d'hier | qui est déjà passé,
comme une seule veille | au milieu de la nuit.
5 Tu balaies les humains | comme un peu de sommeil | qui s'efface à l'aurore.
Ils sont pareils à l'herbe
6 qui fleurit le matin, | qui passe
et qui, le soir, | se fane et se flétrit.

7 Nous sommes consumés | par ta colère,
ta fureur nous effraie :
8 tu as mis devant toi | tous nos péchés,
et tu mets en lumière | tout ce qui est caché.
9 Tous nos jours disparaissent | par ta colère,
et nos années s'effacent | comme un murmure...
10 Le temps de notre vie ? | C'est soixante-dix ans,
au mieux : quatre-vingts ans | pour les plus vigoureux ;
et leur agitation | n'est que peine et misère.
Car le temps passe vite | et nous nous envolons.
11 Qui peut connaître | l'intensité de ta colère,
qui te respecte assez | pour tenir compte | de ton courroux ?
12 Apprends-nous donc | à bien compter nos jours,
afin que notre cœur | acquière la sagesse !
13 Tourne-toi de nouveau vers nous, | ô Eternel ! | Jusques à quand | tarderas-tu encore ?
Aie pitié de tes serviteurs !
14 Rassasie-nous tous les matins | de ton amour,
et nous crierons de joie, | pleins d'allégresse, | tout au long de nos jours.
15 Rends-nous en jours de joie | les jours de nos épreuves,
et en années de joie | nos années de malheur !
16 Que ton œuvre apparaisse | envers tes serviteurs !
Et que leurs descendants | découvrent ta grandeur !
17 Que la tendresse | du Seigneur, notre Dieu, | repose sur nous tous !
Fais prospérer pour nous | l'ouvrage de nos mains !
Oh oui ! fais prospérer | l'ouvrage de nos mains !

Page suivante : « Rassasie-nous tous les matins de ton amour, et nous crierons de joie, pleins d'allégresse, tout au long de nos jours. »

de l'intemporalité de Dieu, notre vie est *pareille à l'herbe*, qui fleurit le matin et se fane quand vient le soir, desséchée par le soleil et le vent. Ce thème revient constamment dans l'Ecriture, qui multiplie les métaphores pour souligner la brièveté de notre passage sur la terre. Notre vie est comparée à de l'eau répandue sur le sol, à une ombre chassée par le soleil et à de la fumée ou de la brume dissipée par le vent.

La colère de Dieu (v. 7-11)

De l'éternité de Dieu, le psalmiste en vient à évoquer sa colère. La transition, abrupte à première vue, s'explique par le fait qu'il considère la nature mortelle de l'homme dans la sombre perspective de la haine divine à l'égard du péché. Il faut savoir que le pays traversait une série de malheurs qui étaient pour le psalmiste la conséquence du jugement de Dieu ; il reconnaît par ailleurs que la mort est le châtiment du péché de l'homme (Gn 2.17 ; 3.19 ; Rm 5.12). Nos *péchés* et *tout ce qui est caché* sont dévoilés devant Dieu (v. 8) et *tous nos jours disparaissent par sa colère* (v. 9). Même les quelque soixante-dix ans que dure notre vie ne sont *que peine et misère.* Il n'y a dans cette constatation aucune amertume, mais un réalisme tranquille et sobre. Chaque être humain est appelé à mourir et, à moins que nous n'implorions sa miséricorde, et jusqu'à ce jour, notre courte vie est placée sous le jugement de Dieu. Cette réalité inspire plusieurs prières, qui concluent le psaume.

La miséricorde de Dieu (v. 12-17)

Dès que nous prenons conscience de notre péché et de notre nature mortelle, nous demandons à Dieu : *Apprends-nous donc à bien compter nos jours, afin que notre cœur acquière la sagesse* (v. 12). La sagesse est la connaissance et la crainte de Dieu. La vie est tellement courte que c'est une folie que de ne tenir aucun compte de Dieu. Il a traité d'insensé le riche propriétaire de la parabole racontée par Jésus, qui formait des projets et parlait comme si la vie ne devait jamais s'arrêter.

Dans un deuxième temps, nous prions : *Rassasie-nous tous les matins de ton amour* ; en effet si, dès le début de la journée nous trouvons notre paix dans l'amour de Dieu, *nous crierons de joie (...) tout au long de nos jours* (v. 13, 14). De plus, la joie de Dieu nous aidera à tenir bon pendant les années de malheur (v. 15).

La troisième prière concerne notre *ouvrage.* Un des aspects tragiques de la mort est qu'elle interrompt notre travail et nous empêche de mener à bien nos projets. Cela n'est vrai cependant que pour ce que l'homme entreprend avec ses propres forces. Lorsque Dieu montre ses œuvres à ses serviteurs, qu'il nous donne sa force pour les accomplir et nous bénit, c'est lui qui fait prospérer *l'ouvrage de nos mains* (v. 16, 17). La seule œuvre durable est celle que Dieu affermit.

La brièveté de la vie devrait nous encourager à acquérir la sagesse, c'est-à-dire à faire de Dieu notre refuge, à trouver le repos dans son amour et à accomplir un travail utile avec sa bénédiction.

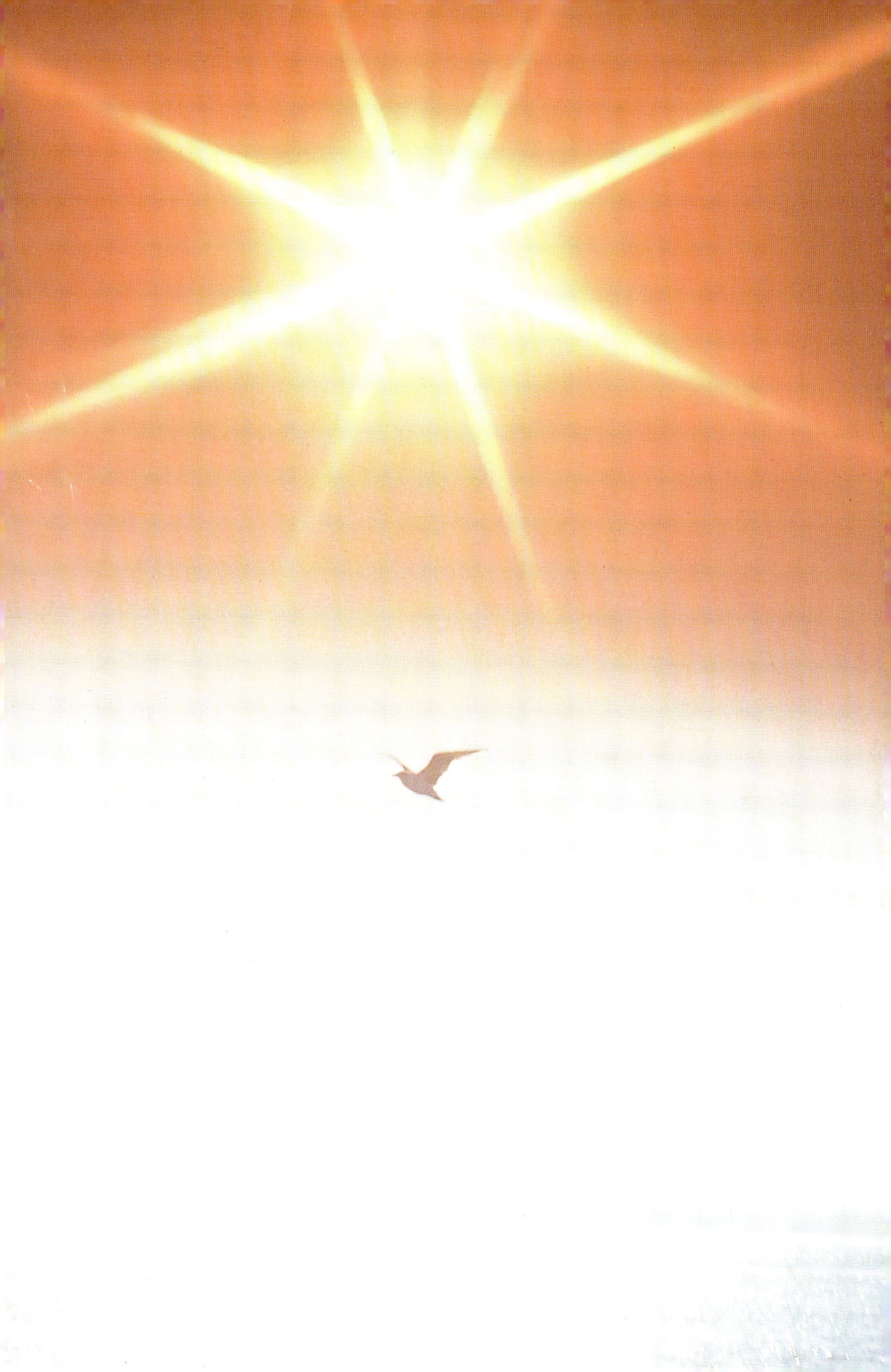

Psaume 91

La protection du Très-Haut

La particularité de ce psaume est d'être le seul passage de l'Écriture (du moins du canon) à avoir été cité par le diable ! (cf. Mt 4.6 et Lc 4.10, 11). C'est plus important qu'il n'y paraît car, en fait, sa citation était inexacte, ou plutôt il en avait forcé le sens, en demandant au Fils de Dieu de se jeter du haut du Temple et de compter sur la promesse divine d'envoyer ses anges pour le protéger. Le diable n'est pas le seul à avoir fait une mauvaise interprétation du psaume 91, comprenant à tort qu'il promettait une protection inconditionnelle dans quelque circonstance que ce soit.

Notre Seigneur savait cependant que c'était tenter Dieu que de sauter du sommet du Temple sur la base de la promesse de ce psaume. Seuls les enfants de Dieu qui vivent selon sa volonté peuvent prétendre à sa protection. Et même là, rien ne leur garantit qu'ils seront à l'abri de tout malheur (voir v. 15). Par contre, ils sont assurés, quelles que soient les circonstances, d'être toujours environnés de l'amour de Dieu. Le texte qui fait écho à ce psaume dans le Nouveau Testament est Romains 8.31-39.

Pour comprendre le cheminement de la pensée, il faut voir que, dans un premier temps, le croyant parle à Dieu (v. 1, 2), ensuite le psalmiste s'adresse au croyant (v. 3-13) et enfin, Dieu intervient à l'intention du lecteur et met son sceau sur la promesse de protection qu'il a faite au croyant (v. 14-16).

1 Celui qui s'abrite | tout près du Très-Haut
repose en lieu sûr, | à l'ombre du Tout-Puissant.
2 Je dis : « Eternel, | tu es mon refuge | et ma forteresse,
oui, tu es mon Dieu | en qui j'ai confiance. »

3 Car c'est lui qui te délivre | du filet de l'oiseleur,
de la peste et du fléau.
4 Il t'abrite de son aile
et, caché sous son plumage, | tu trouves un refuge sûr.
Sa fidélité | est un bouclier, | elle est une armure.
5 Tu n'as plus à craindre, | ni terreurs la nuit,
ni flèches qui volent | durant la journée,
6 ni peste rôdant | dans l'obscurité,
ni insolation | qui frappe à midi.
7 Qu'un millier tombe à ta gauche
et dix milliers à ta droite,
tu ne seras pas atteint.
8 Ouvre seulement les yeux,
et tu pourras contempler | le châtiment des méchants.
9 L'Eternel est mon refuge.
Si tu as fait du Très-Haut | ton abri,
10 aucun mal ne t'atteindra,
nul malheur n'approchera | de la tente où tu demeures,
11 car il chargera ses anges
de veiller sur tes chemins,
12 de te porter sur leurs mains,
de peur que ton pied | ne heurte une pierre.
13 Tu pourras marcher sans crainte | sur le lion et la vipère
et tu fouleras aux pieds | le lionceau et le serpent.

14 « Parce qu'il m'est attaché | à moi, le Seigneur, | je vais le sauver
et le protéger | car il me connaît.
15 Il m'invoquera, | je lui répondrai,
oui, je serai avec lui | au moment de la détresse,
et je le délivrerai, | je le couvrirai de gloire.
16 Je le comblerai de jours
et je lui ferai connaître | mon salut. »

Le croyant (v. 1, 2)

Le croyant fonde sa foi sur la personne de Dieu. Il est le *Très-Haut* et le *Tout-Puissant* (v. 1), infiniment grand et puissant, mais il est aussi l'*Éternel* (v. 2), Yahvé, le Dieu de l'alliance avec Israël, lié à son peuple par un engagement solennel. C'est signe de sagesse que de reposer *à l'ombre* d'un tel Dieu ; il est le *refuge* et la *forteresse* du croyant.

L'église du Saint Sépulcre, à Jérusalem, qui attire des foules de touristes, a probablement été érigée sur le site de la crucifixion de Jésus, à Golgotha. « Si tu fais du Très-Haut ton abri, aucun mal ne t'atteindra. »

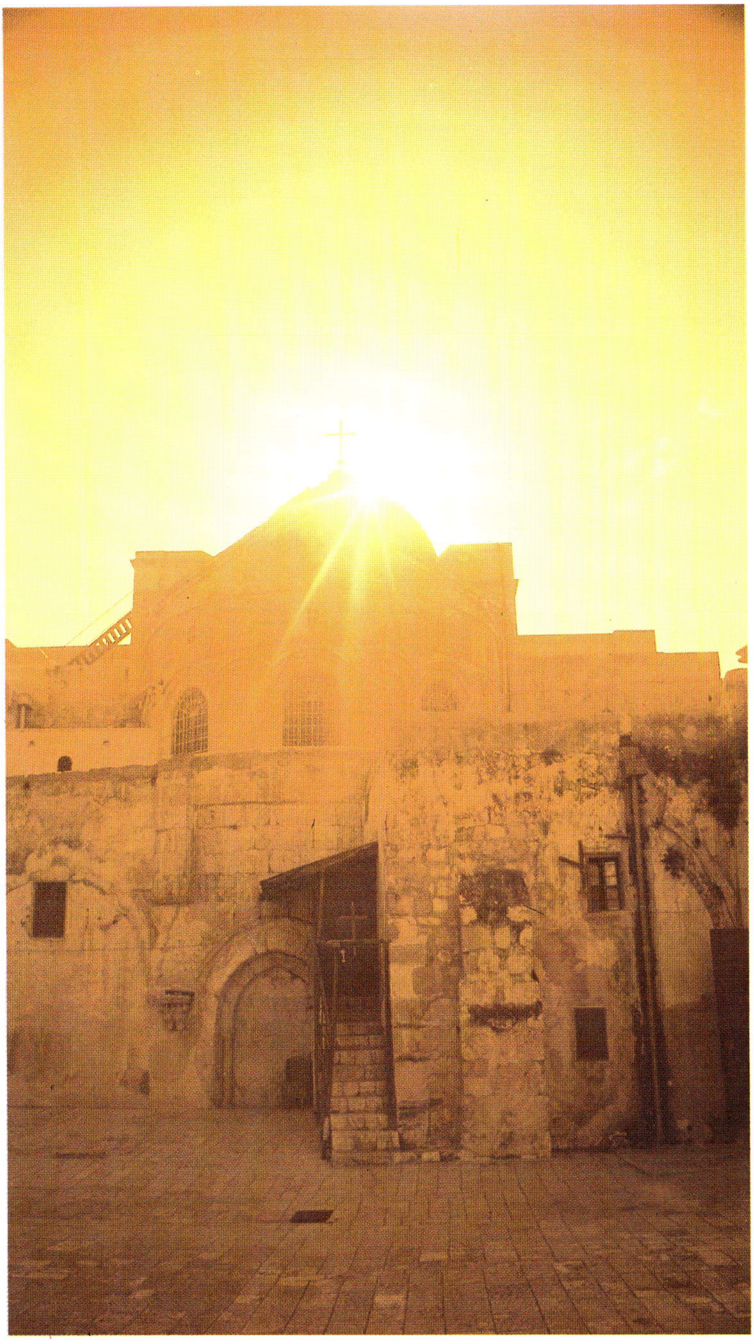

Le psalmiste (v. 3-13)

Le psalmiste va développer cette confession de foi, source d'encouragement et de sécurité pour les croyants. Plusieurs images éloquentes viennent illustrer cette protection divine. Dieu protège les croyants comme une poule abrite ses poussins sous son aile ; sa *fidélité* est pour eux comme un *bouclier* (v. 4). Quels sont ces dangers auxquels sont arrachés les croyants ? Ils sont multiples et variés : le *filet de l'oiseleur (...) la peste et* le *fléau* (v. 3), les *terreurs la nuit (...)* les *flèches (...) durant la journée* (v. 5), la *peste* et l'*insolation* (v. 6).

On peut très bien comprendre ces exemples au sens propre. Certains commentateurs y voient cependant la menace de véritables démons, peut-être d'origine babylonienne.

Quoi qu'il en soit, la promesse de délivrance est claire. Même si *dix milliers* y succombent (v. 7) et que les *méchants* récoltent *le châtiment* que méritent leurs péchés (v. 8), le psalmiste promet à ceux dont l'Eternel est le refuge qu'*aucun mal ne* les *atteindra* (v. 9, 10). Les anges de Dieu les protègeront (v. 11, 12 ; cf. Ps 34.7 et He 1.14), de sorte que pas même *le lion et la vipère (...) et le serpent* (v. 13) ne pourront leur nuire. Lorsqu'on sait que le serpent est l'animal le plus rusé et le lion, le plus fort, le fait que Satan soit appelé *le serpent ancien* et que Pierre dise qu'*il rode comme un lion rugissant* prend tout son sens (Ap 12.9 ; 20.1 ; 1 P 5.8).

L'Éternel (v.14-16)

C'est l'Éternel lui-même qui apporte la conclusion. Ce n'est pas au croyant, ni au psalmiste qu'il s'adresse, mais directement au lecteur, pour confirmer le bien-fondé de la foi du croyant et approuver le psalmiste. Le psalmiste a-t-il affirmé que *c'est lui qui te délivre* ? C'est la vérité et Dieu répète à deux reprises : *je vais le sauver (...) je le délivrerai* (v. 14, 15). Pourquoi ? *Parce qu'il m'est attaché.* Dieu est l'objet suprême de l'amour et de la foi du croyant et la promesse que « l'Esprit fait concourir toutes choses au bien de ceux qui l'aiment » (Rm 8.28) est pour lui. Cela ne veut en aucun cas dire que les croyants peuvent se permettre d'être paresseux et de rester sans rien faire. Mais s'il font confiance à Dieu et expriment leur foi par la prière, ils sont assurés que Dieu leur répondra. Il n'est pas dit qu'ils échapperont à tous les problèmes ; la délivrance de Dieu peut parfois se manifester par sa présence aux côtés des croyants *au moment de la détresse* (v. 15). La promesse ultime que Dieu fait à ses serviteurs confiants est de les combler *de jours* et de leur faire *connaître* son *salut* (v. 16). Il n'est pas impossible que ces paroles du psalmiste, à l'instar de celles des prophètes, aient dépassé sa compréhension. La sécurité, en effet, n'atteint la perfection que dans la vie éternelle et le salut que seul Jésus-Christ peut accorder.

Psaume 95

Venez chanter et écouter !

Ce psaume exhorte le peuple de Dieu à louer et à écouter Celui qui est leur rocher et leur Sauveur (v. 1). On chantait déjà ce psaume dans les églises au quatrième siècle de notre ère, où même avant, pour introduire le moment d'adoration.

Une invitation à chanter la louange de Dieu (v. 1-7)

Le livres de prières du roi Henri VIII définit le psaume 95 comme « un chant qui invite à louer Dieu . » Quelle invitation pressante, en effet ! Les versets 1, 2 et 6 ne contiennent pas moins de cinq exhortations les unes à la suite des autres. Depuis les parvis du Temple, où ils sont réunis, les membres de l'assemblée s'exhortent mutuellement à adorer Dieu et à chanter ses louanges, l'adoration publique étant essentiellement le fait de la communauté.

En même temps que ce psaume nous invite à louer Dieu, il nous donne aussi des raisons de le faire. S'il nous dit : *crions... louons... acclamons...*, il ne manque pas d'ajouter *car il est...* pour alimenter notre louange. Ce n'est que lorsque nous comprenons vraiment qui est l'Eternel que la louange peut monter de notre cœur.

Qui est-il ? D'après ce cantique, il est à la fois *le grand Dieu* (v. 3) et *notre Dieu* (v. 7).

Il est tout d'abord *le grand Dieu,* souverain dans le ciel, *le grand roi au-dessus de tous les dieux* (v. 3), auxquels l'auteur ne prêtait certainement aucune réalité objective, car « tous les dieux des peuples ne

1 Venez, crions notre joie | en l'honneur de l'Eternel !
Louons le Seigneur ! | Acclamons notre rocher | car il est notre Sauveur !
2 Présentons-nous devant lui | avec des prières | de reconnaissance.
Acclamons-le en musique.
3 L'Eternel est le grand Dieu,
il est le grand Roi | au-dessus de tous les dieux.
4 C'est lui qui tient dans sa main | les profondeurs de la terre,
et les cimes des montagnes | sont aussi à lui.
5 A lui appartient la mer : | c'est lui qui l'a faite ;
à lui est la terre : | ses mains l'ont formée.
6 Venez et prosternons-nous,
ployons les genoux | devant l'Eternel | qui nous a créés.
7 Il est notre Dieu,
nous sommes le peuple | de son pâturage,
le troupeau | que sa main conduit.
Aujourd'hui, | si vous entendez sa voix,
8 ne vous endurcissez pas | comme à Mériba,
comme au jour de l'incident | de Massa dans le désert :
9 « Vos ancêtres m'ont défié | voulant me forcer la main,
bien qu'ils m'aient vu à l'action.
10 Pendant quarante ans, | j'ai éprouvé du dégoût | pour cette génération,
et j'ai dit alors : | C'est un peuple qui s'égare,
et qui ne fait aucun cas | des voies que je lui prescris.
11 C'est pourquoi, dans ma colère, | j'ai fait ce serment :
Ils n'entreront pas dans mon repos. »

Coup de vent sur la mer de Galilée. « À lui appartient la mer : c'est lui qui l'a faite ; à lui est la terre : ses mains l'ont formée. »

sont que du néant » (Ps 96.5). Dieu est aussi souverain sur la terre (v. 4, 5). Pour bien montrer que rien n'échappe à la suprématie de Dieu, le psalmiste ne néglige aucune dimension. Les profondeurs de la terre, les sommets des montagnes, les vastes étendues de la mer et de la terre, tout lui appartient. Tout cela est *dans sa main* (v. 4), car *ses mains l'ont formé* (v. 5), ces mains qui ont créé l'univers au commencement et qui le tiennent encore aujourd'hui. Dieu contrôle l'ordre naturel, parce qu'il en est l'auteur.

Ensuite, *il est notre Dieu* (v. 7). Infiniment au-dessus de nous par sa grandeur, il est cependant près de nous par sa bonté. Sa majesté se tempère de miséricorde et sa gloire, de grâce. Ce Dieu qui a créé le monde a aussi créé Israël. C'est lui *l'Éternel qui nous a créés* (v. 6 ; voir aussi Ps 100.3 ; 149.2 ; Es 51.13 ; 54.5). Le Créateur de toutes choses est le Rédempteur de ceux qui lui appartiennent. Il est aussi notre berger, et nous appelle *le peuple de son pâturage* (v. 7).

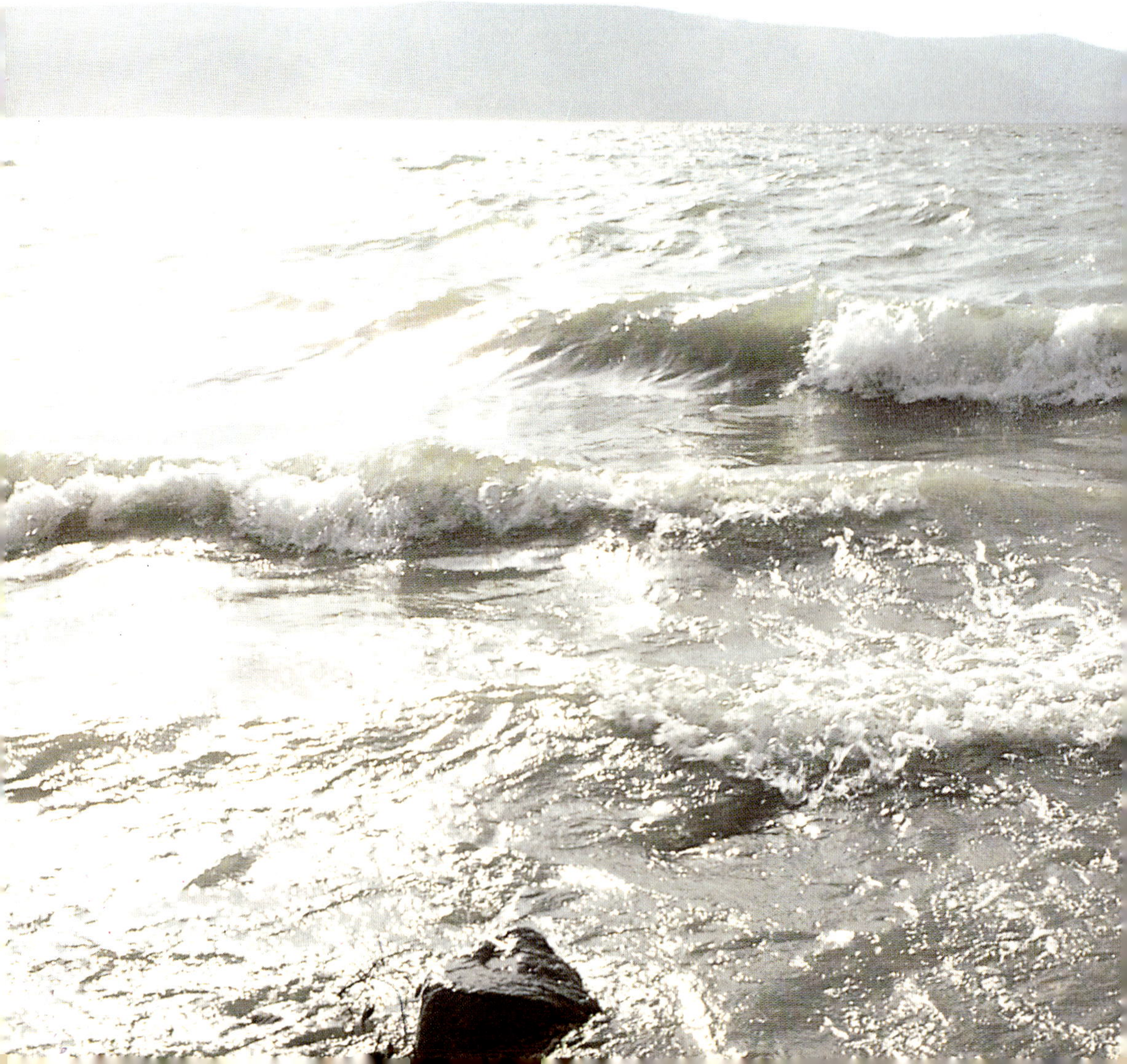

Il est clair d'après ce psaume que notre louange ne sera pas la même selon que nous considérons tel aspect de la personne de Dieu ou un autre. Les versets 1 à 3, qui le décrivent comme *le grand Dieu*, nous invitent à faire monter une joyeuse clameur vers l'Éternel et à venir devant lui avec des actions de grâce. Rien ne nous empêche de nous réjouir de la grandeur de sa création en poussant des cris de joie. Le verset 6, au contraire, nous convie à ployer *les genoux devant l'Éternel*. Pourquoi ? Parce qu'*il est notre Dieu* (v. 7). Ce grand Dieu a accepté de devenir notre Dieu, d'être notre berger et de nous appeler son troupeau. L'attitude alors n'est plus l'exultation, mais plutôt la crainte et l'émerveillement, tandis que, dans le calme, nous nous prosternons devant lui avec respect et humilité.

Le ton change après le verset 7 et ce n'est plus la même personne qui parle. Jusqu'ici, c'étaient les membres de l'assemblée qui s'exhortaient mutuellement ; maintenant, Dieu intervient et s'adresse directement à son peuple.

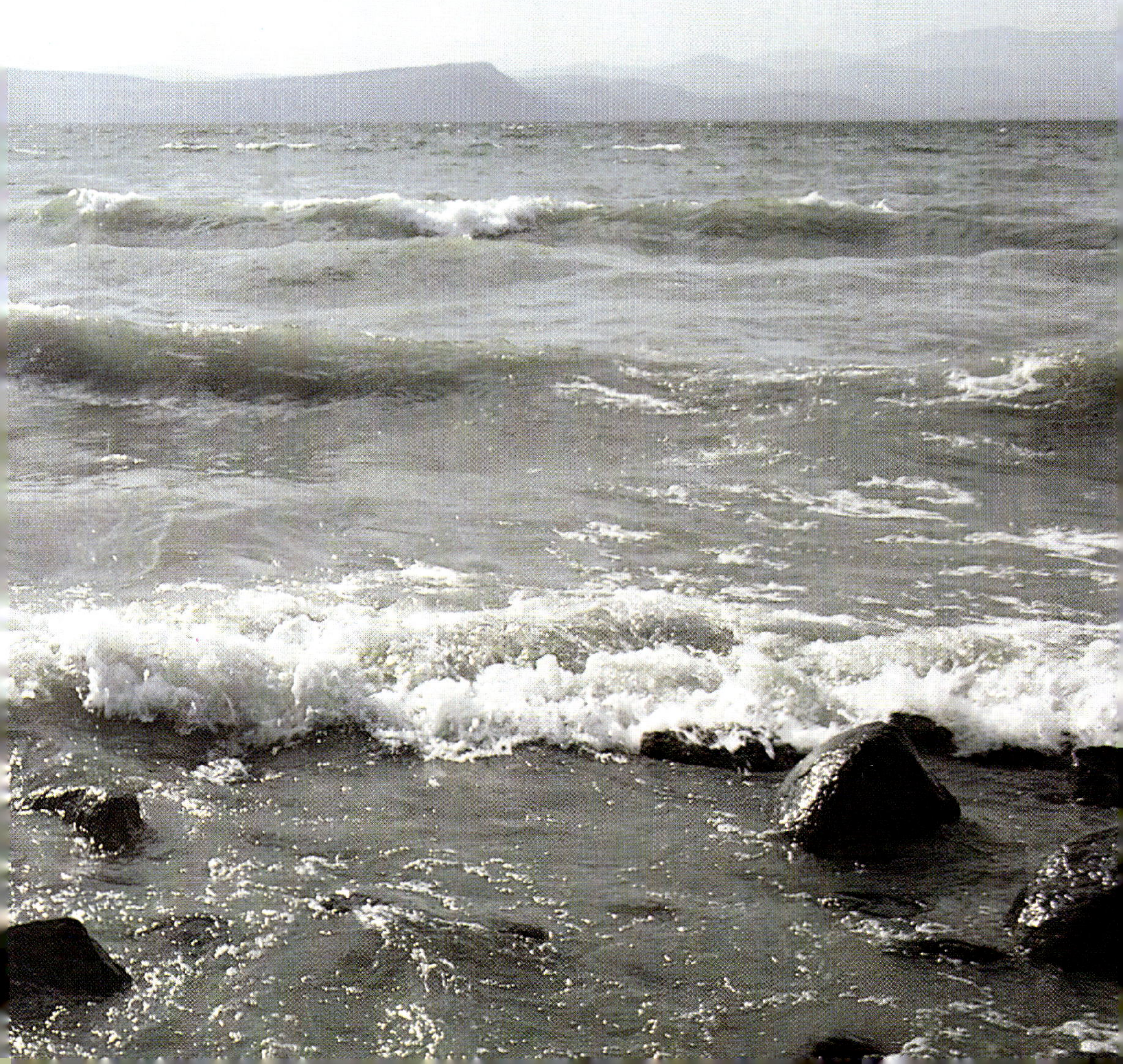

Une invitation à écouter la Parole de Dieu (v. 8-11)

Il ne suffit pas d'ouvrir nos bouches pour chanter les louanges de Dieu, il nous faut aussi ouvrir nos oreilles pour entendre sa Parole. Il est intéressant de remarquer que ce sont ceux qui font partie du *troupeau que sa main conduit* qui sont conviés à entendre la voix de Dieu ; une brebis doit en effet reconnaître la voix du berger. (cf. Jn 10.2-4).

Dieu prend comme exemples des moments marquants de l'histoire d'Israël. Un ou deux mois avant la sortie d'Égypte, juste avant d'atteindre le mont Sinaï, les enfants d'Israël campèrent à Rephidim. Il n'y avait pas d'eau. Le peuple s'en prit à Moïse : « Donne-nous de l'eau à boire ! (...) Pourquoi nous as-tu fait quitter l'Égypte ? Est-ce pour nous faire mourir de soif ici, nous, nos enfants et nos troupeaux ? » Moïse pria Dieu, qui lui ordonna de frapper le rocher avec son bâton, et l'eau en jaillit. Moïse nomma alors ce lieu Massa, qui signifie épreuve ou tentation, et Meriba, qui veut dire querelle ou provocation. Cet épisode est rapporté dans Exode 17.1-7.

Quarante années plus tard, il survint une crise identique à Qadech. Le peuple s'étant à nouveau plaint à Moïse, Dieu intervint une nouvelle fois pour faire jaillir l'eau. Ce lieu prit le nom de Meriba Qadech, pour le distinguer de Meriba à Rephidim. Cette deuxième histoire se trouve dans Nombres 20.1-13.

Les Israélites avaient défié leur Dieu. Ils l'avaient mis à l'épreuve. Ils l'avaient vu à l'œuvre et pourtant ils n'avaient pas foi en lui. Il les avait miraculeusement libérés de leur esclavage en Égypte. Plus tard, il établit une alliance avec eux, leur accorda une révélation toute particulière de sa personne et prit soin d'eux dans le désert, et voilà qu'ils se rebellaient contre lui, mettant en doute son amour et sa bonté. Rien d'étonnant à ce que *pendant quarante ans* Dieu ait *éprouvé du dégoût pour cette génération* et qu'il les qualifie de *peuple qui s'égare* (v. 10). Son errance dans le désert était à l'image de son cœur égaré. Le péché, l'incrédulité et la rébellion d'Israël étaient tels, que Dieu prit de sévères mesures à son égard (v. 11). L'Écriture nous révèle Dieu comme un Dieu d'amour et de colère, de bonté et de sévérité. Il hait le péché d'une haine implacable, tout en aimant le pécheur d'un amour infini.

L'Épître aux Hébreux reprend ces paroles dans un message urgent aux chrétiens d'aujourd'hui. « C'est pourquoi, prenez à cœur ce que dit l'Esprit Saint : "Aujourd'hui, si vous entendez la voix de Dieu, ne vous endurcissez pas, comme l'ont fait vos ancêtres lorsqu'ils se sont révoltés et m'ont provoqué dans le désert..." » (He 3.7, 8). C'est aujourd'hui le jour du salut. Prenons garde de ne pas nous laisser tromper par le péché et de ne pas fermer notre cœur à Dieu (He 3.13).

Psaume 98

Yahvé, le Roi Sauveur

Il faut certainement voir à l'origine de ce psaume une grande victoire nationale, remportée aux yeux de tous les peuples par la puissance du Dieu suprême. Quel qu'ait été l'ennemi vaincu, l'Égypte, Babylone ou autre, cette victoire préfigure certainement celle, plus glorieuse encore, sur le péché, Satan et la mort, que Dieu nous a acquise par Jésus-Christ son Fils. C'est là la plus merveilleuse des *merveilles* de Dieu (v. 1), qui inspire à son peuple *un cantique nouveau,* nouveau parce que sa grâce ne cesse jamais de nous émerveiller. Les chants de louange des chrétiens sont avant tout l'expression de leur joie devant les merveilles de Dieu.

Ce ne sont pas seulement les interventions puissantes de Dieu par le passé qui méritent la louange ; sa souveraineté est aussi manifeste aujourd'hui et constitue un gage du royaume de justice qu'il établira un jour sur la terre. Dieu est donc à la fois le Sauveur, le Roi et le Juge. Le psalmiste exhorte son peuple à chanter son Sauveur (v. 1-4), il encourage la *terre tout entière* à célébrer le Roi (v. 4-6) et enfin la nature (la mer, l'univers, les rivières et les montagnes) à rendre hommage au Juge qui vient (v. 7-9).

Dieu le Sauveur (v. 1-3)

Dieu est l'artisan unique de la victoire qui a dicté ce psaume, aucun homme n'y a participé. Il l'a remportée par *sa puissance, par son pou-*

Chantez à l'Eternel | un cantique nouveau
car il fait des merveilles.
Par sa puissance, | par son pouvoir divin, | il a sauvé.
2 L'Eternel fait connaître son salut ;
aux nations il révèle sa justice.
3 L'Eternel se souvient | de son amour
et de sa bienveillance | à l'égard d'Israël.
Jusqu'au bout de la terre,
on a vu le salut | qui vient de notre Dieu.

4 Acclame l'Eternel, | ô terre tout entière, | avec des cris de joie,
au son de la musique !
5 Au son de la cithare, | célébrez l'Eternel,
au son de la cithare, | de tous les instruments !
6 Au son de la trompette | et aux accents du cor,
exultez en présence | de l'Eternel, du Roi !
7 Que la mer retentisse | et tout ce qui la peuple !
Que l'univers résonne | avec ses habitants !
8 Que les rivières | battent des mains,
que les montagnes, | à l'unisson, | chantent de joie.
9 Que tous louent l'Eternel : | car il vient pour juger la terre !
Il jugera le monde | selon ce qui est juste,
il jugera les peuples | selon ce qui est droit.

Page suivante : Un jeune juif lit le Livre de la Loi, lors de sa bar-mitsvah, devant le Mur Occidental, à Jérusalem.

voir divin (v. 1). Certaines versions traduisent « sa droite et son bras saint ». Puisque « Dieu est esprit » (Jn 4.24), il n'a ni mains ni bras. Mais cette comparaison anthropomorphique est là pour souligner sa force et son intervention directe en faveur de son peuple. L'Écriture attribue de même les délivrances hors d'Égypte ou de Babylone au bras fort ou à la main puissante de Dieu (voir par ex. Ex 15.6, 12 ; Ps 44.1-3 et Es 52.10 ; 59.16 ; 63.5).

En outre, la victoire de Dieu n'a pas été remportée en cachette, mais au vu et au su de tous. Il l'a « révélée » aux yeux des nations, qui ont vu son *salut* et sa *justice* (v. 2).

Dieu se souvient aussi de *son amour et (...) sa bienveillance* (ou « sa fidélité ») *à l'égard d'Israël* (v. 3), le peuple élu de Dieu, avec qui il a conclu une alliance solennelle, qu'il ne rompra ni n'oubliera jamais. De fait, cette délivrance est une preuve de son engagement. Il convient donc de le louer, tant pour sa puissance victorieuse que pour sa fidélité qui l'a poussé à agir. Cette victoire, remportée pour Israël par le Dieu d'Israël (*notre* Dieu), a cependant pu être contemplée *jusqu'au bout de la terre*, selon la prophétie d'Ésaïe 52.10, que Jean-Baptiste appliquera au salut en Jésus (Lc 3.6). D'autres passages (Ps 89, Ps 92.2 et 100.5, ainsi que Mi 7.20), associent également *amour* et *bienveillance* (ou fidélité).

Dieu le Roi (v. 4-6)

Après le peuple d'Israël, ce sont les habitants de la *terre tout entière* (v. 4 ; cf. Ps 100.1) qui sont conviés à louer Dieu. Certes, ils n'ont pas vécu le salut d'Israël, mais ils peuvent néanmoins s'associer au peuple de Dieu pour reconnaître sa royauté. Il est *l'Éternel*, le *Roi* (v. 6). La délivrance glorieuse qu'il a opérée en faveur de son peuple est une preuve tangible de sa souveraineté dans la vie des hommes et des nations. Il convient de l'adorer, non seulement *avec des cris*, mais aussi avec des chants et au son des instruments de musique (v. 5, 6).

Ces manifestations de joie étaient celles qui accompagnaient généralement l'avènement ou le couronnement d'un nouveau roi. Lorsque Tsadoq oignit Salomon, on sonna du cor alors que le peuple criait de joie et se réjouissait au son des instruments (1 R 1.39, 40). De même lorsque le prêtre Yehoyada couronna et oignit le jeune Joas, tout le peuple applaudit (2 R 11.12-14). Il est donc juste que le règne de Yahvé soit célébré lui aussi avec des chants, des cris, des applaudissements et au son des cors (cf. Ps 47). C.S. Lewis dira que la célébration hébraïque était empreinte d'une certaine « fougue ».

Dieu le Juge (v. 7-9)

C'est l'univers entier, animé et inanimé, qui est invité à présent à se joindre à ce concert de voix et d'instruments célébrant Dieu. La mer et ce qu'elle contient, la terre et ses habitants, les flots comme les montagnes, s'unissent pour louer *l'Éternel* (v. 6, 9). Le mugissement

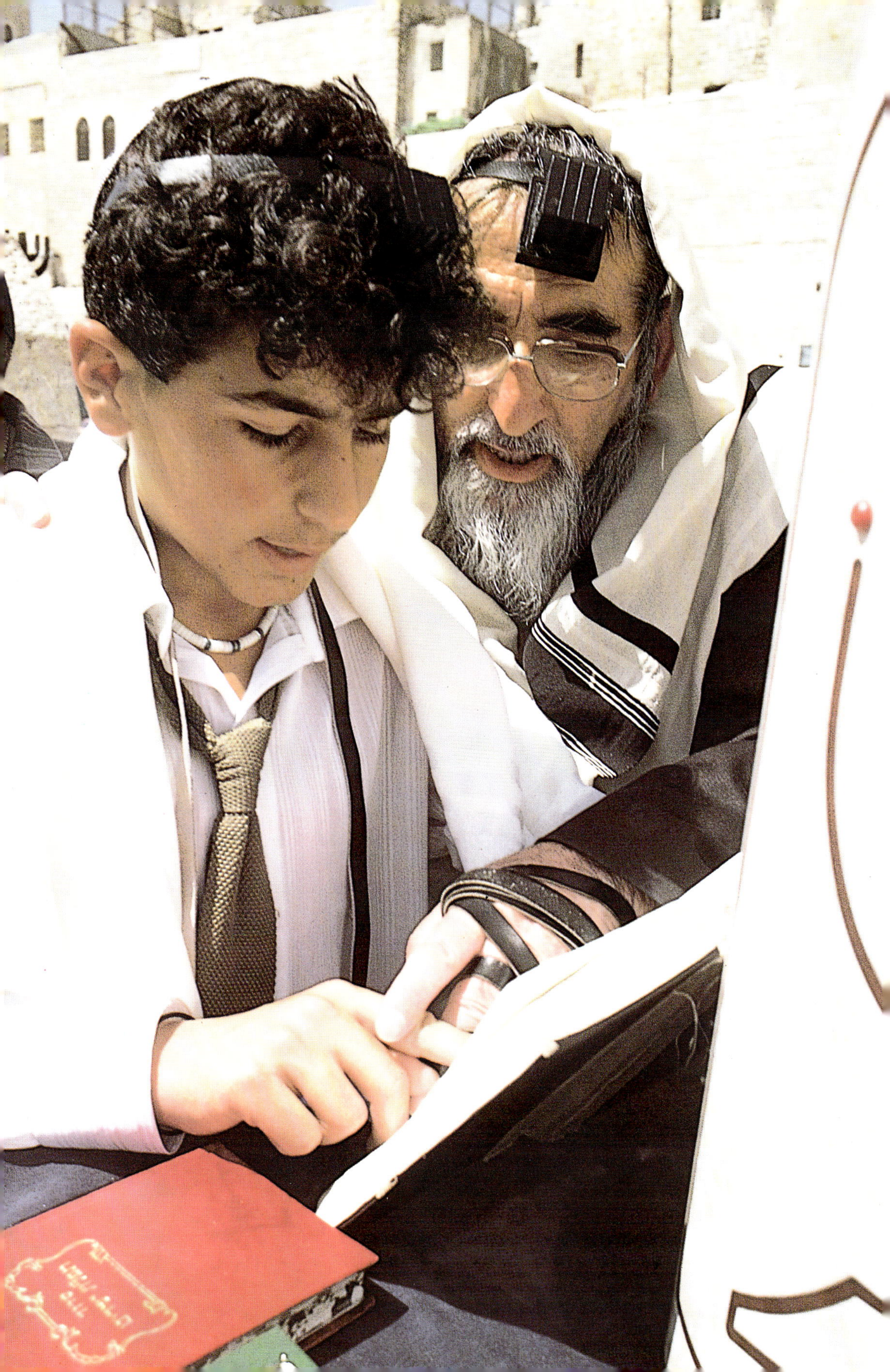

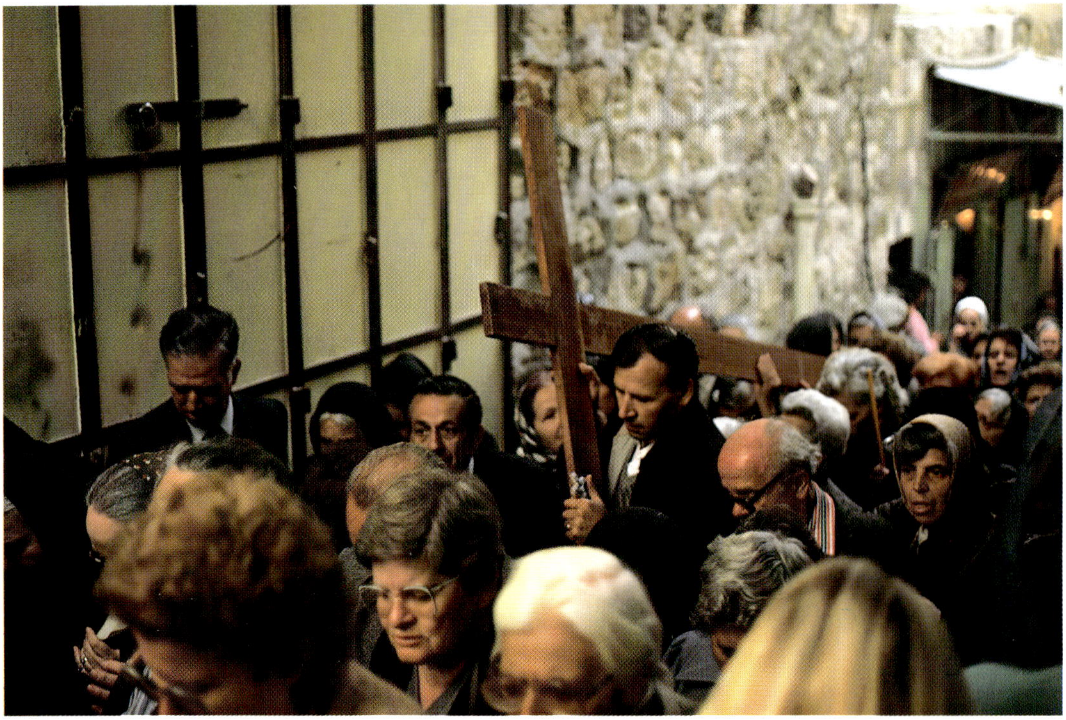

À l'occasion du vendredi saint, des pèlerins défilent en procession le long de la Via Dolorosa, dans la vieille ville de Jérusalem.

des flots est leur chant d'adoration, le clapotis des rivières est un applaudissement. La raison de leur joie est cependant encore à venir. Il semble que la nature supporte encore un joug, comme le dira Paul dans Romains 8.18-25, dont elle ne sera délivrée que lorsque Dieu viendra pour établir son règne. Il est déjà Roi (v. 6), mais la terre ne le reconnaît pas encore en tant que tel et il viendra donc pour juger la terre et ses peuples (v. 9). Lorsque son règne sera établi (ce qui a commencé avec le Christ, bien que ce psaume présente le règne messianique comme celui de Yahvé lui-même), les peuples et la nature seront soumis et gouvernés avec justice. Celui qui a déjà révélé sa justice en sauvant son peuple (v. 2) la manifestera à nouveau en jugeant le monde. Même le châtiment des méchants, qui est clairement annoncé dans Ésaïe 11.1-5, nous remplira de joie, car nous reconnaîtrons que « ses jugements sont vrais et justes » et nous nous écrierons « Amen ! Alléluia ! » (Ap 19.1-5).

Psaume 100

L'Éternel est Dieu et l'Éternel est bon

Ce psaume était chanté par les Israélites, d'abord dans le Temple, puis lors du service quotidien dans les synagogues. Au Moyen Âge, il faisait partie de l'office appelé Laudes. Th. De Bèze l'a adapté pour en faire un cantique bien connu, intitulé « Vous qui sur la terre habitez. »

Bien que très court, cinq versets seulement, il est une invitation éloquente à la louange, qui doit revêtir deux aspects.

Deux aspects de la louange

Ce psaume est souvent appelé le « Jubilate », ce qui signifie « réjouissez-vous » ou « poussez des cris de joie. » La joie doit caractériser notre louange. Le psaume 100 fait partie d'un groupe de huit psaumes, dits royaux, qui célèbrent la souveraineté royale de Yahvé et dont il est la doxologie. « L'Éternel règne, revêtu de majesté (...). Dès l'origine, ton trône est ferme. » « L'Éternel est le grand Dieu, il est le grand Roi au-dessus de tous les dieux. » « Proclamez aux nations que l'Éternel est roi ! » « L'Éternel règne ! Ô terre exulte ! » « Exultez en présence de l'Éternel, du Roi ! » « L'Éternel règne. Les peuples sont dans l'effroi. » (Ps 93.1, 2 ; 95.3 ; 96.10 ; 97.1 ; 98.6 ; 99.1).

En effet, si Dieu est Roi, notre louange peut-elle être autre que pleine de joie ? Fini les figures d'enterrement et les hymnes lugubres ! La louange est indissociable de la joie, de l'allégresse et des chants.

La louange doit aussi être universelle. *Acclame l'Éternel, ô terre tout entière* (v. 1). Certes, ce psaume parle de Yahvé, le Dieu d'Israël,

Acclame l'Eternel,
ô terre tout entière !
2 Servez l'Eternel avec joie !
Entrez en sa présence | avec des chants joyeux !
3 Sachez que c'est lui seul, | l'Eternel, qui est Dieu !
C'est lui qui nous a faits, | nous lui appartenons,
et nous sommes son peuple, | le troupeau de son pâturage.

4 Entrez sous ses portiques | avec reconnaissance !
Entrez dans ses parvis | en chantant ses louanges !
Rendez-lui votre hommage | et louez-le pour ce qu'il est !
5 Car l'Eternel est bon, | car son amour dure à toujours
et sa fidélité | s'étendra d'âge en âge.

La Porte Dorée, à Jérusalem, domine la vallée du Kidron. Les Juifs et les Musulmans s'accordent pour penser que c'est là qu'aura lieu le Jugement dernier.

mais le psalmiste sait que son peuple n'en a pas l'exclusivité. N'a-t-il pas promis à Abraham : « Tous les peuples de la terre seront bénis à travers toi » ? N'est-il pas écrit dans Ésaïe 56.6, 7 : « Et tous ceux qui sont étrangers et qui s'attacheront à l'Éternel pour le servir, pour l'aimer (…) je les ferai venir à ma montagne sainte et je les réjouirai au Temple où l'on me prie (…) Car on appellera mon Temple "maison de prière en faveur de tous les peuples". » ? Aucune nation ne devrait donc rester à l'écart de cet appel à la louange. Yahvé n'est pas la divinité tribale d'Israël, mais le Roi souverain de toute la terre, c'est pourquoi nous devrions aspirer à ce que toutes les nations participent à notre adoration et à nos manifestations de joie communautaires.

La suite de ce psaume développe les raisons pour lesquelles les nations devraient nous rejoindre dans l'adoration. Si la louange véritable est joyeuse et universelle, elle est aussi fondée.

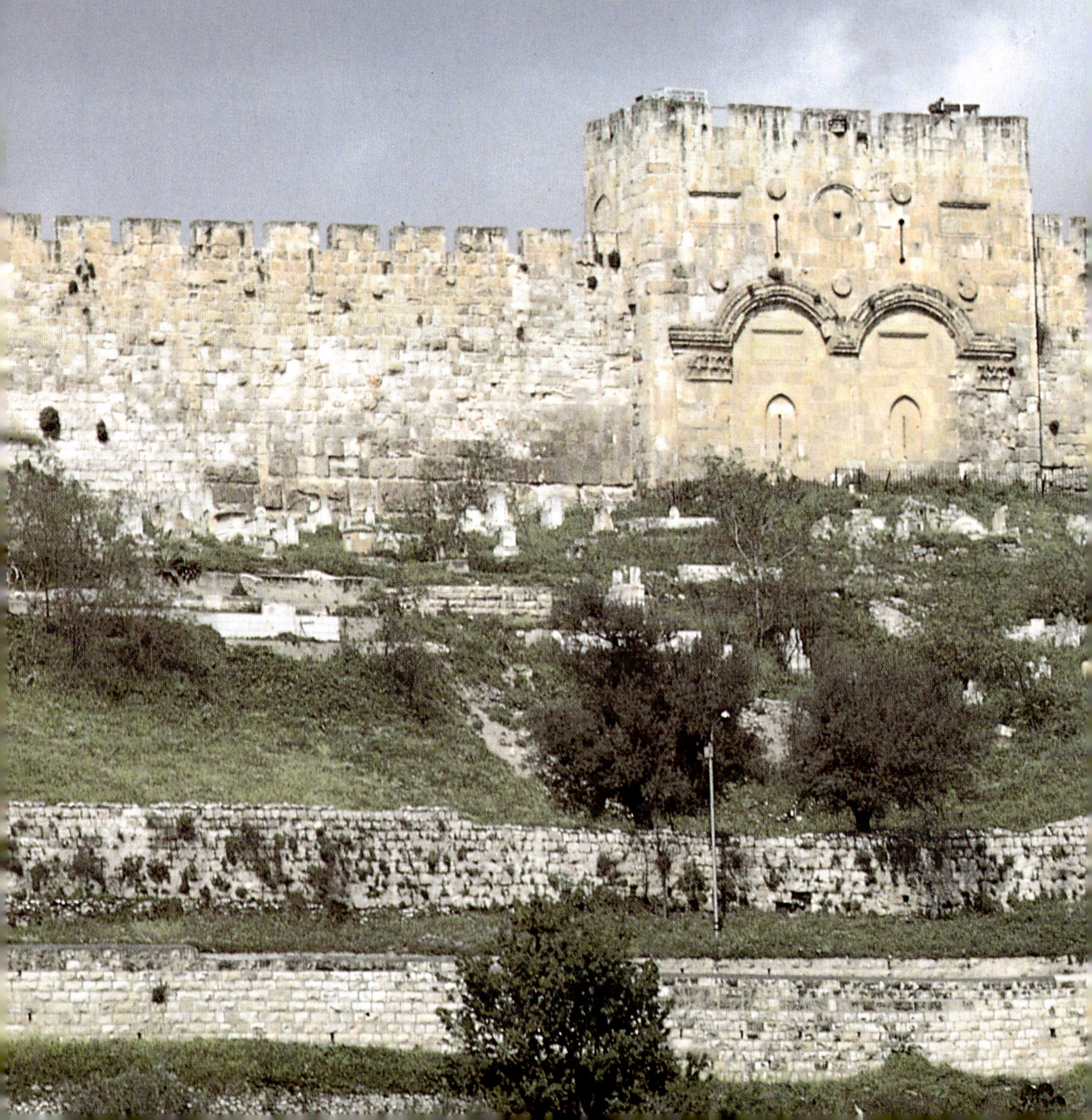

La grandeur de Dieu

Sachez que c'est lui seul, l'Éternel, qui est Dieu (v. 3). Notre louange dépend de ce que nous connaissons et de l'étendue de notre compréhension. Les chrétiens n'adorent pas « un Dieu inconnu », comme les Athéniens, mais un Dieu qui s'est révélé.

Que devons-nous donc connaître ? Les dieux des païens sont des idoles qui ne peuvent ni voir, ni parler, ni agir. Notre Dieu à nous est un Dieu vivant et agissant, ce dont l'histoire d'Israël est la meilleure preuve. Il a libéré son peuple de l'esclavage, a conclu une alliance avec lui sur le mont Sinaï, l'a guidé dans le désert et établi en Terre Promise. En un mot, il l'a « fait » (cf. Dt 32.6, 15 et Ps 95.6). *C'est lui qui nous a faits, nous lui appartenons* (v 3). Deux images éloquentes illustrent la souveraineté de Dieu et son intervention dans notre vie.

Premièrement, Dieu est le potier. *C'est lui qui nous a faits*, tel un artisan. Ce verset se place à l'échelle de la nation, que Dieu appelle parfois « l'ouvrage de ses mains » dans l'Ancien Testament, et non à celle de l'individu (voir par ex. Es 60.21).

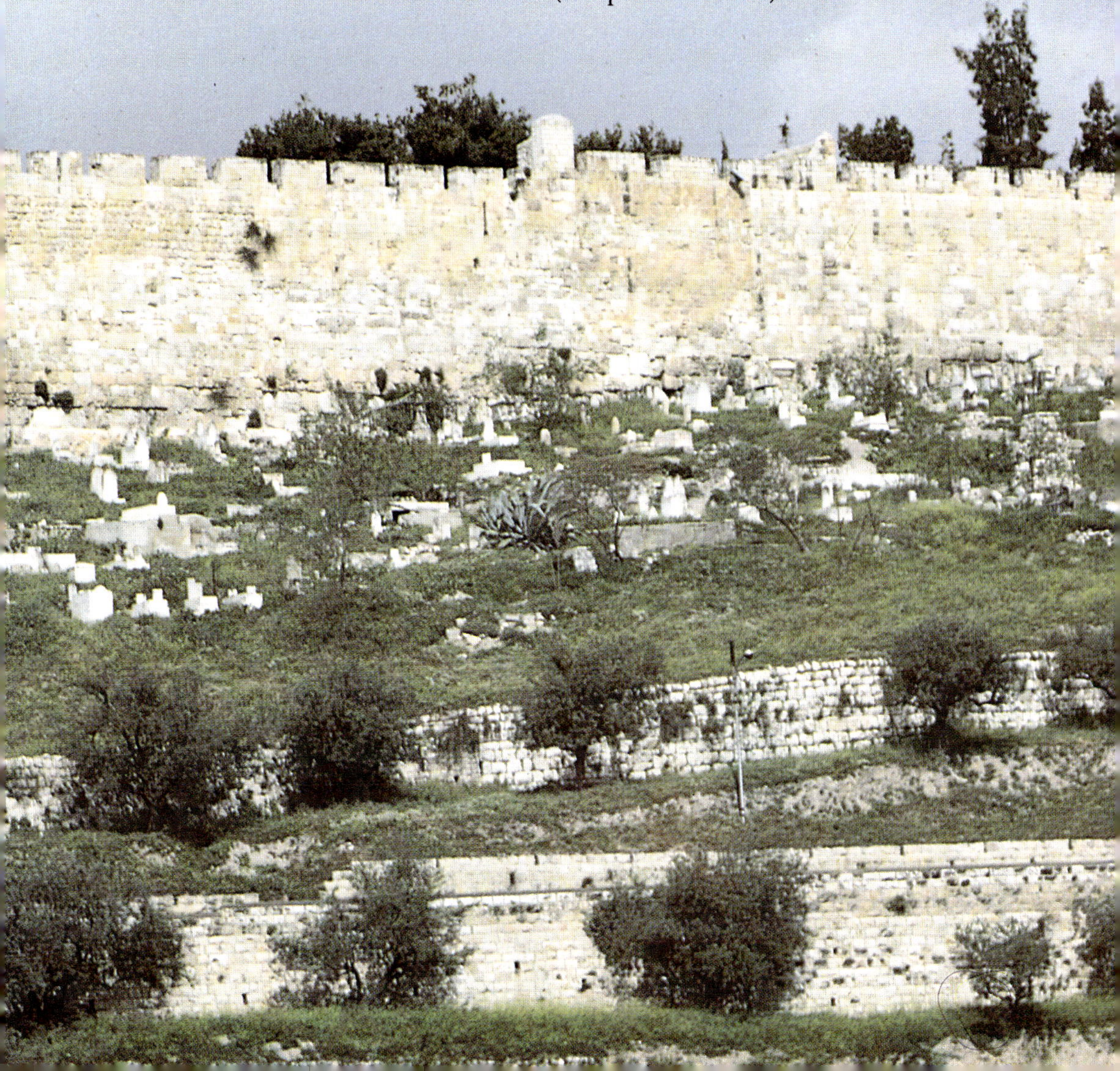

Combien il fallut de talent et de patience au divin potier ! Sa matière première était toujours ingrate, souvent récalcitrante. D'autres auraient depuis longtemps abandonné tout espoir de réussite. Mais lui persévéra. Bravant les échecs et refusant de se laisser abattre, il façonna patiemment Israël pour en faire un vase d'honneur qui lui plaise.

Deuxièmement, Dieu est le berger. *Nous sommes son peuple, le troupeau de son pâturage.* Le potier qui les façonna était aussi le berger qui les fit paître. Il les protégea et les guida à travers toutes les péripéties de leur marche mouvementée. Il veilla sur eux avec la tendresse scrupuleuse propre aux bergers orientaux.

Il en va de même pour nous. Dieu nous a rachetés et attirés à lui. Nous pouvons confesser qu'il est notre potier et notre berger. Quelle autre comparaison pourrait exprimer de façon aussi claire et puissante ce que nous devons à la grâce de Dieu ? C'est lui qui nous a faits et nous sommes son peuple. Nous ne nous sommes pas créés nous-même, pas plus que nous n'avons décidé de notre propre chef de devenir son peuple. « Par la grâce de Dieu nous sommes ce que nous sommes. » Il convient de louer Dieu et non de glorifier l'homme.

Le psalmiste nous y invite une nouvelle fois. *Entrez sous ses portiques avec reconnaissance ! Entrez dans ses parvis en chantant ses louanges* (v. 4). C'est notre reconnaissance qui met de la joie dans notre louange.

La bonté de Dieu

Si l'Éternel est grand, il est aussi *bon* (v. 5). Il y a donc lieu de le louer, tant pour ce qu'il a fait que pour ce qu'il est.

En quoi consiste sa bonté ? Elle réside dans son amour *qui dure à toujours* et dans *sa fidélité* (v. 5). Nous avons un Dieu fidèle à son alliance, il n'est ni inconstant ni déloyal, sa Parole est sûre et ses promesses sont dignes de confiance. D'âge en âge il demeure le même. D'éternité en éternité il est Dieu.

Louons-le donc, non seulement parce qu'il nous a faits et que nous lui appartenons, mais aussi parce qu'il ne nous laissera pas. Le potier céleste ne renoncera jamais à parfaire son œuvre, mais continuera à la façonner pour en faire un vase agréable à regarder et utile. Le berger céleste n'abandonnera jamais ses brebis. Il les fera paître dans de verts pâturages et les mènera près des eaux paisibles. Sa bonté et sa miséricorde les accompagneront tous les jours de leur vie. Le vase est en sécurité entre les mains du potier, comme les brebis le sont dans les bras du berger.

Psaume 103

Les bienfaits de la grâce de Dieu

Le psaume 103 compte sans doute parmi les préférés. Il a été repris dans de nombreux cantiques. Un enfant de Dieu racheté donne libre cours à sa gratitude envers le Dieu de grâce. Ici, le psalmiste développe sa louange en trois cercles concentriques. Il commence par s'exhorter lui-même à louer Dieu comme il le mérite : *Que tout mon être loue l'Éternel* (v. 1-5). Puis il rappelle la miséricorde de Dieu à tout le peuple de son alliance (v. 6-18), pour finir par la création tout entière, qu'il invite à se joindre au chœur des louanges (v. 19-22).

Les bienfaits de Dieu envers moi (v. 1-5)

Les cinq premiers versets ont un ton très personnel, où l'auteur se place face à son propre devoir et encourage son âme paresseuse à adorer Dieu, à louer *le Dieu saint* (v. 1), transcendant, et à se souvenir de tous *ses bienfaits.* Il veut en effet que sa louange soit à la mesure des bénédictions de Dieu à son égard : *tout ce que je suis* en réponse à tous *ses bienfaits,* bienfaits qui profitent au corps comme à l'âme, car *c'est lui qui pardonne tous* mes *péchés, c'est lui qui* me *guérit de toute maladie* (v. 3). De surcroît, il m'arrache *à la tombe* (v. 4). Mais Dieu ne se contente pas de délivrer le psalmiste du péché, de la maladie et de la

Que tout mon être | loue l'Eternel !
Que tout ce que je suis | loue le Dieu saint !
2 Que tout mon être | loue l'Eternel,
sans oublier | aucun de ses bienfaits.
3 Car c'est lui qui pardonne | tous tes péchés,
c'est lui qui te guérit | de toute maladie,
4 qui t'arrache à la tombe.
C'est lui qui te couronne | de tendresse et d'amour,
5 et qui te comble de bonheur | tout au long de ton existence ;
et ta jeunesse, comme l'aigle, | prend un nouvel essor.
6 L'Eternel intervient | pour redresser les torts
et il défend les droits | de tous les opprimés.
7 Il a manifesté | ses desseins à Moïse
et montré ses hauts faits | au peuple d'Israël.
8 L'Eternel est plein de pitié | et miséricordieux.
Il est plein de patience | et débordant d'amour.
9 Il ne tient pas rigueur sans cesse
et son ressentiment | ne dure pas toujours.
10 Il ne nous traite pas | selon le mal | que nous avons commis,
il ne nous punit pas | comme le méritent nos fautes.
11 Autant le ciel est élevé | au-dessus de la terre,
autant l'amour de Dieu dépasse | tous ceux qui le révèrent.
12 Autant l'Orient | est loin de l'Occident,
autant il éloigne de nous | nos mauvaises actions.
13 Et, comme un père | est plein d'amour | pour ses enfants,
l'Eternel est rempli d'amour | pour ceux qui le révèrent :
14 il sait de quelle pâte | nous sommes façonnés,
il se rappelle bien | que nous sommes poussière.
15 L'homme... | sa vie ressemble à l'herbe,
à une fleur des champs : | la voici qui fleurit !
16 Qu'un vent souffle dessus, | la voilà disparue !
Le lieu qu'elle occupait | ne la reconnaît plus.
17 Eternel, ton amour | est là depuis toujours |
et durera toujours | pour ceux qui te révèrent.
Ta loyauté demeure | à l'égard des enfants |
de leurs enfants.
18 Elle est pour ceux qui restent | fidèles à ton alliance,
pour ceux qui se souviennent | de tes commandements | pour les mettre en pratique.
19 Dans les cieux, l'Eternel | a établi son trône :
il est le Roi, le Maître | de l'univers entier.
20 Louez donc l'Eternel, | vous tous ses anges
vaillants et forts | qui faites ce qu'il dit
dès qu'il vous le demande !
21 Oui, louez l'Eternel, | vous toutes ses armées célestes,
vous qui, à son service, | exécutez sa volonté.
22 Oui, louez l'Eternel, | toutes ses créatures,
partout où il gouverne !
Que tout mon être | loue l'Eternel !

mort, il le comble en plus de cadeaux. Il le *couronne* (v. 4), faisant de son enfant un roi (cf. Ps 8.5).

Le *bonheur* que Dieu lui accorde permet à sa *jeunesse, comme l'aigle,* de prendre *un nouvel essor* (v. 5). Peut-être faut-il voir là une allusion à une ancienne légende selon laquelle l'aigle s'approchait parfois tellement près du soleil qu'il s'y brûlait les ailes et tombait dans la mer, d'où il ressortait miraculeusement rajeuni ; il peut aussi s'agir de la mue annuelle de l'oiseau après la période de reproduction, qui réapparaît au printemps suivant avec un plumage tout neuf. Comme dans Ésaïe 40.31, l'aigle symbolise ici la jeunesse et la force.

Tels sont les bienfaits personnels que Dieu accorde au psalmiste. Libéré du péché, de la maladie et de la mort, il est heureux comme un roi et vigoureux comme un aigle.

La miséricorde de Dieu envers les siens (v. 6-18)

Le psalmiste élargit sa vision, pour évoquer, non plus les bienfaits de Dieu à son seul égard, mais la grâce plus vaste de Dieu qui s'étend à tout le peuple de son alliance, dont il a redressé *les torts* et défendu *les droits* à chaque fois qu'il était opprimé (v. 6). La meilleure preuve est donnée par sa sollicitude à l'égard de Moïse et des enfants d'Israël (v. 7). Les soins dont il entoura son peuple étaient une expression de sa grâce.

Le psalmiste nous conduit alors dans une sorte de méditation sur cette révélation glorieuse du nom de Dieu faite à Moïse. « L'Éternel, l'Éternel, un Dieu plein de compassion et de grâce, lent à se mettre en colère, et riche en amour et en fidélité » (Ex 34.6). Il la cite au verset 8, puis la développe par deux remarques restrictives, trois illustrations et une opposition frappante.

Dieu a fixé deux limites à sa juste colère contre le péché, à la fois dans le temps, car *il ne tient pas rigueur sans cesse*, et dans la sévérité du châtiment, puisque, au lieu de nous punir comme nous le méritons, *il ne nous traite pas selon le mal que nous avons commis* (v. 9, 10). Viennent ensuite trois illustrations de la grâce de Dieu. Son amour inébranlable est aussi grand que le ciel est élevé, son pardon éloigne nos transgressions jusqu'au bout du monde et sa compassion est celle d'un père pour ses enfants, parce qu'il sait de quoi nous sommes faits (v. 11-14).

Cette évocation de la faiblesse humaine permet de souligner la miséricorde de Dieu et, comme dans le psaume 90, la vie éphémère de l'homme s'oppose à l'éternité de l'amour de Dieu. L'homme fleurit comme l'herbe et périt comme elle dès que souffle le vent chaud du désert, mais à ceux qui le craignent, qui gardent son alliance et se souviennent de ses commandements, Dieu conserve son *amour* et sa *loyauté,* de même qu'à leurs enfants après eux (v. 15-18). Nombre d'hommes et de femmes, qui regardaient en pleurant un cercueil descendre au fond de la tombe, ont trouvé leur consolation dans leur confiance en cet amour immuable de Dieu de génération en génération.

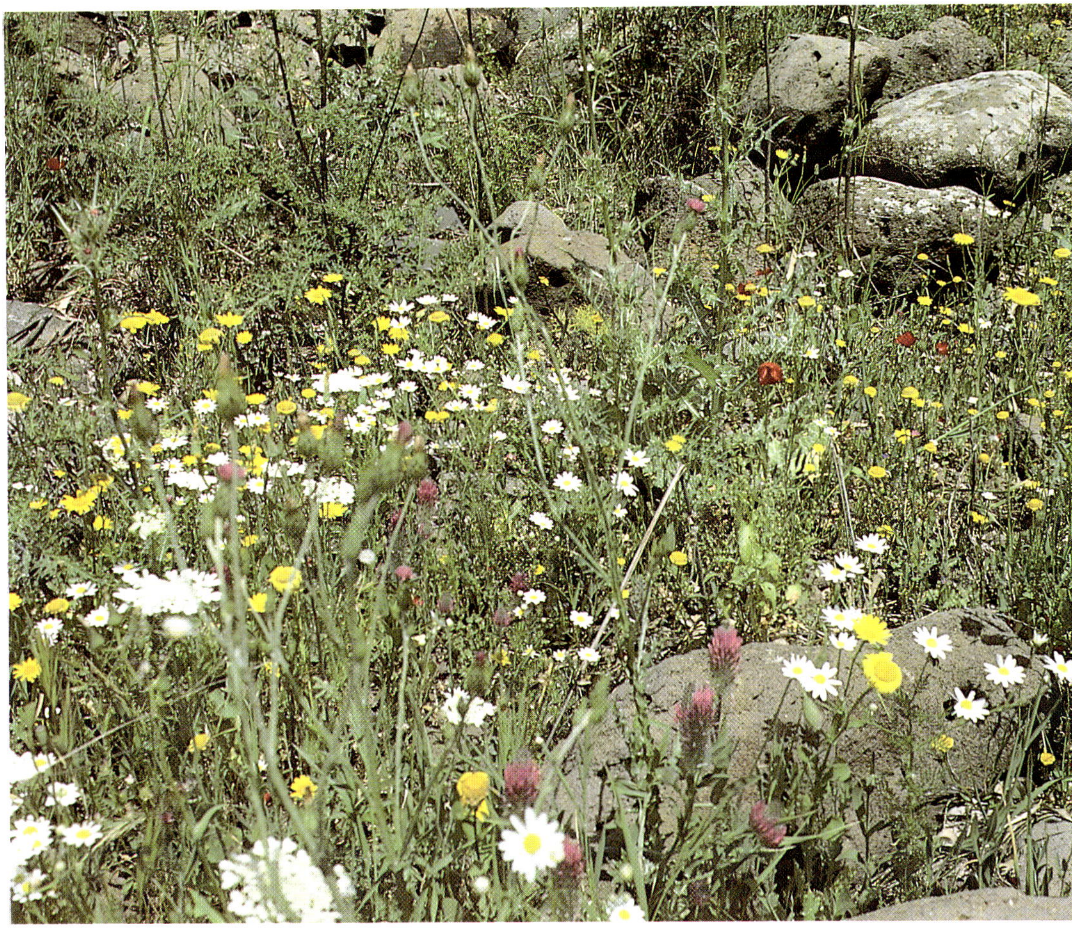

Des fleurs sauvages poussent librement sur les bas-côtés de la route, près de Samarie. « L'homme... sa vie ressemble à l'herbe, à une fleur des champs. »

La domination de Dieu sur toute la création (v. 19-22)

L'auteur conclut en évoquant la souveraineté de Dieu sur toute sa création. *Dans les cieux, l'Éternel a établi son trône : il est le Roi, le Maître de l'univers entier* (v. 19). Le psalmiste appelle toute la création à louer ce Dieu qui règne sur la terre. Il s'adresse d'abord aux *anges*, aussi appelés *ses armées célestes (...) à son service,* dont le rôle est « d'exécuter sa volonté » (v. 20, 21). Puis il se tourne vers les catégories moins élevées de sa création, conviant *toutes ses créatures* à l'adorer. Il terminera ce psaume comme il l'a commencé, par cette exhortation personnelle, *que tout mon être loue l'Éternel* (v. 22).

Psaume 104

Les merveilles de Dieu dans la nature

Les psaumes 103 et 104 se complètent à merveille et illustrent bien l'équilibre du message biblique. Tous deux commencent et se terminent par les mots : *Que tout mon être loue l'Éternel.* Alors que le premier exalte la bonté du Dieu du salut, le second chante la grandeur du Dieu de la création. Le psaume 103 décrit l'attitude du Père céleste envers ses enfants et le psaume 104, celle du Créateur envers sa création. L'un énumère ses *bienfaits* (v. 2) et l'autre ses *œuvres* (v. 13, 24, 31).

L'auteur s'inspire de toute évidence du récit du premier chapitre de la Genèse, dont il suit à peu près le même ordre, depuis l'apparition de la lumière jusqu'à la création de l'homme. Il raconte en termes poétiques comment Dieu a créé les cieux et la terre (v. 1-9) et comment il donne le manger, le boire et le gîte aux animaux (v. 10-23), avant de considérer les œuvres nombreuses et variées de Dieu, qui crée et fait vivre « des plus petits jusqu'aux plus grands » (v. 24-30). En guise de conclusion, il prie que la gloire de Dieu subsiste et décide pour sa part de louer Dieu toute sa vie. Quant aux méchants, qui altèrent sa création, il souhaite qu'ils ne soient plus (v. 31-35).

Si le psalmiste, selon les termes de C.S. Lewis, « savoure la nature », il convient cependant de considérer sa motivation profonde. Il n'exalte pas la nature pour elle-même, « les psaumes ne sont pas des hymnes à la nature. Il n'y est fait mention de la nature que dans la mesure où elle renvoie à Celui qui a fait toutes choses » (C.S. Lewis).

Dieu a créé les cieux et la terre (v. 1-9)

La plupart des verbes de ce paragraphe devraient probablement se conjuguer au passé, comme se référant à la création des cieux (v. 1-4) et de la terre (v. 5-9). Il ne faut pas comprendre ces versets au sens propre, car l'auteur est un poète, et non un homme de science. Il ne veut pas dire que Dieu se déplace sur un char de nuages, ou qu'il a édifié le monde, tel une maison, sur de véritables fondements de pierre. Ce sont là des images.

Par contre, ce passage nous enseigne que Dieu a créé l'univers, dans lequel il s'est révélé. Invisible de par sa nature même, il se fait connaître par l'ordre visible qu'il a établi. La lumière est son manteau, l'étendue des cieux sa tente, le ciel ses chambres et les nuées lui sont un char ; il fait du vent ses messagers et des éclairs ses serviteurs (v. 2-4). « En comparant la lumière à un manteau », commente le

1 Que tout mon être | loue l'Eternel !
O Eternel, mon Dieu, que tu es grand !
Tu es revêtu de splendeur, | et de magnificence,
2 tu as pour manteau la lumière,
et tu déploies les cieux | comme une tente,
3 tu construis au-dessus des eaux du ciel | tes hauts palais inaccessibles.
Des nuées, tu te fais un char,
tu te déplaces | sur les ailes du vent,
4 tu fais des vents tes messagers,
les éclairs sont tes serviteurs.

5 Tu as établi notre terre | sur de solides fondements
pour qu'elle reste inébranlable | à tout jamais.
6 Tu l'as couverte d'océans | comme d'un vêtement,
les eaux recouvraient les montagnes.
7 Lorsque tu les as menacées, | les eaux se sont enfuies au loin
et se sont élancées | au bruit de ton tonnerre,
8 franchissant des montagnes, | dévalant vers des plaines
jusqu'à l'endroit | que tu leur avais assigné.
9 Tu as fixé une limite | que les eaux ne franchiront plus,
et elles ne reviendront plus | pour submerger la terre.

10 C'est toi qui fais jaillir des sources | dans les ravins.
Et les torrents | s'écoulent entre les montagnes.
11 Là viennent s'abreuver les bêtes | qui peuplent les champs et les bois,
là viennent boire les onagres.
12 Les oiseaux nichent sur leurs rives,
chantant à l'abri du feuillage.
13 Du haut de ses palais, | Dieu verse la pluie sur les monts,
la terre est remplie des bienfaits | du fruit de ton ouvrage.
14 C'est toi qui fais pousser | le foin pour le bétail,
et qui fais prospérer | les plantes pour les hommes
afin qu'ils tirent de la terre | le pain pour se nourrir.
15 Le vin réjouit le cœur de l'homme
et fait resplendir son visage, | le rendant brillant plus que l'huile.
Le pain restaure sa vigueur.
16 Les arbres, qui sont ton ouvrage, | ô Eternel, sont pleins de sève.
Tels sont les cèdres du Liban | que ta main a plantés.
17 C'est là que nichent les oiseaux
et la cigogne a sa demeure | là, sur les branches des cyprès.
18 Les bouquetins ont leurs retraites | aux sommets des monts élevés,
et les rochers sont le refuge | où les petits damans se cachent.

19 C'est toi qui as formé la lune | pour marquer les dates des fêtes.
Le soleil sait quand il se couche.
20 Tu fais descendre les ténèbres, | et c'est la nuit.
Alors les hôtes des forêts | se mettent tous en mouvement :
21 les lionceaux rugissent | après leur proie,
ils demandent à Dieu | leur nourriture.
22 Mais dès que paraît le soleil, | ils se retirent
pour se coucher dans leurs tanières.
23 Et l'homme sort pour son ouvrage,
qu'il poursuivra jusqu'à la nuit.

24 Combien tes œuvres sont nombreuses, | ô Eternel,
tu as tout fait avec sagesse,
la terre est pleine | de tout ce que tu as créé :
25 voici la mer immense | qui s'étend à perte de vue,
peuplée d'animaux innombrables,
des plus petits jusqu'aux plus grands,
26 les bateaux la parcourent,
ainsi que le monstre marin | que tu as fait pour qu'il y joue.

27 Ils comptent sur toi, tous ces êtres,
pour recevoir leur nourriture, | chacun au moment opportun.
28 Tu la leur donnes : ils la prennent,
ta main s'ouvre, et ils sont comblés.
29 Tu te détournes, | ils sont épouvantés.
Tu leur ôtes le souffle, | les voilà qui expirent,
redevenant poussière.
30 Si tu envoies ton souffle, | ils sont créés,
tu renouvelles l'aspect de la terre.

31 Gloire à jamais à l'Eternel !
Qu'il se réjouisse de ses œuvres !
32 Son regard fait trembler la terre,
il touche les montagnes | et, déjà, elles fument.

33 Je veux chanter pour l'Eternel | ma vie durant,
célébrer mon Dieu en musique | tant que j'existerai.
34 Que mon poème lui soit agréable !
Moi, j'ai ma joie en l'Eternel.
35 Que les pécheurs soient ôtés de la terre !
Que les *méchants n'existent plus !

Que tout mon être | loue l'Eternel !
Oui, louez l'Eternel !

réformateur Jean Calvin, « le psalmiste veut souligner que, si Dieu est invisible, sa gloire, elle, est manifeste. »

Il est dit de même que la terre a été établie sur des fondements solides, puis recouverte par les eaux. C'est le chaos initial, quand « la terre était...informe et vide » et que « l'Esprit de Dieu planait au-dessus des eaux » (Gn 1.2). Puis vient, décrite avec force images (cf. Gn 1.9, 10), la séparation des eaux d'avec la terre ferme. Les eaux *se sont élancées (...) franchissant des montagnes, décalant vers des plaines, jusqu'à l'endroit que tu leur avais assigné* (v. 8).

. **Dieu fait vivre les animaux** (v. 10-23)

La plupart des verbes de ce paragraphe sont au présent ; les chrétiens ne sauraient être déistes. Les déistes du XIXe siècle croyaient en effet que Dieu avait fabriqué l'univers comme une gigantesque horloge, l'avait mis en mouvement puis livré à son libre cours. Mais la

Bible enseigne que Dieu est un Dieu vivant, qui garde la maîtrise de ce qu'il a fait et ne cesse d'en prendre soin. Il pourvoit aux besoins des *bêtes qui peuplent les champs et les bois* et des *oiseaux* (v. 11, 12). Le terme d'« écologie » a une connotation trop pompeuse et trop scientifique pour être employé ici, mais c'est pourtant bien ce dont il s'agit. Le psalmiste est émerveillé de voir comment Dieu a adapté les ressources de la terre aux besoins des animaux et vice versa.

Les animaux sauvages peuvent ainsi boire aux torrents qui coulent dans les vallées (v. 10, 11) tandis que la pluie de Dieu arrose les montagnes (v. 13) et les arbres (v. 16). De même, hommes et bétail tirent leur nourriture de la terre ; rien ne manque, pas même le vin, l'huile et le pain (v. 14, 15). Même les lions, animaux carnivores par excellence, demandent leur nourriture à Dieu (v. 21).

Mais le manger et le boire ne suffisent pas à la vie ; les animaux ont aussi besoin d'un abri qui les protège de la fureur des éléments et où ils puissent se reproduire. Ainsi les oiseaux, qui chantent *à l'abri du feuillage* (v. 12) y *nichent* aussi (v. 17). La cigogne s'installe *sur les branches des cyprès* (v. 17), tandis que les monts élevés sont un refuge pour *les bouquetins,* et les rochers, pour les *damans* (v. 18). Sous le couvert de la nuit, *les hôtes de la forêt se mettent tous en mouvement.* Puis, *dès que paraît le soleil, ils se retirent pour se coucher dans leurs tanières.* Les êtres humains, par contre, travaillent le jour et dorment la nuit (v. 19-23).

Dieu a créé tous les êtres et les maintient en vie (v. 24-30)

Une explosion de louange vient interrompre la description du psalmiste (v. 24). La terre comme la mer fourmillent des animaux qu'il a créés, *des plus petits jusqu'aux plus grands* (v. 25). La mer, sillonnée de bateaux, est aussi le repaire du *monstre marin* (v. 26), ou Léviathan (version Segond). Il s'agit certainement d'un grand animal marin, « pour certains la baleine, pour d'autres le marsouin ; dans Job 41, il est probablement question du crocodile. » Quoi qu'il en soit, le Talmud nous dit que Dieu joue avec le Léviathan.

Qui plus est, si Dieu, dans sa sagesse a créé tous les êtres, dans sa fidélité il veille sur eux. Ils *comptent sur toi, tous ces êtres* (v. 27). Ils dépendent de lui pour leur nourriture et le souffle de la vie. Ils ne restent cependant pas passifs, leur rôle étant de « prendre » la nourriture, mais c'est Dieu qui la *donne,* comme le souligne l'image de la main de Dieu. Tout comme un enfant, au zoo ou à la ferme, tend de la nourriture aux animaux dans sa main ouverte, ainsi Dieu ouvre sa main, pour que les êtres qu'il a créés soient *comblés.* Mais dès qu'il se détourne, *ils sont épouvantés* et lorsqu'il leur ôte le souffle, ils *expirent, redevenant poussière.* Par contre, son *souffle,* non seulement leur donne la vie, mais la renouvelle constamment.

La nourriture et la vie, qui sont les besoins fondamentaux de toute créature, proviennent donc ici de la main ouverte, du souffle et du regard de Dieu, tandis que leur absence est signe que Dieu cache sa face. Cela peut paraître très naïf à des lecteurs modernes. Pouvons-nous croire de telles choses à notre époque de progrès scientifiques et technologiques ? Est-il besoin de rappeler que les descriptions sont imagées et que l'auteur puise largement dans le langage poétique et les comparaisons anthropomorphiques ?

Mais il n'en reste pas moins vrai que Dieu le Créateur est le maître de sa création. Il n'a pas abdiqué, il règne sur ce qu'il a fait. Un chrétien ne saurait avoir une conception mécaniste de la nature. L'univers n'est pas une machine qui fonctionnerait selon des règles rigides, pas plus que Dieu n'a créé de lois dont il serait maintenant esclave. L'expression « lois naturelles » n'est qu'une formulation commode pour désigner la cohérence de l'activité de Dieu. Il est vivant et il agit dans son univers, et nous dépendons de lui pour « la vie, le souffle et toutes choses » (Ac 17.25). Il est bon que nous le remerciions, non seulement de nous avoir créés, mais aussi de nous maintenir en vie.

En conclusion, le psalmiste souhaite de tout son cœur que la gloire de Dieu, révélée dans ses œuvres, dure à jamais et que Dieu continue à se réjouir de sa création, comme il l'a fait au tout début (v. 31 ; cf. Gn 1.31), de peur qu'il ne jette un regard de jugement et non plus de bienveillance sur la terre (v. 32). L'auteur est résolu à passer sa vie entière à louer Dieu et espère que ce psaume, dans lequel il a considéré toutes les œuvres divines, lui plaise (v. 33, 34). Il reconnaît cependant qu'il existe des *pécheurs* et des *méchants* qui ne rendent pas au Dieu qui les a créés et les maintient en vie la gloire qui lui est due (v. 35). Ils n'honorent pas le Dieu qui tient leur souffle de vie dans sa main (Dn 5.23). Le psalmiste souhaite vivement que Dieu ne permette plus à ces pécheurs de défigurer sa création.

Psaume 121

L'Éternel est celui qui nous garde

Les psaumes 120 à 134 inclus constituent une collection distincte et il est probable qu'à une certaine époque ils aient formé un recueil séparé. Ce sont les cantiques *pour la route vers la demeure de l'Éternel*, littéralement les « cantiques des montées », probablement nommés ainsi parce que chantés par des groupes de pèlerins qui « montaient » vers Jérusalem à l'occasion de l'une des trois grandes fêtes annuelles. Ce sont donc des chants de pèlerinage. Ils sont courts et la plupart d'entre eux témoignent d'un amour sincère pour Sion et son Temple et d'un désir profond de paix et de prospérité pour Jérusalem. Il se dégage de tous ces petits psaumes une foi tranquille, solide dans le Dieu d'Israël, *qui a fait le ciel et la terre* (Ps 121.2 ; 124.8 ; 134.3).

Je lève les yeux vers les monts :
d'où le secours me viendra-t-il ?
2 Mon secours vient de l'Eternel
qui a fait le ciel et la terre.
3 Il te gardera des faux pas,
ton gardien ne dormira pas.
4 Non, jamais il ne dort, | jamais il ne sommeille,
le gardien d'Israël.
5 L'Eternel sera ton gardien,
l'Eternel est à ton côté | comme une ombre qui te protège,
6 et, durant le jour, le soleil | ne te causera aucun mal
ni, au cours de la nuit, la lune.
7 Oui, l'Eternel te gardera | de tout malheur :
il gardera ta vie.
8 L'Eternel veillera sur toi | de ton départ à ton retour,
dès maintenant et à jamais.

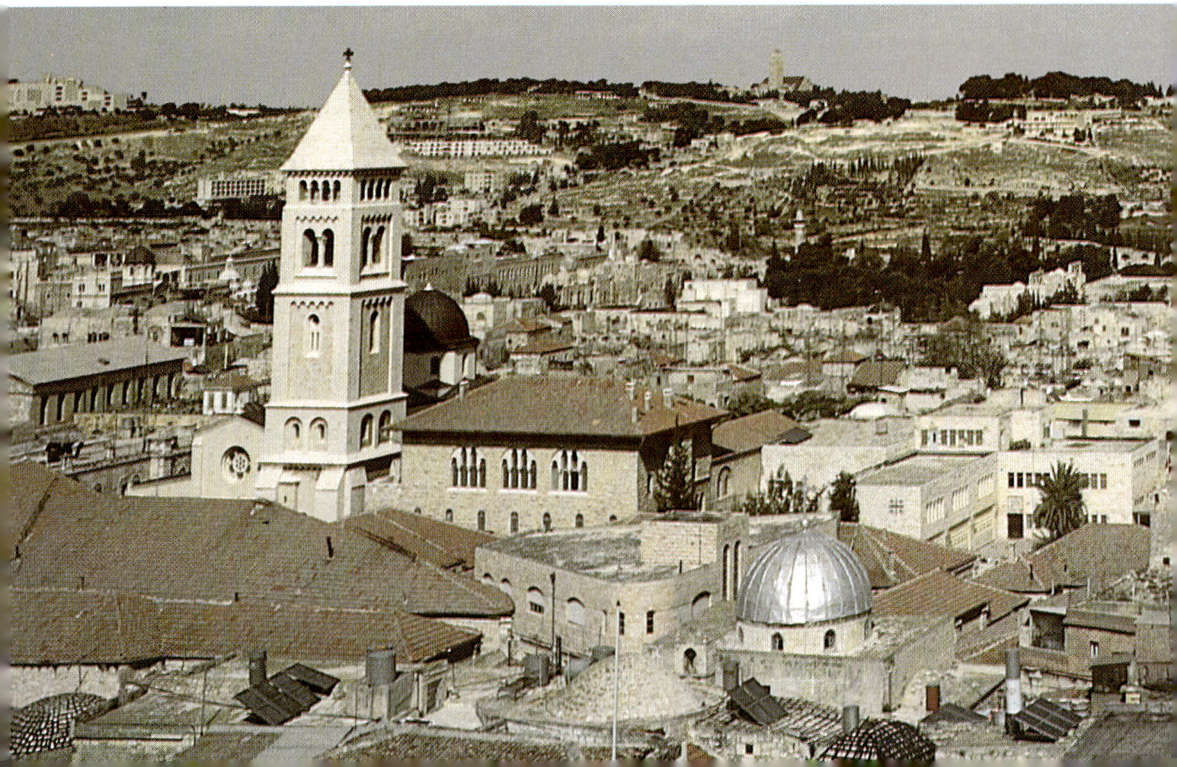

Le mont des Oliviers, vu de Jérusalem. Lorsque les pèlerins arrivaient au sommet de cette colline, la ville de Jérusalem se déployait sous leurs yeux.

Le psaume 121 convenait parfaitement pour être entonné par les pèlerins s'approchant des collines de Jérusalem.

Dans les deux premiers versets, le psalmiste parle en son nom propre et pose une question sur la provenance du secours, à laquelle il répond aussitôt : *Mon secours vient de l'Éternel qui a fait le ciel et la terre* (v. 2). Ce verset affirme tout à la fois que Yahvé est le Dieu de l'alliance avec Israël et qu'il est le Créateur de l'univers. Le verset 4 ajoute qu'il est *le gardien d'Israël*, qui ne sommeille ni ne dort. Le pouvoir souverain du Créateur du monde, ainsi que la vigilance sans faille du gardien d'Israël sont les deux fondements de la foi du psalmiste en la protection divine.

Se tournant alors vers un compagnon de pèlerinage, il va développer ce thème de la protection divine. Les termes « garder » et « gardien » sont répétés six fois dans ce psaume et reviennent presque à chaque verset. Celui qui garde la nation d'Israël garde aussi l'individu (v. 4, 5). Il le gardera *de tout malheur,* il gardera sa *vie* de son *départ* à son *retour (...) dès maintenant et à jamais* (v. 7, 8).

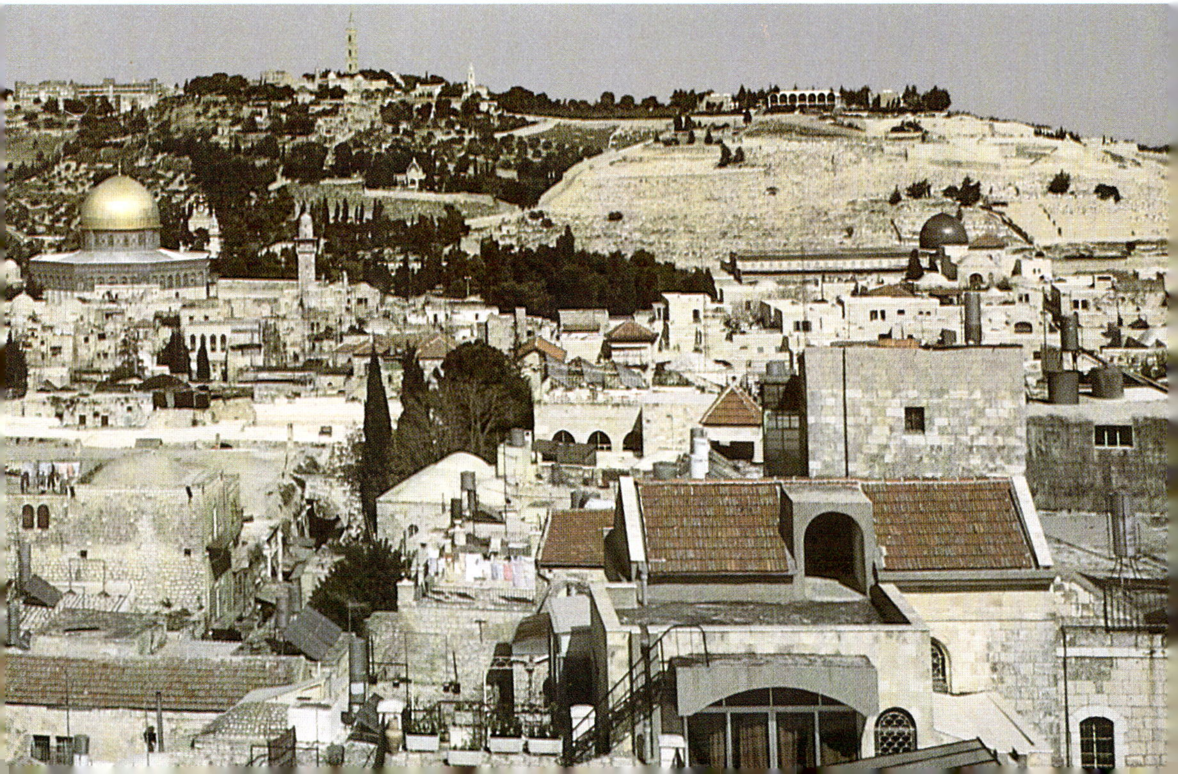

Page suivante : Le Dôme du Rocher, vu de l'intérieur de la chapelle Dominus Flevit, rappelle que Jésus pleura sur Jérusalem lors de sa dernière visite.

Psaume 122

La paix de Jérusalem

De tous les « cantiques des montées » ce psaume est celui qui convenait le mieux à des pèlerins se rendant à Jérusalem pour l'une ou l'autre des fêtes.

Le premier verset exprime l'émotion ressentie par le psalmiste, invité à se joindre au pèlerinage. Au verset 2, il est arrivé à destination, avec tous ses compagnons. Alors qu'il regarde autour de lui, différentes pensées se bousculent dans sa tête. Il remarque par exemple que la cité forme *un tout bien uni* (v. 3). Il se souvient aussi de l'ordre que Dieu a donné aux tribus d'Israël de s'y rendre chaque année pour les fêtes ; *c'est la loi en Israël,* dit-il, faisant certainement allusion au commandement rapporté dans Exode 23.17. Il se rappelle que Jérusalem est le centre de la vie politique et religieuse de la nation, où le peuple peut venir, soit pour louer l'Éternel, soit pour s'approcher des trônes de ceux *qui exercent la justice,* en cas de litige ou de procès (v. 4, 5).

Ces réflexions achevées, le psalmiste exhorte vivement le peuple à prier pour la paix de Jérusalem et lui propose un modèle de prière (v. 6, 7). Il donne l'exemple en priant lui-même. Pour l'amour de ses compagnons de pèlerinage et *pour l'amour de la demeure de l'Éternel notre Dieu,* qui donne toute sa valeur à Jérusalem, il souhaite le *bonheur* de la ville (v. 8, 9).

Je suis dans la joie | lorsque l'on me dit :
« Nous allons monter | à la demeure de l'Eternel. »
2 Voici que nos pas s'arrêtent
à tes portes, | ô Jérusalem !
3 O Jérusalem, | cité bien bâtie,
formant un tout bien uni !
4 C'est là qu'affluent les tribus, | les tribus de l'Eternel
–c'est la loi en Israël –
pour y louer l'Eternel.
5 C'est là que sont établis les trônes | pour ceux qui exercent la justice
et les trônes | pour les descendants du roi David.

6 Priez pour la paix | de Jérusalem :
oui, que ceux qui t'aiment, | ô Jérusalem, | vivent en sécurité !
7 Que la paix soit dans tes murs
et que la sécurité | règne en tes palais !
8 Pour mes frères, mes amis,
je me plais à dire : | « La paix soit chez toi ! »
9 Pour l'amour de la demeure | de l'Eternel notre Dieu,
je souhaite ton bonheur.

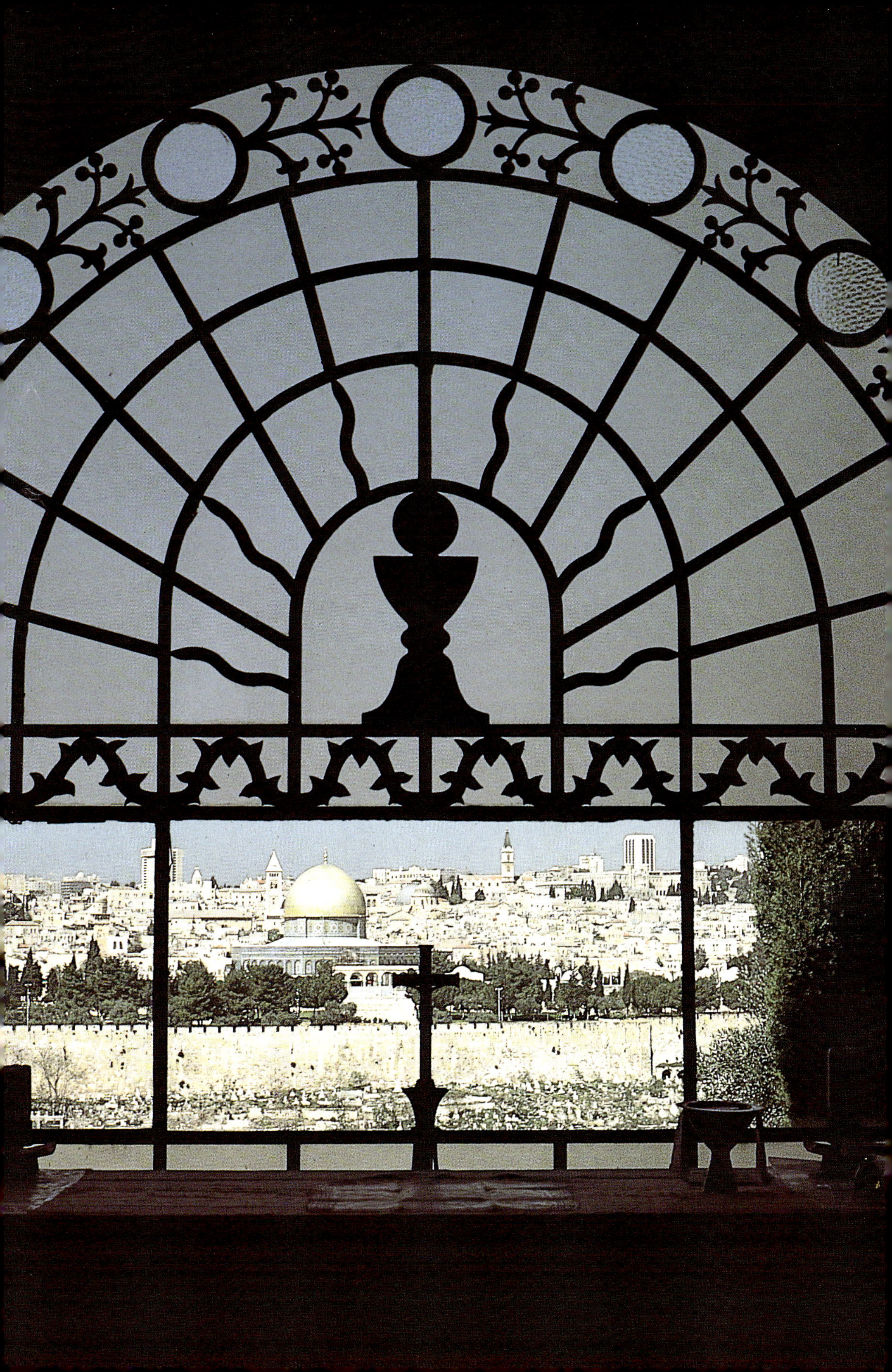

La neige recouvre le sommet du mont Hermon, situé dans le Nord du pays.

Psaume 123

Le regard de la foi

Le point de départ de ce psaume est l'opposition méprisante des *repus* et des *hautains* (v. 4). On ne peut dire avec certitude à qui ces termes font allusion ; ils peuvent désigner n'importe quel ennemi d'Israël, mais plus probablement Sanballat, le Horonite, Tobiya l'Ammonite et Guéchem, l'Arabe, qui avaient accablé les Juifs de leurs moqueries et de leur mépris en apprenant qu'ils voulaient reconstruire la muraille de la ville (Ne 2.19 ; 4.1-5).

Le psaume commence sur un ton de confiance paisible et patiente au Dieu qui siège dans les cieux (v. 1). Comme le serviteur regarde la main de son maître, et la servante, celle de sa maîtresse, *ainsi nos regards*

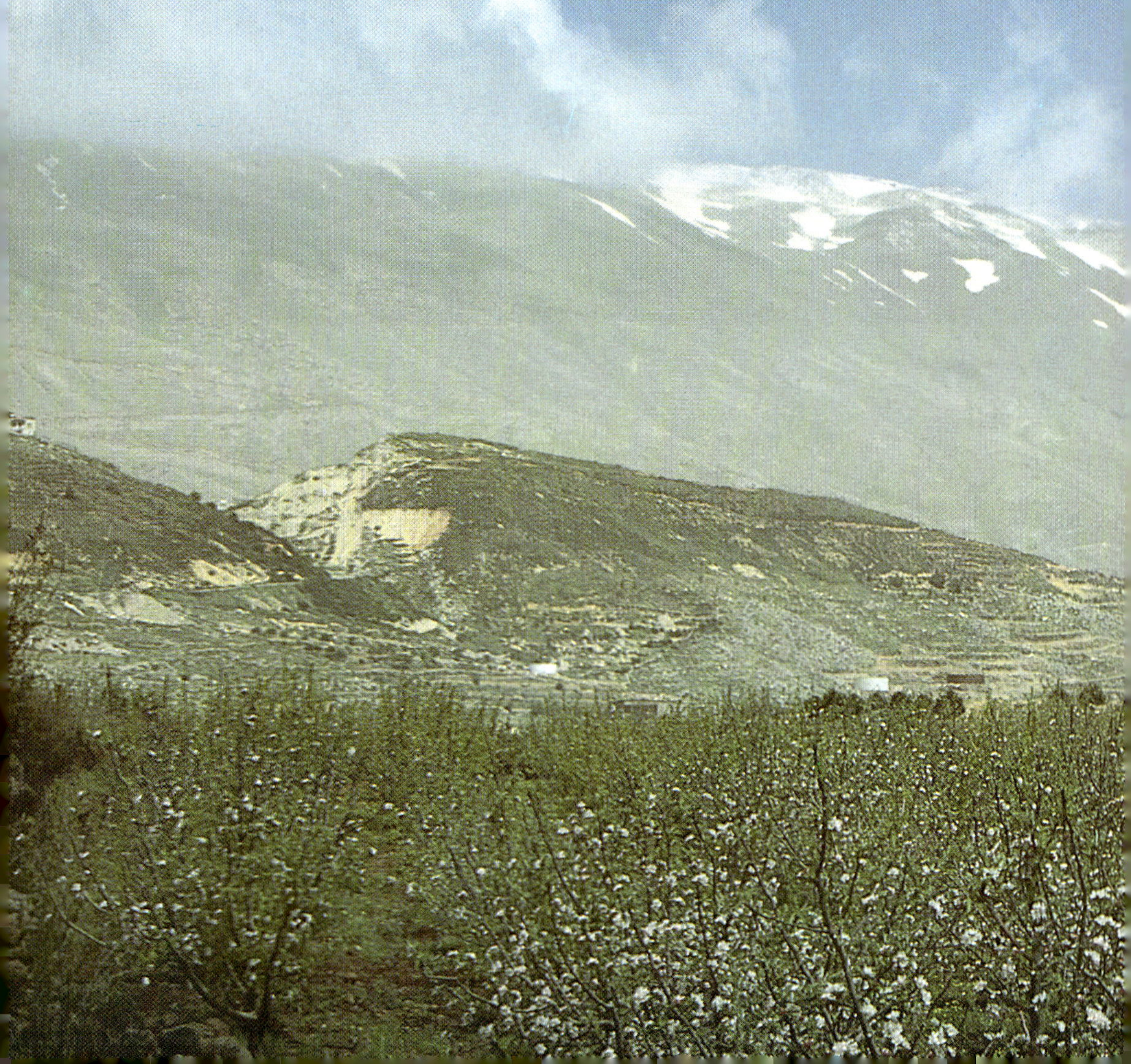

se tournent vers l'Éternel, notre Dieu (v. 2). Ce n'est pas le regard de quelqu'un qui attend des ordres, mais de quelqu'un qui espère une réponse à un besoin. Il exprime la dépendance, plutôt que l'obéissance.

Le psalmiste en appelle à présent à cette miséricorde divine sur laquelle il compte tant. Sa prière n'est pas une prière individuelle, il s'identifie au contraire à la nation lorsqu'il dit : *nous sommes saturés des insultes des repus.*

J'ai levé les yeux vers toi,
toi qui règnes dans les cieux.

2 Oui, comme les serviteurs | fixent leurs regards
sur la main du maître,
comme la servante | fixe ses regards | sur la main de sa maîtresse,
ainsi nos regards se tournent | vers l'Eternel, notre Dieu,
dans l'attente de sa grâce.

3 Fais-nous grâce, ô Eternel ! | Aie pitié de nous !
Car nous sommes saturés | du mépris qu'on nous témoigne.
4 Oui, nous sommes saturés
des insultes des repus | et du mépris des hautains.

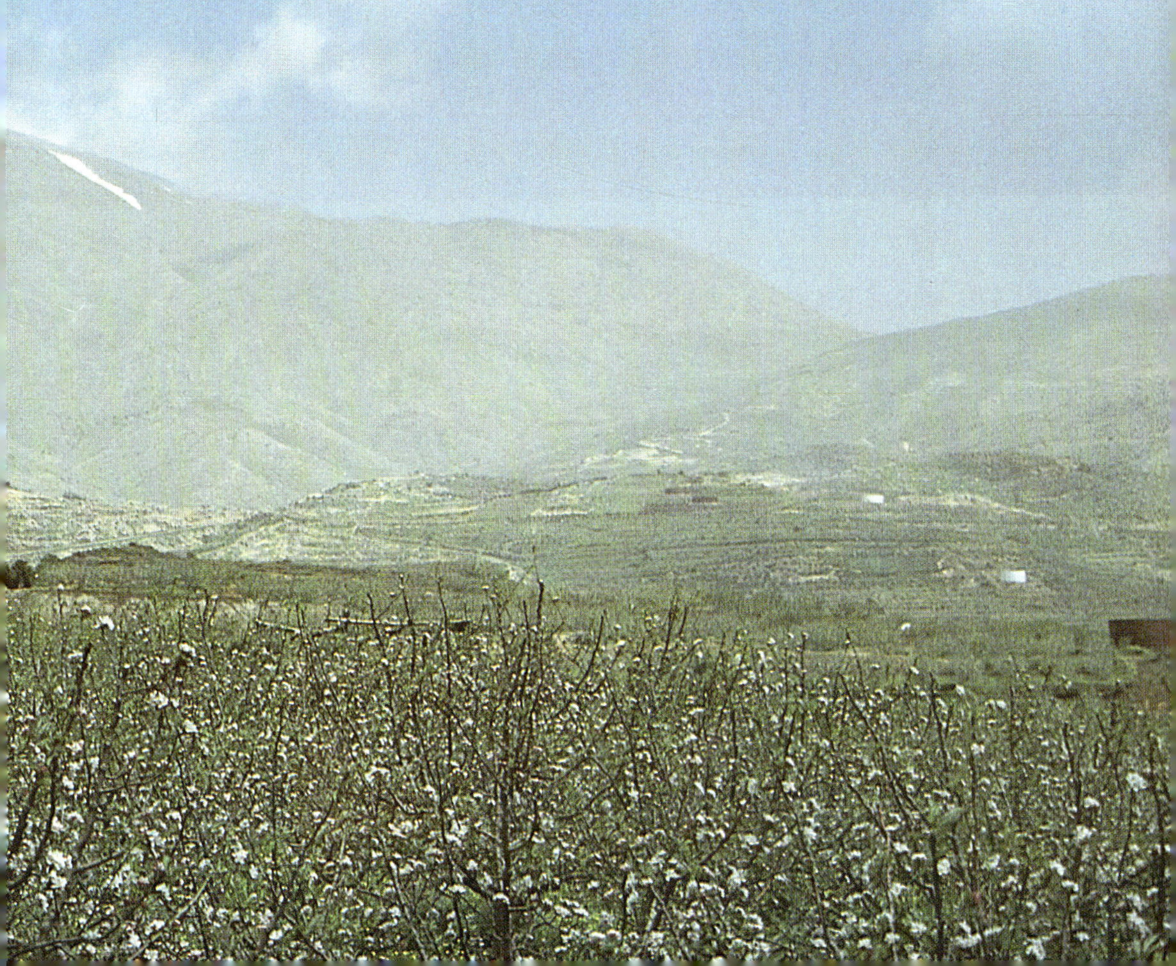

Page suivante : Le monastère orthodoxe grec est accroché aux flancs du mont de la Tentation, près de Jéricho. La tradition situe la tentation de Jésus dans ce lieu.

Psaume 125

Les montagnes qui entourent le mont de Sion

La Palestine est une région principalement montagneuse et le relief a joué un rôle important dans l'histoire d'Israël. Rien d'étonnant donc à ce que les chants des pèlerins qui s'approchaient de Jérusalem parlent de montagnes (voir aussi Ps 121.1).

Le thème de la montagne suggère deux comparaisons au psalmiste. D'une part, les croyants sont inébranlables, comme le mont de Sion. D'autre part, la protection de Yahvé les environne comme les montagnes entourent Jérusalem. Ceux qui appartiennent à Dieu sont donc semblables à une montagne entourée d'autres montagnes, tout à la fois inébranlables et imprenables (v. 1, 2).

Replacées dans le contexte historique, ces images signifient que Dieu ne permettra pas qu'un *injuste pouvoir* (v. 3) gouverne *le pays des justes*, de peur que ceux-ci en viennent *eux aussi à prêter la main à des actions coupables*. Bien au contraire, le psalmiste prie avec confiance que Dieu soit *bon (...) pour celui qui est bon*, mais qu'il éloigne ceux qui font le mal (v. 4, 5). Il faut peut-être voir là une allusion aux agissements des Samaritains sous l'emprise des Perses.

Ceux qui ont placé leur confiance | en l'Eternel
sont comme le mont de Sion : | il n'est pas ébranlé
et demeure à jamais.
2 Comme Jérusalem | se trouve entourée de montagnes,
de même l'Eternel | entoure aussi son peuple,
dès maintenant | et à jamais.
3 Un injuste pouvoir | ne pourra subsister
dans le pays des justes,
sinon ils en viendraient | eux aussi à prêter la main | à des actions coupables.

4 Sois bon, ô Eternel, | pour celui qui est bon,
pour celui qui a le cœur droit !
5 Mais ceux qui se détournent | vers des voies tortueuses,
que l'Eternel les chasse
avec tous ceux qui font le mal !

Que la paix soit sur Israël !

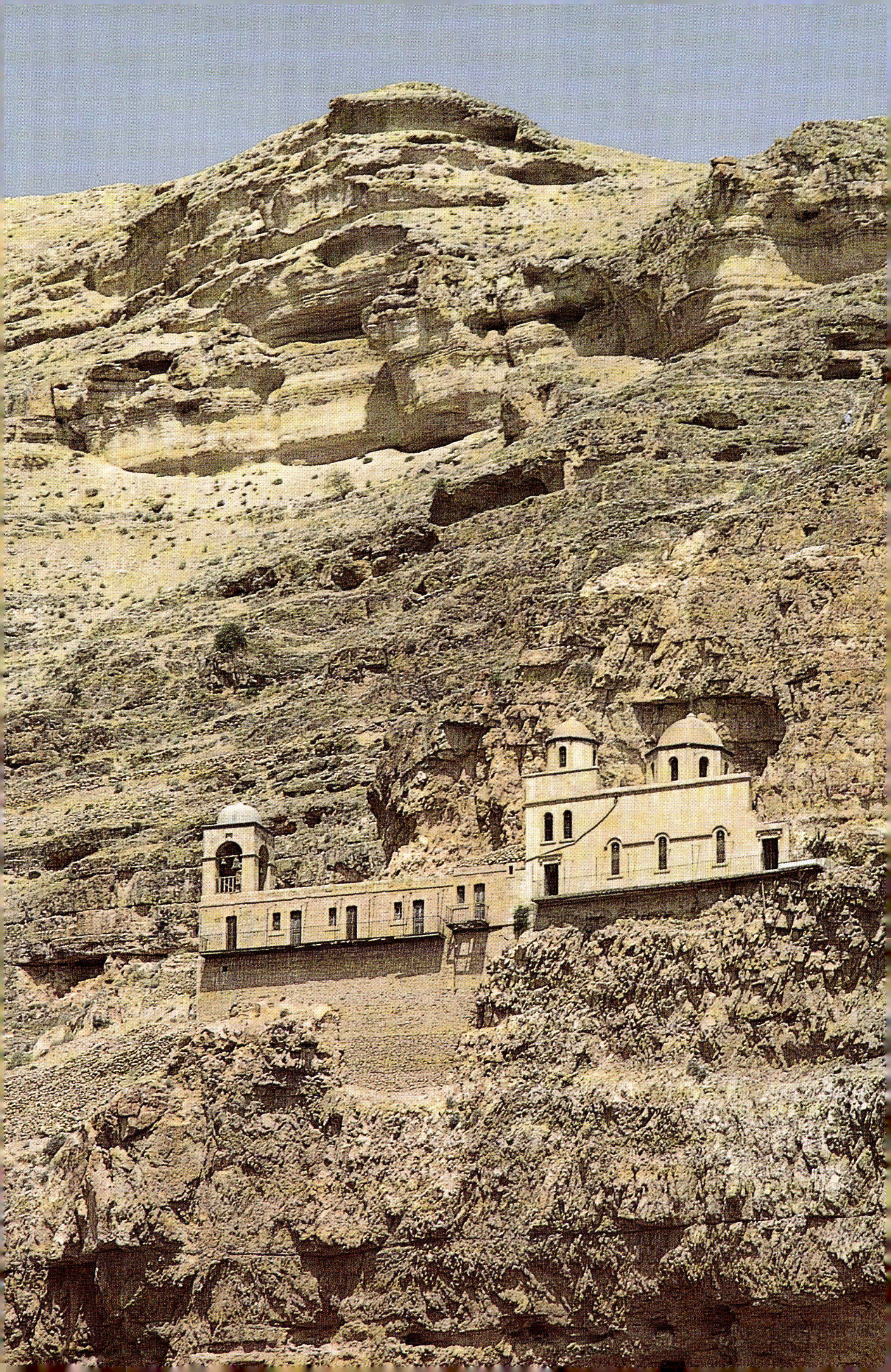

Un rabbin orthodoxe fait traverser la cour du Temple, en face du Mur Occidental, à un groupe d'enfants juifs.

Psaume 127

Le travail que l'Éternel ne bénit pas est vain

Il ne sert à rien de se lancer dans un nouveau projet ou d'essayer de faire prospérer une ancienne entreprise, si l'Éternel ne bénit pas le travail (v. 1). Le bâtisseur travaille en vain si ce n'est pas l'Éternel qui bâtit, de même que le guet de la sentinelle est inutile si l'Éternel ne veille pas sur la ville. Nous pouvons travailler dur, jusqu'à nous surmener, nous lever tôt et nous coucher tard, mais n'oublions pas que *Dieu en donne autant à ceux qui lui sont chers pendant qu'ils dorment* (v. 2). Il est évident que Dieu ne condamne pas le travail, pas plus que dans Matthieu 6.25-34 notre Seigneur n'interdit la prévoyance sage. Ce qui est mauvais c'est, d'une part l'inquiétude, d'autre part une activité fiévreuse qui dénoterait une trop grande confiance en soi. Les deux attitudes dévoilent le manque de foi en Dieu.

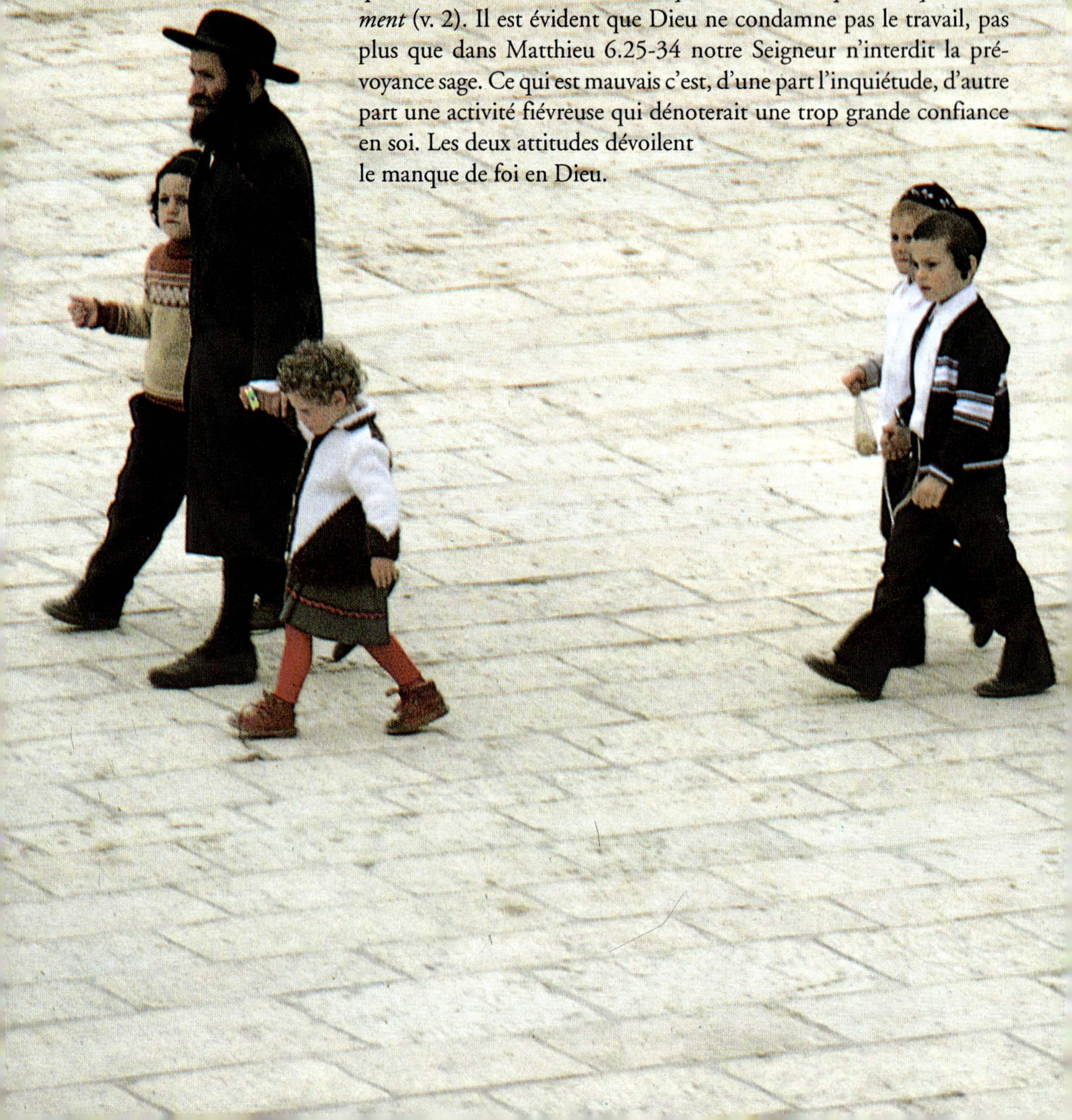

Nous devons considérer les enfants comme *l'héritage que donne l'Éternel* (v. 3), un des cadeaux les plus précieux que Dieu puisse nous faire. *Ils sont pareils aux flèches (…) les fils de la jeunesse* (v. 4) ; en effet, lorsque leur père sera devenu vieux, ils seront eux-mêmes en âge de le défendre et de le protéger. De plus, si *le carquois en est rempli,* il pourra tenir ferme dans toutes les discussions *aux portes de la ville*, c'est-à-dire là où se traitaient les affaires et où se déroulaient les procès.

Si l'Eternel | ne bâtit la maison,
en vain les bâtisseurs travaillent.
Si l'Eternel | ne garde pas la ville,
en vain la sentinelle veille.
2 Oui, il est vain | de vous lever très tôt | et de vous coucher tard,
et de vous donner tant de peine | pour gagner votre pain.
Car Dieu en donne autant | à ceux qui lui sont chers | pendant qu'ils dorment.
3 Des fils : | voilà bien l'héritage | que donne l'Eternel,
oui, des enfants | sont une récompense.
4 Ils sont pareils aux flèches | dans la main d'un archer,
les fils de la jeunesse.
5 Heureux est l'homme | dont le carquois en est rempli !
Il ne connaîtra pas la honte
quand il plaidera contre l'ennemi | aux portes de la ville.

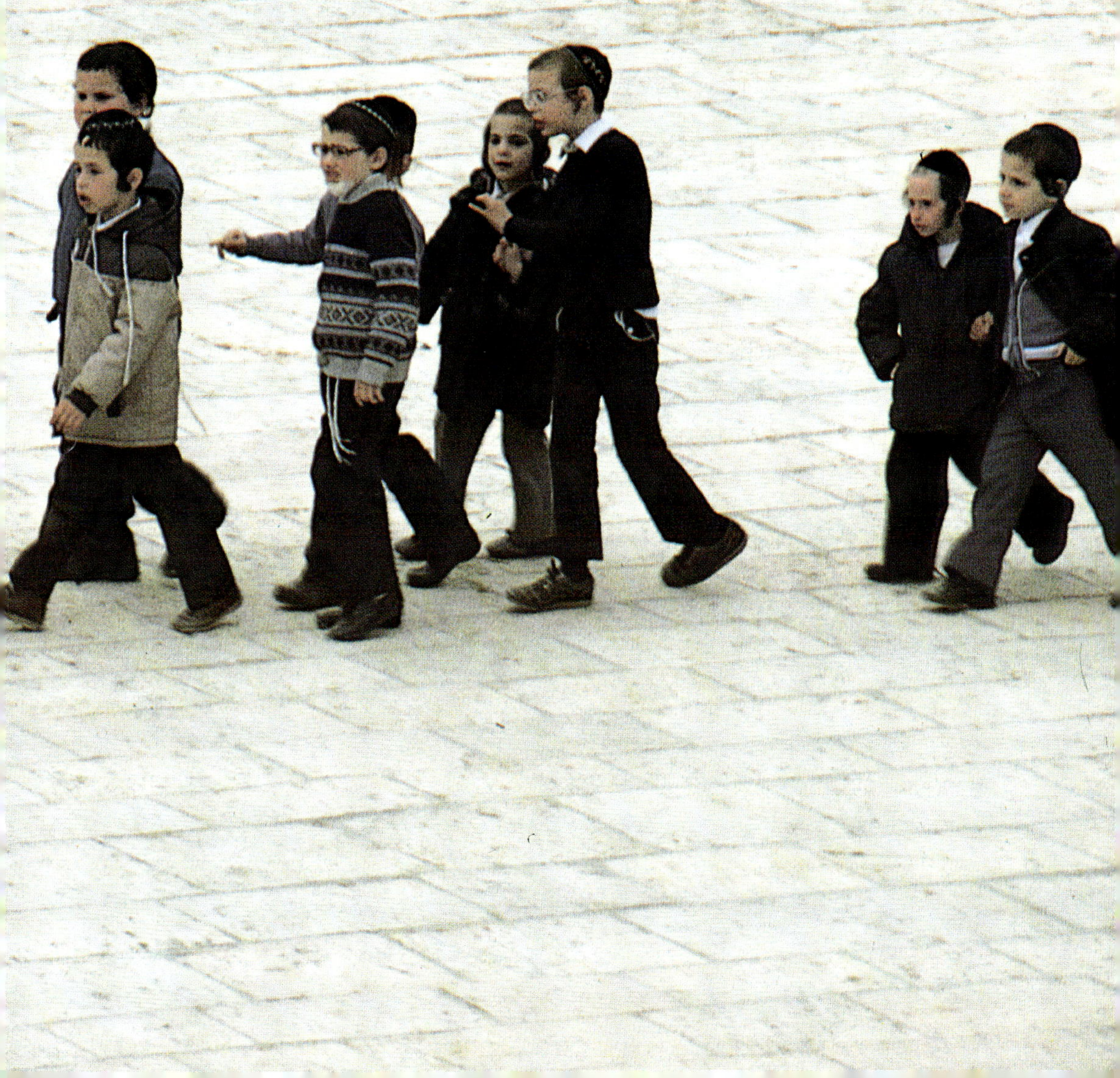

Page suivante : Ces tours de guet en pierres sèches se rencontraient fréquemment dans les champs de la rive occidentale du Jourdain, près de Samarie. Les fermiers venaient y dormir pendant la moisson, pour protéger leurs récoltes des voleurs.

Psaume 130

Du fond de la détresse

Si le psalmiste a obtenu le pardon divin, pourquoi Israël ne pourrait-il pas aussi faire confiance à Dieu pour sa rédemption ?

L'auteur se débat dans des eaux profondes et il appelle Dieu au secours *du fond de la détresse* (v. 1, 2). Ces eaux profondes sont une image du péché, de la culpabilité, du jugement mérité de Dieu, pour l'auteur ou pour toute la nation à laquelle il s'identifie (cf. Ne 1.4-7). Il sait que si Dieu prend *en compte nos fautes,* c'est-à-dire s'il en garde le souvenir et nous en tient rigueur, ni lui ni personne ne *subsistera* (v. 3). *Mais,* ajoute-t-il aussitôt, *le pardon se trouve auprès de toi* (v. 4).

C'est parce qu'on y trouve cette notion de pardon par la grâce, sans les œuvres, que Luther a qualifié ce psaume de pénitence de « paulinien ». Le verset 4 est aussi un de ceux qui ont encouragé John Bunyan, l'auteur du *Voyage du pèlerin,* alors qu'il était déclaré coupable de péché. Il est remarquable d'équilibre, dans la mesure où, après avoir donné une assurance aux désespérés, il met en garde les présomptueux. Loin de conforter les pécheurs dans leur péché, le pardon divin suscite la crainte de l'Eternel, le respect devant sa présence, qui conduisent les hommes et les femmes à se détourner du mal (cf. Pr 16.6).

Confiant dans la miséricorde et le pardon de Dieu pour les pécheurs, l'auteur fait alors deux choses. Premièrement, il affirme sa propre détermination de s'attendre à lui pour son pardon, sur la base de sa promesse (v. 5). Sereine, son âme *guette le Seigneur* (v. 6). Sa conscience chargée l'a plongé dans les ténèbres, mais il attend fermement de voir poindre l'aube du pardon divin. Deuxièmement, il exhorte Israël à en faire autant. Assuré de son propre pardon (v. 4) il peut affirmer que l'amour que l'on trouve *auprès de lui* délivrera aussi Israël de ses péchés (v. 7).

Du fond de la détresse | je t'appelle, Eternel.
2 Seigneur, écoute-moi !
Sois attentif
à mes supplications !
3 O Eternel, si tu retiens nos fautes,
Seigneur, qui donc subsistera ?
4 Mais le pardon | se trouve auprès de toi
afin qu'on te révère.
5 Moi, je m'attends à l'Eternel, | oui, je m'attends à lui, | de tout mon être,
j'ai foi en sa parole.
6 Je guette le Seigneur
bien plus que les guetteurs | n'attendent le matin,
oui, plus que les guetteurs | n'attendent le matin.
7 O Israël, | place ta foi en l'Eternel,
car c'est auprès de lui | que l'on trouve l'amour :
on trouve auprès de lui | une parfaite délivrance,
8 et c'est lui qui délivrera | Israël de tous ses péchés.

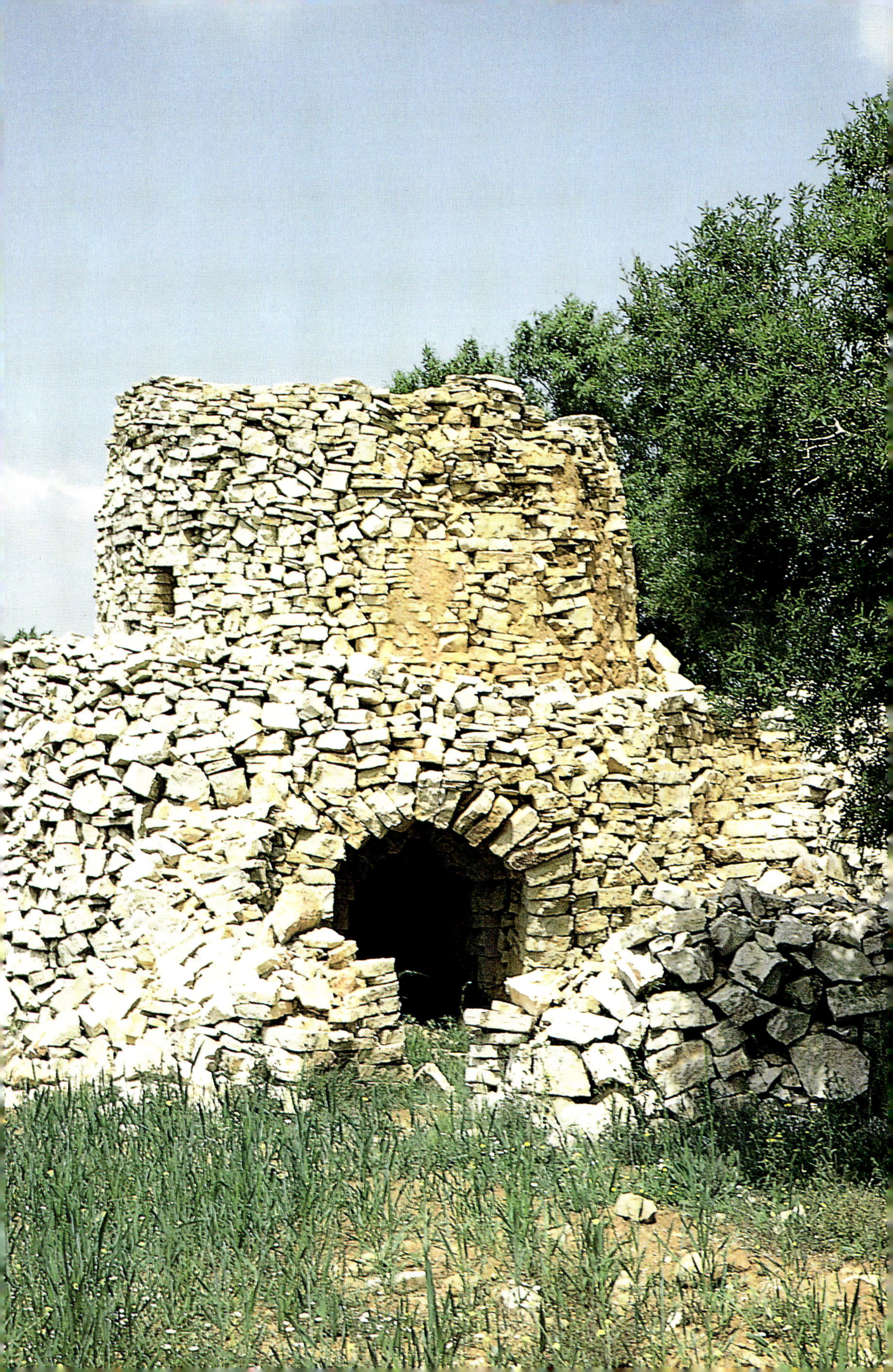

Un jeune garçon arabe de Bethléhem. Ce psaume nous demande d'être humble comme un petit enfant.

Psaume 131

Comme un petit enfant

Les quelques versets de ce psaume, qui évoquent la dépendance paisible d'un nourrisson vis-à-vis de sa mère, annoncent déjà l'enseignement de notre Seigneur sur la nécessité de ressembler à un petit enfant.

Le psalmiste se décrit tel qu'il est et oppose deux états d'esprit. Son cœur n'est pas hautain et ses yeux ne visent pas trop haut. Il ne s'engage pas *dans des projets trop grands* (v. 1). Il a renoncé à ses ambitions de prestige et de pouvoir, tant pour lui-même que pour la nation d'Israël après la Restauration, pour l'heure encore humiliée sous un joug étranger. Il désire plutôt être *comme un nourrisson rassasié*, qui, après avoir été allaité, se repose, apaisé, dans les bras de sa mère (v. 2). Cette attitude est celle d'une personne (ou d'une nation) qui, libre d'ambitions trop élevées, trouve sa pleine satisfaction en Dieu. C'est une belle image, non seulement d'une foi humble, mais aussi de ce que nous pouvons appeler « le cœur de mère » de Dieu.

Comme dans le psaume 130, l'auteur exhorte Israël à apprendre la même leçon que lui. *Israël, mets ton espérance en l'Éternel, dès maintenant et pour toujours* (v. 3).

O Eternel, | mon cœur ne s'enfle pas d'orgueil, |
mes yeux n'ont pas visé trop haut,
je ne me suis pas engagé | dans des projets trop grands,
trop élevés pour moi.
2 Bien au contraire : | je suis resté tranquille | et dans le calme.
Je me sentais | comme un nourrisson rassasié |
dans les bras de sa mère,
comme un nourrisson apaisé.

3 Israël, mets ton espérance | en l'Eternel,
dès maintenant et pour toujours.

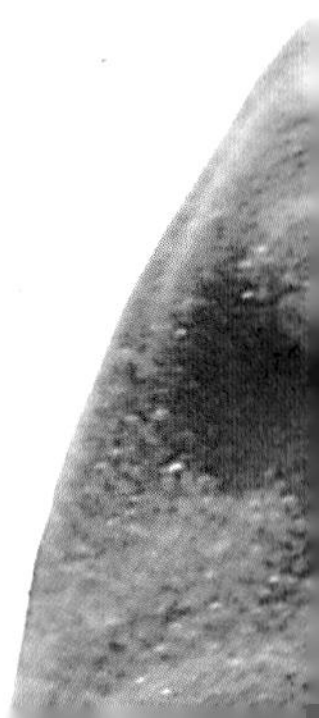

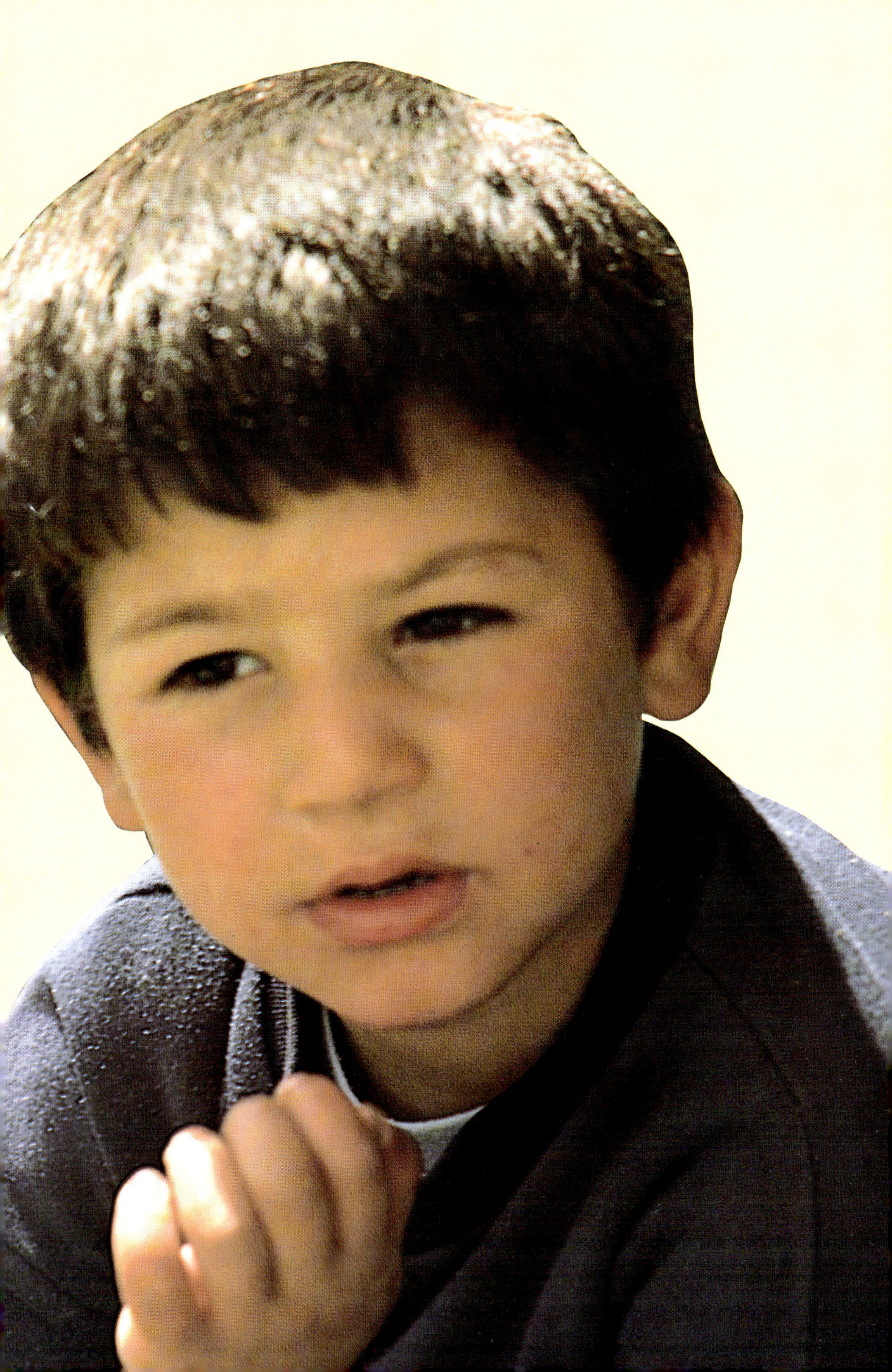

Page suivante : Un vieil homme juif étudie les Écritures à l'ombre du Mur Occidental, à Jérusalem.

Psaume 133

L'unité entre frères

Dieu, tout comme le peuple lui-même, a toujours désiré l'unité de la nation. Si ce psaume se situe après l'Exil, il traduit la joie et la solidarité des pèlerins réunis à Jérusalem pour adorer Dieu, une fois guérie la blessure de la division du royaume.

Les enfants de l'alliance sont déjà *des frères*, mais *quel plaisir (...) quel bonheur* si, en plus, ils sont *ensemble* (v. 1 ; « unis » selon la version synodale). Deux comparaisons illustrent cette unité. Elle est comme l'huile de l'onction *qui descend sur la barbe, la barbe d'Aaron* (depuis le sommet de la tête), et *coule jusqu'au bord de ses habits*, et comme *la rosée qui descend de l'Hermon*, connue pour être abondante (v. 2, 3).

Le texte ne nous dit pas pourquoi l'unité des croyants est semblable à l'huile de l'onction et à la rosée de l'Hermon. Certains commentateurs font remarquer que dans les deux cas il s'agit d'un liquide coulant de haut en bas, tout comme l'influence d'une entente véritable entre frères se fait ressentir partout et sanctifie tout le corps. En outre, de même que l'huile répand son parfum et que la rosée est indispensable pour fertiliser le sol aride de la Palestine, l'unité des croyants est de bonne odeur comme l'huile et rafraîchissante comme la rosée pour Jérusalem. C'est là que Yahvé *accorde sa bénédiction et la vie pour toujours* (v. 3).

Oh ! Quel plaisir c'est, pour des frères, | et quel bonheur
que d'être ensemble !
2 C'est comme l'huile parfumée
répandue sur la tête,
qui descend sur la barbe, | la barbe d'Aaron,
et coule jusqu'au bord
de ses habits.
3 C'est comme la rosée | qui descend de l'Hermon
sur le mont de Sion.
C'est là que l'Eternel | accorde sa bénédiction
et la vie pour toujours.

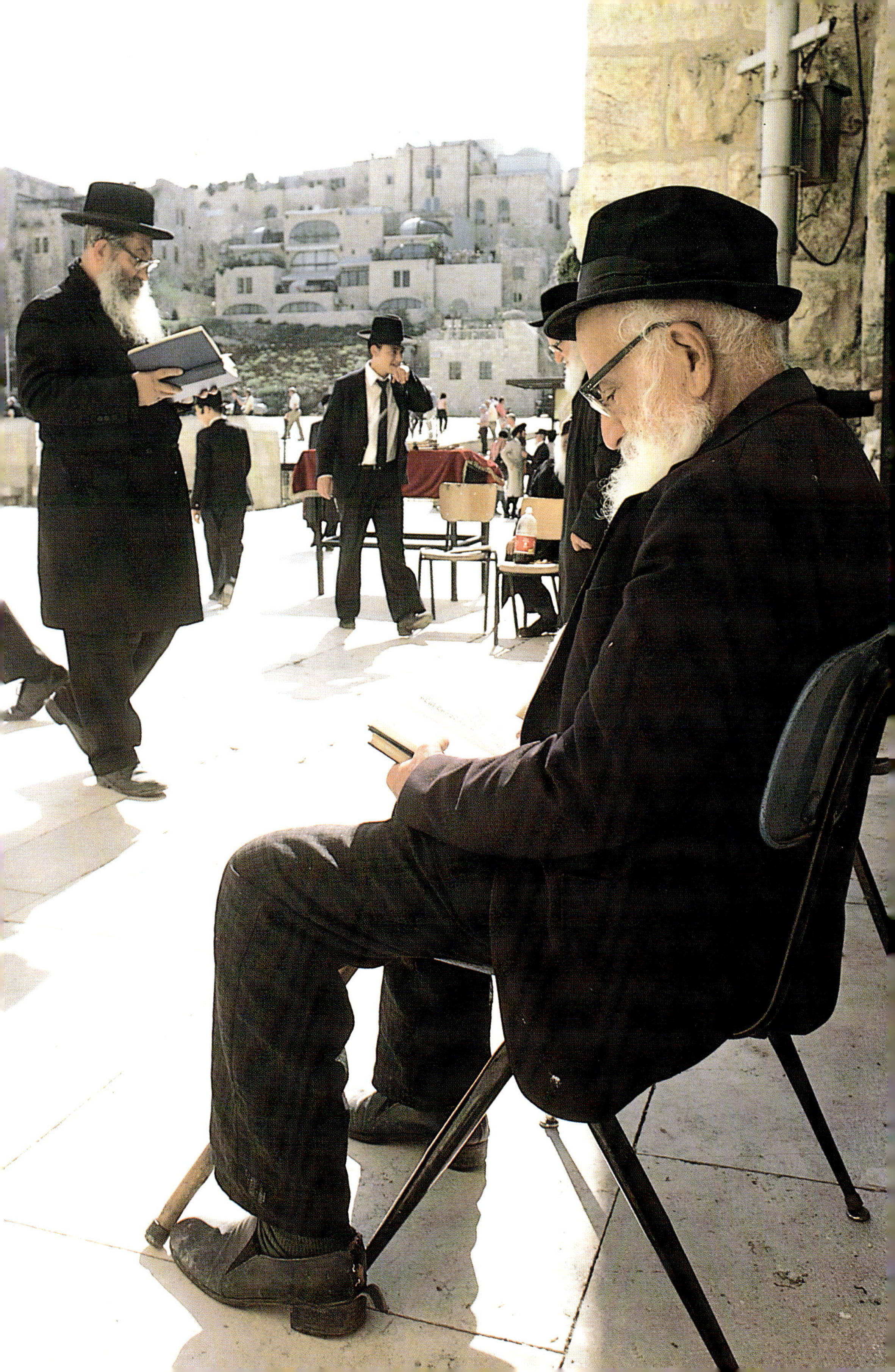

Coucher de soleil sur la mer de Galilée. « Pour toi, les ténèbres deviennent lumière et la nuit est claire comme le plein jour : lumières ou ténèbres pour toi sont pareilles. »

Psaume 139

L'omniscience de Dieu

Ce psaume, appelé par certains « la couronne de tous les psaumes », est une méditation, extraordinaire de profondeur, sur le savoir sans bornes de Dieu et sa présence universelle, tels que les a compris un homme. On connaît surtout les versets 6 à 11, qui développent l'impossibilité dans laquelle se trouve l'être humain d'échapper à Dieu.

L'omniscience de Dieu (v. 1-6)

L'auteur utilise toute une palette de verbes qui montrent à quel point Dieu connaît l'homme. Il « sonde, connaît, discerne, sait » et tout ce qui nous concerne lui est « familier » (v. 1-3). Cette connaissance divine s'étend à nos pensées, nos actes et nos paroles. Tout d'abord, Dieu discerne nos pensées *de loin* (v. 2). Comme l'a dit Perowne, « l'espace et le temps n'existent pas pour Dieu » et toutes les pensées humaines sont dévoilées à ses yeux. Dieu voit aussi *tous mes chemins*, aussi bien les activités de la journée que le repos de la nuit (v. 2, 3). Enfin, il connaît toutes nos paroles avant même que nous ne les prononcions (v. 4).

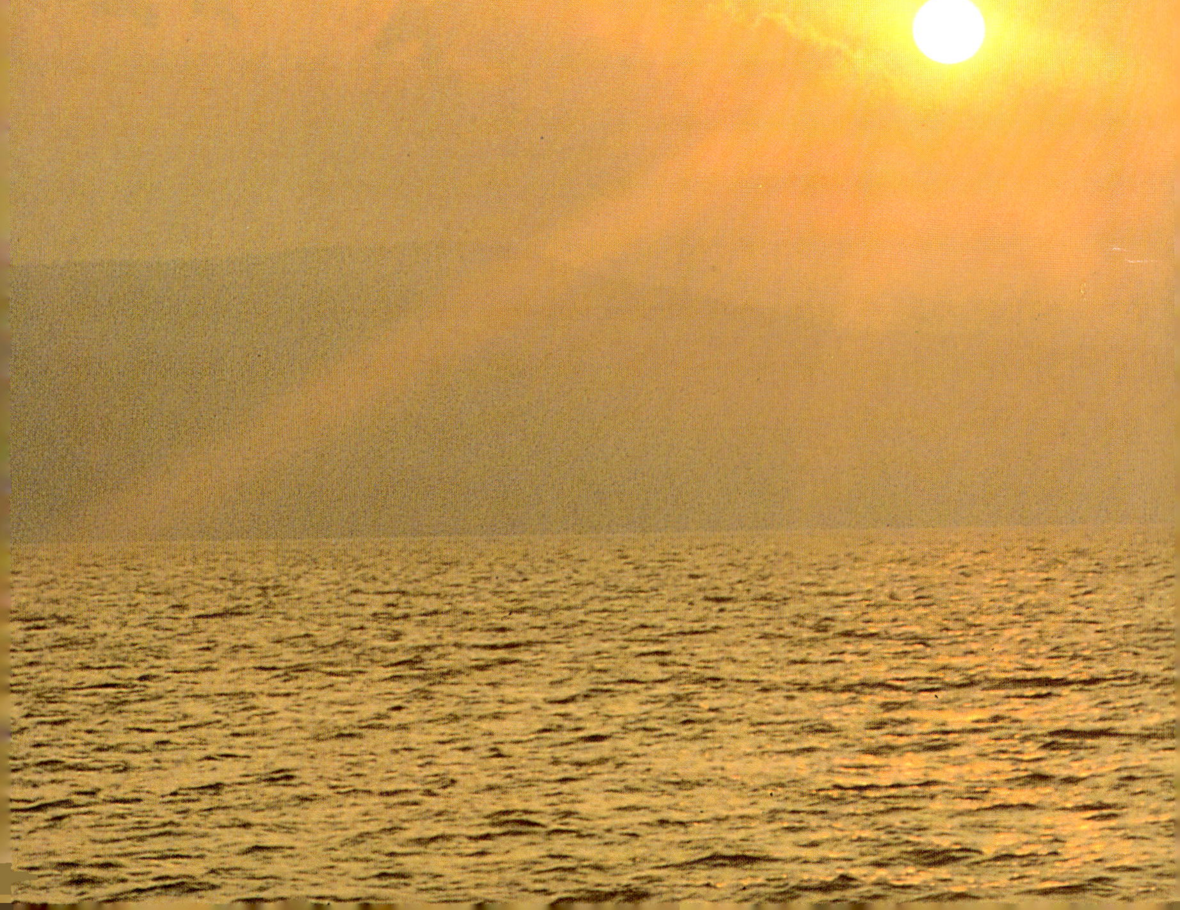

Eternel, | tu me sondes | et tu me connais.
2 Quand je suis assis | et quand je me lève, | tu le sais.
De loin, tu discernes | tout ce que je pense.
3 Tu sais quand je marche | et quand je me couche,
et tous mes chemins | te sont familiers.
4 Bien avant qu'un mot | vienne sur mes lèvres,
Eternel, | tu sais déjà tout | ce que je vais dire.
5 Tu es devant moi | et derrière moi :
tu m'entoures ; | ta main est sur moi.
6 Merveilleux savoir | hors de ma portée,
savoir trop sublime | pour que je l'atteigne.

7 Où pourrais-je aller | loin de ton Esprit ?
Où pourrais-je fuir | hors de ta présence ?
8 Si je monte au ciel | tu es là,
et si je descends | au séjour des morts, | t'y voilà !
9 Et si j'empruntais | les ailes de l'aube
pour me réfugier | aux confins des mers,
10 là aussi ta main | me dirigerait,
ton bras droit | me tiendrait.
11 Et si je me dis : | « Du moins les ténèbres | m'envelopperont »,
alors la nuit même | se change en lumière | tout autour de moi.
12 Pour toi, les ténèbres | deviennent lumière
et la nuit est claire | comme le plein jour :
lumière ou ténèbres | pour toi sont pareilles.

13 Tu m'as fait ce que je suis,
et tu m'as tissé | dans le ventre de ma mère.
14 Merci d'avoir fait de moi | une créature | aussi merveilleuse :
tu fais des merveilles,
et je le reconnais bien.
15 Mon corps n'était pas caché | à tes yeux
quand, dans le secret, | je fus façonné
et tissé | comme dans les profondeurs | de la terre.
16 Je n'étais encore | qu'une masse informe, | mais tu me voyais
et, dans ton registre, | se trouvaient déjà inscrits
tous les jours | que tu m'avais destinés
alors qu'aucun d'eux | n'existait encore.

17 Combien tes desseins, ô Dieu, | sont, pour moi, impénétrables,
et comme ils sont innombrables !
18 Si je les comptais,
ils seraient bien plus nombreux | que les grains de sable | sur les bords des mers.
Voici : je m'éveille, | je suis encore avec toi.

19 Puisses-tu, ô Dieu, | faire mourir le méchant !
Que les hommes sanguinaires | partent loin de moi !
20 Ils se servent de ton nom | pour leurs desseins criminels,
eux, tes adversaires, | l'utilisent pour tromper.
21 Eternel, | comment donc ne pas haïr | ceux qui te haïssent,
et ne pas prendre en dégoût | ceux qui te combattent ?
22 Eh bien, je leur voue | une haine extrême,
et les considère | comme mes ennemis mêmes.

23 Sonde-moi, ô Dieu, | pénètre mon cœur,
examine-moi, | et pénètre les pensées | qui me bouleversent !
24 Considère si je suis | le chemin du mal
et dirige-moi | sur la voie | de l'éternité !

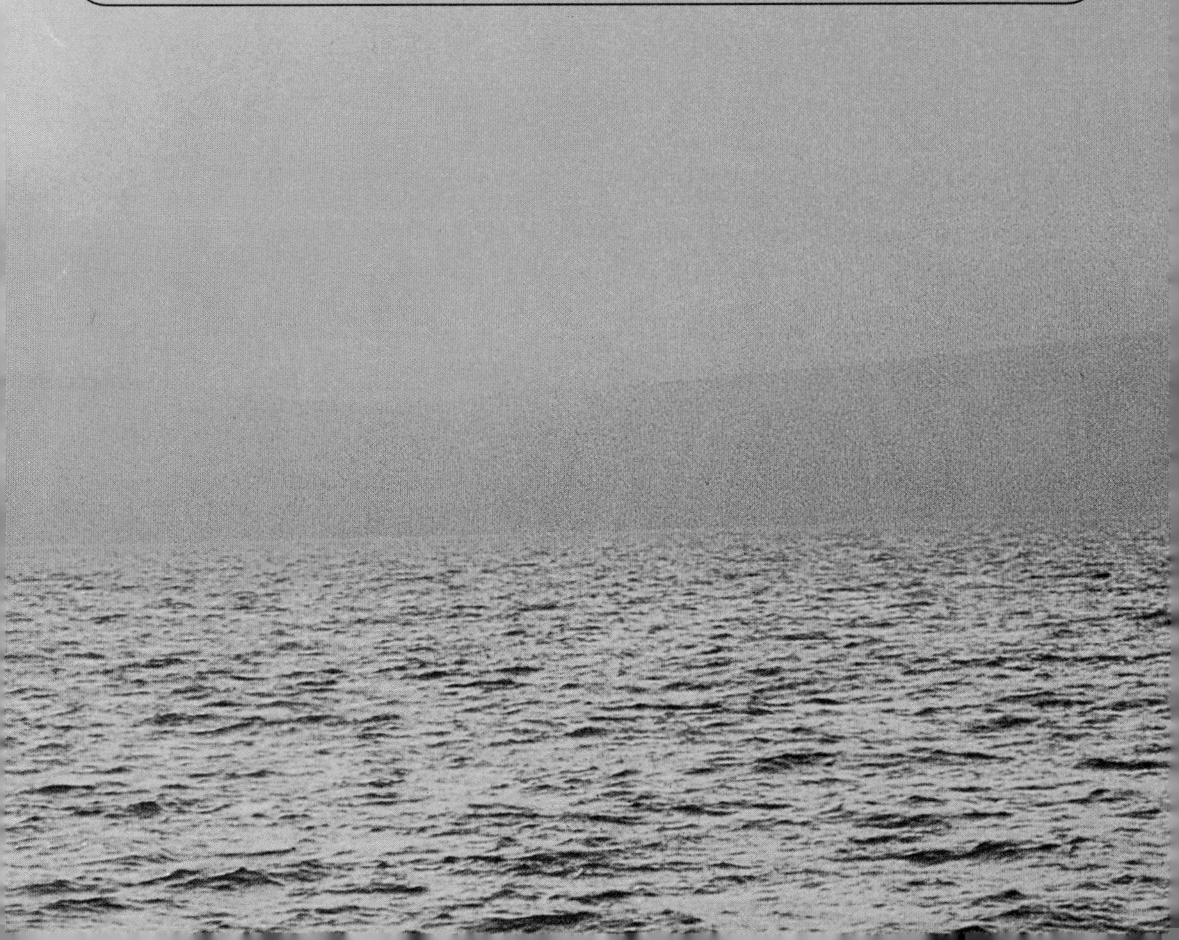

Cette connaissance s'explique par la présence incessante de Dieu *devant* et *derrière* (v. 5), qui sera le thème du paragraphe suivant. Le psalmiste se sent comme une ville assiégée, mais loin d'éprouver de la crainte face à cette présence, il est au contraire émerveillé et loue Dieu pour son savoir prodigieux, inaccessible (v. 6).

L'omniprésence de Dieu (v. 7-12)

La question du psalmiste, *Où pourrais-je aller loin de ton Esprit* (v. 7) ne traduit aucune révolte. L'auteur est au contraire heureux de ce que toute fuite soit impossible et la main de Dieu toujours là pour le diriger et le tenir (v. 10). Pour bien souligner cette impossibilité d'échapper à Dieu, il mentionne trois portes de sortie ou cachettes possibles, qu'il élimine l'une après l'autre parce que, même là, Dieu serait présent. En effet, s'il montait au ciel ou descendait au séjour des morts, Dieu y serait (v. 8). S'il empruntait *les ailes de l'aube* pour atteindre *les confins des mers* – une façon poétique de désigner la vitesse de la lumière – là aussi, il Le rencontrerait. En effet, la distance qui sépare le levant du couchant ne suffirait même pas à le séparer de Dieu (v. 9, 10). S'il essayait, enfin, de se cacher dans les ténèbres, il découvrirait que Dieu perce l'obscurité, car pour Dieu *lumières ou ténèbres (...) sont pareilles* (v. 11, 12).

La toute-puissance de Dieu (v. 13-18)

Si Dieu sait tout, c'est d'une part parce qu'il est omniprésent, comme nous venons de le voir, d'autre part parce qu'il est tout-puissant. S'il est capable de sonder un homme, ce n'est pas uniquement parce qu'il le voit, mais parce que c'est lui qui l'a fait. Le Créateur connaît ses créatures à fond. C'est par la puissance créatrice de Dieu que l'embryon se développe dans le sein de la mère. Dieu a créé la « personnalité » (version en Français courant) comme le *corps* (v. 13, 15). Il s'agit de l'homme dans son ensemble, corps et esprit, émotion et volonté. Ce Dieu créateur merveilleux voyait déjà le psalmiste alors qu'il n'était encore *qu'une masse informe* (v. 16). Qui plus est, avant même sa naissance, tous les jours de sa vie étaient prévus et inscrits dans le livre de Dieu (v. 15, 16). Subjugué par cette connaissance et cette prescience divines, le psalmiste laisse éclater sa louange, car les desseins de Dieu, *impénétrables* et *innombrables*, sont *bien plus nombreux que les grains de sable* (v. 17, 18).

La fin de ce paragraphe n'est pas très claire. *Voici : je m'éveille, je suis encore avec toi* (v. 18) reprend, selon certains commentateurs, l'idée du début, à savoir la présence constante de Dieu, alors que d'autres y voient le sommeil de la mort.

Le jugement de Dieu (v. 19-24)

Puisses-tu, ô Dieu, faire mourir le méchant ! (v. 19). Pour beaucoup de chrétiens, cette prière inattendue jette une note discordante dans ce psaume. Elle s'inscrit pourtant dans la même logique. Celui pour qui Dieu est tout ne supporte pas le mal. Ces méchants sont des *hommes sanguinaires* (v. 19) qui se servent du nom de Dieu pour *tromper* (v. 20), par le blasphème ou la rébellion. Ils se rendent coupables à la fois envers Dieu et envers leurs semblables. Ils bafouent les deux principaux commandements sur l'amour de Dieu et l'amour du prochain et ne reculent devant rien, ni le sang (violence, meurtre), ni le blasphème.

Une première remarque s'impose. Le psalmiste ne parle pas par animosité ou par désir de vengeance personnels, mais il en est venu à considérer les ennemis de Dieu (v. 20) comme ses ennemis propres (v. 22). Il s'indigne à juste titre là où nous aurions tort d'être indulgents. Son cœur est enflammé d'une haine divine à l'égard du péché.

On peut objecter que cet homme n'a pas su faire la différence entre le péché et le pécheur. Ne devrait-il pas (et nous avec lui) apprendre à aimer le pécheur et haïr le péché ? S'il y a là une part évidente de vérité, il faut cependant reconnaître que le péché, ou le mal, n'est pas quelque chose d'abstrait, mais qu'il existe dans les cœurs et les actions des pécheurs. Le jugement de Dieu s'exercera sur les pécheurs, non sur la notion abstraite du péché.

Mais, peut-on encore avancer, tant que l'espoir subsiste, ne faudrait-il pas souhaiter le salut des pécheurs et non leur jugement ? Oui, en effet. Mais si les pécheurs refusent de se repentir ? Nous ne pouvons passer outre leur propre refus de recevoir le salut. C'est là le cœur du problème. La Bible enseigne que le pécheur est l'objet tout à la fois de l'amour et de la colère de Dieu (cf. Jn 3.16, 36) et notre attitude devrait, par la grâce, être la plus proche possible de celle de Dieu. Nous devrions désirer de tout notre cœur le salut des pécheurs s'ils se repentent, tout comme nous devrions souhaiter leur destruction (et en fait la nôtre), s'ils ne se repentent pas (ou si nous ne nous repentons pas). Si nous avons du mal à adhérer aux paroles du psalmiste, c'est que nous trouvons difficile, sinon impossible, d'éprouver de tels sentiments dans toute leur pureté divine et sans y mêler notre venin personnel. Mais sachons en reconnaître la raison : nous ignorons ce qu'est une juste indignation.

Page suivante : Une femme guide un aveugle dans les ruelles de la vieille ville de Jérusalem. « L'Éternel est plein de grâce et de compassion, lent à la colère et riche en amour. »

Psaume 145

La louange du règne de Dieu

Ce psaume célèbre le « règne » de Dieu, c'est-à-dire son gouvernement sur l'univers dans son ensemble et dans la vie de chacun de ses enfants. C'est un psaume alphabétique, dont les vers débutent par les lettres successives de l'alphabet hébraïque, consacré tout entier à la gloire et la miséricorde du gouvernement de Yahvé, dont la louange doit être éternelle et raisonnée.

Une louange éternelle (v. 1-7)

Le psalmiste annonce sa détermination à exalter et à louer Dieu, non seulement *tous les jours* (v. 2), mais *jusque dans l'éternité* (v. 1, 2). Parce que l'Eternel est grand, il est *très digne de louanges* (v. 3) ; à sa grandeur *insondable* sied une louange incessante, ce qu'aucun homme sur terre ne peut faire. Il semble donc que l'auteur, parlant au nom d'Israël, demande à chaque génération à venir d'annoncer les œuvres de Dieu à la suivante, de manière à perpétuer sa louange (v. 4). Elles s'attacheront à raconter les *merveilles* (...) la *force redoutable* (...) les *exploits* de Dieu (v. 5-7).

Je t'exalterai,ˡô mon Dieu, mon Roi,
et je te loueraiˡjusque dans l'éternité.
2 Oui, je te loueraiˡtous les jours,
et je te célébreraiˡjusque dans l'éternité.
3 L'Eternel est grandˡet très digne de louanges,
sa grandeur est insondable.
4 Que chaque générationˡdise à celle qui la suitˡcombien tes œuvres sont belles.
Qu'elle publie tes exploits,
5 l'éclat et la gloireˡde ta majesté.
Pour moi, je méditeraiˡle récit de tes merveilles.
6 Qu'elle parleˡde ta force redoutable,
et moi, je proclameraiˡtes exploits.

7 Qu'elle évoqueˡtes bienfaits immenses,
qu'elle chante ton salut !

8 L'Eternel est plein de grâceˡet de compassion,
lent à la colèreˡet riche en amour.
9 L'Eternel est bonˡenvers tous les hommes
et plein de tendresseˡpour toutes les créatures.
10 Que toutes tes œuvresˡte louent, Eternel,
et que tes fidèlesˡte célèbrent !
11 Ils diront la gloireˡde ta royauté
et proclameront ta force.
12 Ils feront connaître aux hommesˡtes exploits,
la gloire et l'éclatˡde ta royauté.

13 Ton règne est un règneˡqui s'étend sur tous les temps,
et ta seigneurieˡdure d'âge en âge.
L'Eternel tient ses promesses,
il est plein d'amourˡdans tout ce qu'il fait.
14 L'Eternel est le soutienˡde tous ceux qui tombent,
il relèveˡtous ceux qui fléchissent.
15 Les regards de tousˡsont tournés vers toi :
tous attendent que tu donnesˡà chacun sa nourritureˡau moment voulu.
16 Tu ouvres ta main
et tu combles les désirsˡde tout ce qui vit.
17 L'Eternel est justeˡdans tous ses desseins,
il est plein d'amourˡdans tout ce qu'il fait.
18 L'Eternel est procheˡde ceux qui l'appellent,
de tous ceux qui sont sincèresˡlorsqu'ils font appel à lui.
19 Il accomplit les désirsˡde tous ceux qui le révèrent,
il entend leur criˡet il les délivre.
20 L'Eternel garde tous ceux qui l'aiment,
mais il détruira tous les méchants.

21 Je proclameraiˡta louange, ô Eternel !
Toute créatureˡte louera, toi le Dieu saint
jusque dans l'éternité.

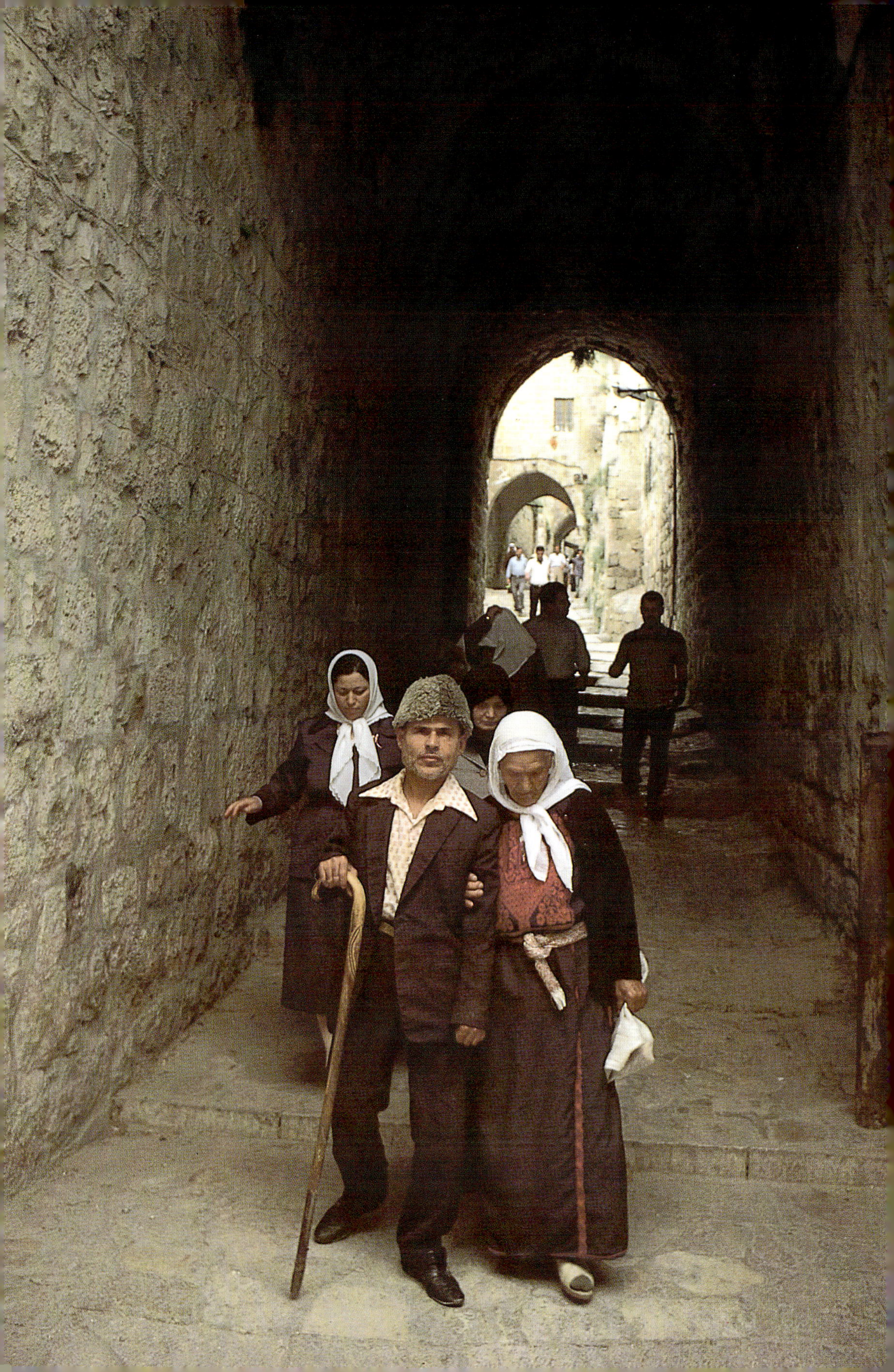

Une louange universelle (v. 8-13)

Dieu mérite une louange universelle, à laquelle participent toutes ses créatures. Ce n'est que justice, car il est *plein de tendresse pour toutes les créatures* (v. 9). La gloire que les hommes rendent à Dieu répond à la miséricorde de Dieu envers eux. Dieu fait miséricorde parce qu 'il est miséricordieux et c'est justement ce caractère miséricordieux de Dieu qui commande à la louange d'être éternelle et universelle. Le verset 8 reprend ce que Yahvé a révélé de lui-même à Moïse dans Exode 34.6 et qui a déjà été mentionné dans le Psaume 103.8. Dieu manifeste sa grâce et sa bienveillance en étant bon envers tous les hommes (v. 9). D'où l'universalité de la louange. Les êtres humains chantent la gloire, la puissance et l'éternité de son règne (v. 11-13). On voit déjà annoncée ici la doxologie du Notre Père : « Car à toi appartiennent le règne la puissance et la gloire à jamais » (Mt 6.13).

Une louange raisonnée (v. 14-21)

La louange qu'il est juste d'adresser à Dieu en tout temps est une louange intelligente ; c'est ce que le Seigneur Jésus appellera « adorer...en vérité » (Jn 4.24). Pour que Dieu agréé notre louange, elle doit venir en réponse à sa révélation. Autrement dit, c'est la louange de son « nom » (version Segond ; v. 1, 2, 21), de sa personne éternelle, révélé par ses paroles et ses œuvres.

Le psalmiste donne à présent quelques exemples concrets de la grâce de Dieu, qui montrent que son gouvernement, quoique puissant, n'est pas arbitraire. Au contraire, son règne est un règne bienfaisant et son trône, un trône de grâce. Il vient en aide à son peuple dans tous ses besoins, soutient ceux qui tombent et relève ceux qui fléchissent (v. 14). Il rassasie ceux qui ont faim et comble *les désirs de tout ce qui vit* (v. 15, 16). Il s'approche de ceux qui l'invoquent, entend leurs prières et y répond (v. 18, 19). Il protège ceux qui l'aiment, mais *il détruira tous les méchants* (v. 20).

On remarquera que dans les versets 19 et 20 la révérence et l'amour vont de pair. Quelqu'un a dit : « La crainte (ou la révérence) et l'amour sont deux composants inséparables de la vraie religion. La crainte empêche l'amour de dégénérer en une familiarité présomptueuse, et grâce à l'amour, la crainte ne se transforme pas en une peur servile. »

Le dernier verset (v. 21) résume les trois aspects de la louange de Yahvé, tels que les a présentés ce psaume. Elle est éternelle (*jusque dans l'éternité*), universelle *(toute créature)* et raisonnée (« la louange de ton nom »).

Psaume 150

La doxologie finale

Quelle belle conclusion au Psautier que cette doxologie et son appel inégalé à la louange ! De même que le Hallel (Ps 113-118) et les quatre psaumes précédents (146-149), celui-ci commence et finit avec les termes *Alléluia* ou *Louez l'Éternel.* Chaque verset est en fait une invitation à la louange, et nous dit où et pourquoi, comment et par qui, Dieu doit être loué.

Où et pourquoi (v. 1, 2)

Louez Dieu dans son sanctuaire, avec des instruments qui font clairement référence aux solennités du temple. Mais il doit aussi être loué *dans l'étendue où éclate sa puissance* (v. 1). Ce verset s'adresse probablement à la fois aux hommes et aux anges, les hommes dans le sanctuaire terrestre, les anges au ciel. Il nous rappelle que la gloire de Dieu est une, la louange de l'Église sur terre se joignant à celle « des anges, des archanges et de l'assemblée céleste. »

Ses œuvres et sa personne, autrement dit ce qu'il fait et ce qu'il est, voilà ce qui va susciter notre louange. Le psalmiste ne précise pas quels sont *ses hauts faits*, mais la création, la préservation de la vie, les soins dont il entoure ses créatures et sa rédemption en font partie. Ils sont l'expression de *sa grandeur infinie.* C'est là le thème éternel de la louange, la grandeur de Dieu, manifestée dans ses œuvres.

1 Louez l'Eternel !

Louez Dieu | dans son sanctuaire !
Louez-le dans l'étendue | où éclate sa puissance !
2 Louez-le pour ses hauts faits,
louez-le | pour sa grandeur infinie !
3 Louez-le au son du cor,
louez-le au son du luth | et de la cithare !
4 Louez-le avec des danses | et au son des tambourins !
Louez-le avec la lyre | et avec la flûte !
5 Louez-le par les cymbales | bien retentissantes !
Louez-le par les cymbales | résonnant avec éclat !

6 Que tout ce qui vit | loue donc l'Eternel !

Louez l'Eternel !

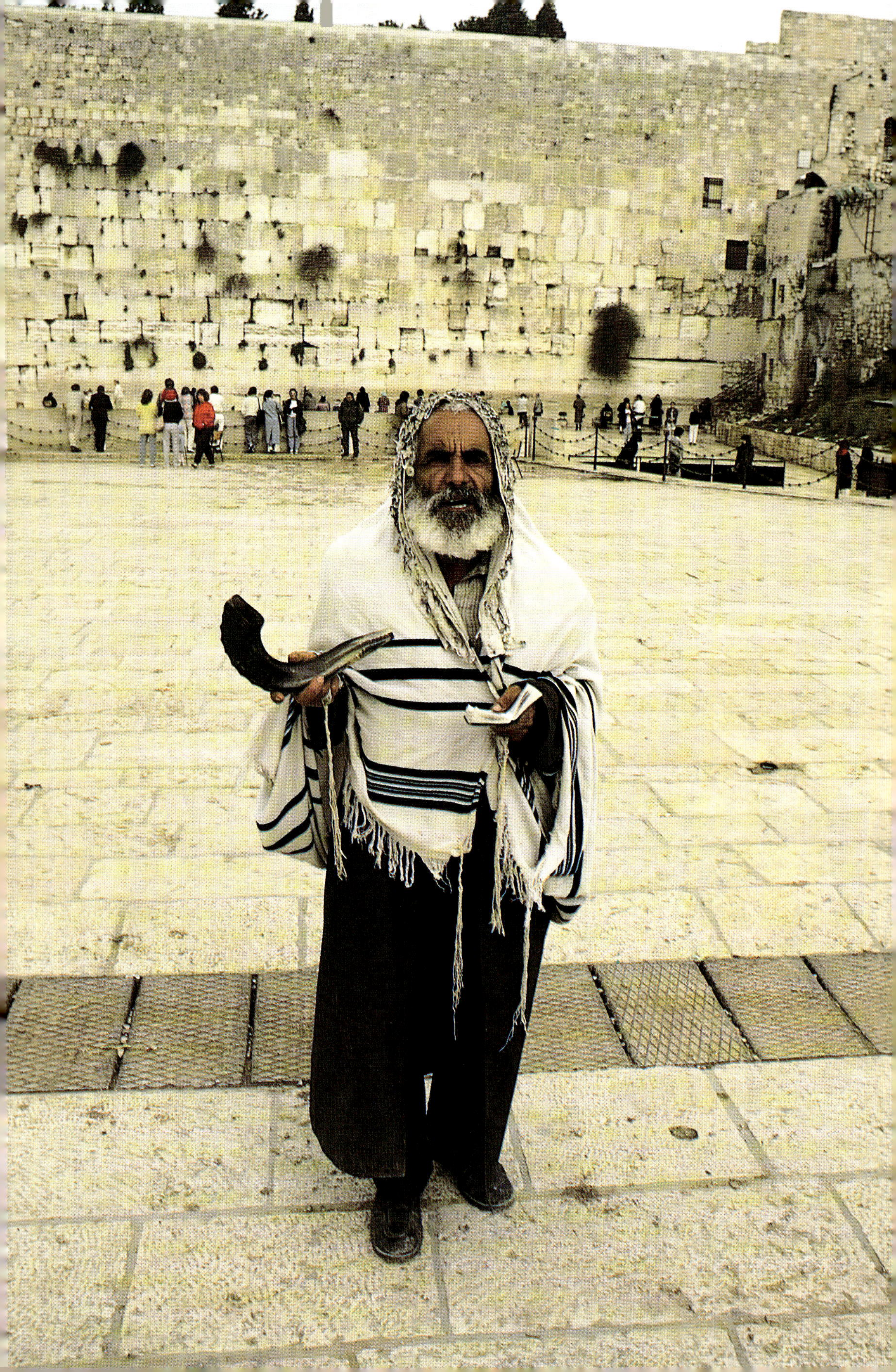

Page précédente : Un chef religieux juif sonne le schofar, c'est-à-dire la corne de bélier traditionnelle. Il servait à appeler les Israélites lors des convocations militaires ou religieuses.

Comment et par qui (v. 3-6)

Tout instrument de musique peut servir à la louange de Yahvé, qu'il soit à vent, à corde ou à percussion (cf. Ps 81.1-3). Le premier est le *cor*, fait d'une corne de bélier à l'extrémité recourbée. C'est, écrit un commentateur, « le seul instrument encore utilisé de nos jours dans les synagogues et il peut faire un bruit prodigieux entre des mains expertes. » Les deux autres instruments mentionnés au verset 3 sont à corde, à savoir le luth et la cithare. Puis viennent les *danses* et les *tambourins* (v. 4) et enfin, *la lyre et (...) la flûte*, cette dernière étant peut-être le simple chalumeau du berger. Il est question de deux sortes de cymbales (v. 5), probablement des espèces de petites castagnettes pour les unes et des instruments plus grands, qui résonnent, pour les autres.

L'orchestre est au complet. Il ne reste plus aux adorateurs qu'à souffler dans la corne et à pincer la harpe, à battre du tambour et à effleurer les cordes, à jouer de la flûte et à frapper les cymbales. « Le terme de musique n'est pas assez fort, il serait plus juste de parler de bruit...Que nos cymbales retentissent, en harmonie, certes, mais surtout *avec éclat*...et n'oublions pas les danses », écrit C.S. Lewis. C'est ainsi que des êtres consacrés à Dieu donnent libre cours à leur joie.

Mais le concert des instruments et les danses, même fort agréables, ne sauraient plaire à Dieu s'ils ne jaillissent d'un cœur et d'un esprit consacrés. En invitant *tout ce qui vit* (v. 6) à louer Dieu, il est possible que le psalmiste inclue les animaux ; l'accent est néanmoins mis sur nous, les êtres humains, couronnement de la création, à qui il a insufflé la vie (Gn 2.7). Que notre adoration ne se cantonne pas aux offices religieux. Au contraire, que toute notre vie, que notre respiration même, louent notre Dieu.